# THE GRIP BOOK

# The Grip Book

By Michael G. Uva

**ELSEVIER**

AMSTERDAM • BOSTON • HEIDELBERG • LONDON
NEW YORK • OXFORD • PARIS • SAN DIEGO
SAN FRANCISCO • SINGAPORE • SYDNEY • TOKYO
Focal Press is an imprint of Elsevier

**Focal Press**

| | |
|---|---|
| Acquisitions Editor: | Elinor Actipis |
| Project Manager: | Brandy Lilly |
| Associate Editor: | Becky Golden-Harrell |
| Marketing Manager: | Christine Degon Veroulis |
| Cover Design: | Cate Barr |
| Interior Design: | SNP Best-set Typesetter Ltd., Hong Kong |

Focal Press is an imprint of Elsevier
30 Corporate Drive, Suite 400, Burlington, MA 01803, USA
Linacre House, Jordan Hill, Oxford OX2 8DP, UK

**Library of Congress Cataloging-in-Publication Data**
Uva, Michael.
    The grip book /c by Michael G. Uva.—3rd ed.
      p.   cm.
    Includes bibliographical references and index.
    ISBN-13: 978-0-240-85233-1 (pbk. : alk. paper)
    ISBN-10: 0-240-85233-8 (pbk. : alk. paper)
    1. Cinematography–Handbooks, manuals, etc.
    2. Grips (Persons)–Handbooks, manuals, etc.  I. Title.
    TR850.U93 2006
    778.5′3—dc22

                                                                        2005036148

**British Library Cataloguing-in-Publication Data**
A catalogue record for this book is available from the British Library.

ISBN 13: 978-0-240-85233-1
ISBN 10: 0-240-85233-8

For information on all Focal Press publications
visit our website at www.books.elsevier.com

05 06 07 08 09 10   10 9 8 7 6 5 4 3 2 1

Printed in the United States of America

This book is dedicated to all the "newbies" who want to learn it all, to all the great production people who work so hard that they can't possibly know it all, and, last but not least, to the old salts who invented it all. Thank you, one and all.

—Mike

# Contents

## Expendables    119

# Notice to All:

Before you decide to use, buy, or order any product listed in this latest book, always check with the manufacturer or supplier for any and all revisions, warnings, or updated requirements. There are cell phones, faxes, the internet, and many other ways to check it out first. Don't be "dead wrong." "We're just making a movie here!" Don't make the news!

*—Mike*

# Contributing Companies and Manufacturers and Suppliers

## Contributing Companies

### Aerocrane
Phone: (818) 252-7700; Phone 2: (888) 766-0650; Fax: (818) 252-7709
*Cranes:* Enlouva IIIA, Felix, Jib Arms, Phoenix, and Super
*Dollies:* Aerobase, Barby, and Magnum
*Accessories:* Power Pod, 3 Axis, Aerohead, Gazelle, Graphite, Kuper, Lynx, Motion
  Control, and Zebra
www.aerocrane.com

### American Grip
8468 Kewen Avenue
Sun Valley, CA 91352
Phone: (818) 768-8922; Fax: (818) 768-0564
*Grip equipment*
www.americangrip.com

### Anytime—Hollywood
755 N. Lillian Way
Hollywood, CA 90038
Phone: (323) 461-8483; Fax: (323) 461-2338
*Equipment rentals*
www.anytime-rentals.com

### Backstage Equipment, Inc.
8052 Lankershim Boulevard
North Hollywood, CA 91605
Phone: (818) 504-6026; Phone 2: (800) 692-2787; Fax: (818) 504-6180
*Electric, grip, and prop carts*
www.backstageweb.com

### Barber Boom/Camera Booms
P.O. Box 248
Sun Valley, CA 91353
Phone: (818) 982-7775
*Booms:* 20-ϕτ Barber Boom and Barber Baby Boom accessories (camera car shock
  mount and remote focus and zoom)
www.ezprompter.com

### Bill Ferrell Co.
14744 Oxnard Street
Van Nuys, CA 91411
Phone: (818) 994-1952; Phone 2: (866) 994-1952; Fax: (818) 994-9670
*Ferrells*
www.billferrell.com

**Branam/West Coast Theatrical**
28210 Constellation Road
Santa Clarita, CA 91355
Phone: (661) 295-3300; Fax: (661) 295-3865
*Trusses, motors, cables*
www.west-coast-theatrical.com

**Bullet Grip, Inc.**
11717 Seminole Circle
Northridge, CA 91326
Phone: (818) 832-8707; Fax: (818) 832-8807
*Grip equipment*

**Cablecam International, Inc.**
17810 Simonds Street
Granada Hills, CA 91344
Phone: (818) 363-5383; Phone 2: (818) 601-6333; Fax: (818) 363-2570
*Accessories:* Cable-suspended camera tracking systems and mounts
www.cablecam.com

**Champion Crane Rental, Inc.**
12521 Branford Street
Pacoima, CA 91331
Phone: (818) 781-3497; Phone 2: (323) 875-1248; Fax: (818) 896-6202
*Cranes:* 40-το. 265-φτ reach
*Accessories:* Camera baskets, light bars, and rain bars
www.championcrane.us.com; e-mail: championcr@aol.com

**Coptervision**
7625 Hayvenhurst Avenue, Suite 41
Van Nuys, CA 91406
Phone: (818) 781-3003; Phone 2: (818) 782-6673; Fax: (818) 782-4070
*Accessories:* Rollvision three-axis remote camera system
www.coptervision.com; e-mail: info@coptervision.com

**Dean Goldsmith/Camera Car Industries**
12473 San Fernando Road
Sylmar, CA 91342
Phone: (818) 998-4798; Fax: (818) 833-5962
*Camera cars*
*Accessories:* Three-axis remote camera systems
www.Cameracarindustries.com

**Doggicam, Inc.**
1500 W. Verdugo Avenue
Burbank, CA 91506
Phone: (818) 845-8470; Fax: (818) 845-8477
*Accessories:* Body-mount, bulldog wireless remote head, doggimount, lightweight
  remote sparrow head, remote follow focus, and rhino clamps
www.doggicam.com

**Filmair**
51 Auckland Street
P.O. Box 537
Milnerton, Capetown 7435
South Africa
Phone: (021) 511-5579; Fax: (021) 511-2812
www.filmairinternational.com

**Filmotechnic International Corp.**
18314 Oxnard Street, Suite 2
Tarzana, CA 91356
Phone: (818) 342-3392; Fax: (818) 342-3572
*Cranes:* Russian arm crane with 14-ft vertical reach, cross country crane with 21-ft reach, and scissor crane with 30-ft reach
*Accessories:* Action arm, Flight Head III and IV, and shock absorber system
www.filmotechnic.net

**Geo Film Group, Inc.**
7625 Hayvenhurst Avenue, Suite
46 Van Nuys, CA 91406
Phone: (818) 376-6680; Phone 2: (877) 436-3456; Fax: (818) 376-6686
*Arms:* Jan Jib and Maxi Jib
*Cranes:* Javelin, M.T.V., Scanner, Skymote, Super Aerocrane, Superskymote, Technocrane, and VIP
*Accessories:* Hot Head II Plus, Libra III, Megamount, Mini Shot, Power Pod Plus, and Pee Pod
www.geofilm.com; e-mail: info@geofilm.com

## *Manufacturers and Suppliers*

**Able Equipment Rental**
8242 Orangethorpe Boulevard
Buena Park, CA 90621
Phone: (714) 521-5602; Fax: (818) 997-0478

**ADCO Equipment, Inc.**
P.O. Box 2100
City of Industry, CA 91746
Phone: (562) 695-0748

**Advanced Camera Systems, Inc.**
7625 Hayvenhurst Avenue
Van Nuys, CA 91406
Phone: (818) 989-5222; Fax: (818) 994-8405
www.advancedcamera.com

**Aero Cam Productions**
6920 Hayvenhurst Avenue, Suite 202
Van Nuys, CA 91406
Phone: (818) 997-0512

**Aerocrane USA, Inc.**
16139 Wyandotte Street
Van Nuys, CA 91406
Phone: (818) 252-7700 or (888) 766-0650; Fax: (818) 252-7709

**Anytime Production Rentals**
755 N. Lillian Way
Hollywood, CA 90038
Phone: (323) 461-8483; Fax: (323) 461-2338
www.anytimerentals.com

**Cablecam Systems, Ltd.**
17070 Simonds Street
Granada Hills, CA 91344
Phone: (818) 601-6333; Fax: (818) 363-2570
jr@cablecam.com

**Chapman/Leonard Studio Equipment, Inc.**
12950 Raymer Street
N. Hollywood, CA 91605
Phone: (818) 764-6726, (888) 883-6559
www.chapman-leonard.com

**Cinema Products**
3211 S. La Cienega Boulevard
Los Angeles, CA 90016-3112
Phone: (310) 836-7991; Fax: (310) 836-9512
www.steadicam.com

**Dexter, Ron**
320 Calle Elegante
Santa Barbara, CA 93108-1809
Phone: (805) 565-3156

**Eagle High Reach**
14241 Alondra Boulevard
La Mirada, CA 90638
Phone: (800) 363-6590 or (714) 522-6590; Fax: (714) 522-6591

**Egripment U.S.A., Inc.**
7240 Valjean Avenue
Van Nuys, CA 91406
Phone: (818) 989-5222
www.egripment.com

**Equipment Express**
11862 Balboa Boulevard, Suite 398
Granada Hills, CA 91344-2789
Phone: (818) 360-8002

**Bill Ferrell Co.**
14744 Oxnard Street
Van Nuys, CA 91411
Phone: (818) 994-1952; Fax: (818) 994-9670
www.billferrell.com

**J.L. Fisher, Inc.**
1000 Isabel Street
Burbank, CA 91506
Phone: (818) 846-8366; Fax: (818) 846-8699
www.jlfisher.com

**Genie Industries**
18340 NE 76th Street
P.O. Box 97030
Redmond, WA 98073-9730
Phone: (425) 556-8620, (877) 436-3456; Fax: (425) 556-6535
www.genielift.com

**Geo Film Group**
7625 Hayvenhurst, Suite 46
Van Nuys, CA 91406
Phone: (818) 376-6680; Fax: (818) 376-6686
www.geofilm.com

**Gyron Systems International, Ltd.**
39 E. Walnut Street
Pasadena, CA 91103
Phone: (626) 584-8722; Fax: (626) 584-4069
www.danwolfe.com

**Hachapi Tees**
(Custom graphics and illustrations by Christi Friesen)
20407 Brian Way
Tehachapi, CA 93581
Phone: (661) 822-6999

**Hollaender Manufacturing Co.**
10285 Wayne Avenue
Cincinnati, OH 45215-6399
Phone: (800) 772-8800 or (513) 772-8800; Fax: (800) 772-8806 or (513) 772-8806
www.hollaender.com

**HydroFlex**
5335 McConnell Avenue
Los Angeles, CA 90066
Phone: (310) 301-8187; Fax: (310) 821-9886
www.hydroflex.com

**Isaia and Company**
4650 Lankershim Boulevard
N. Hollywood, CA 91602
Phone: (818) 752-3104; Fax: (818) 752-3105
www.isaia.com

**Matthews Studio Electronics, Inc.**
6910 Tujunga Avenue
North Hollywood, CA 91605
Phone: (818) 623-1661; Fax: (818) 623-1671
www.camerasystems.com

**Matthews Studio Equipment, Inc.**
2405 Empire Avenue
Burbank, CA 91504
Phone: (818) 843-6715; (800) CE-STAND; Fax: (323) 849-1525
www.msegrip.com

**Modern Studio Equipment**
7428 Bellaire
North Hollywood, CA 91605
Phone: (818) 764-8574; Fax: (818) 764-2958

**Nebekers Motion Picture Video**
1240 E. 2100 South, Suite 300
Salt Lake City, UT 84106
Phone: (801) 467-1920; Fax: (801) 467-0307

**NES Studio Equipment**
11043 Olinda Street
Sun Valley, CA 91352
Phone: (818) 673-0202; Fax: (818) 252-7711
www.nesstudioequipment.com

**Ragtime**
10905 Chandler Boulevard
North Hollywood, CA 91601
Phone: (818) 761-8463; Fax: (818) 761-8483
www.ragtimerentals.com

**Reel EFX**
5539 Riverton Avenue
North Hollywood, CA 91601
Phone: (818) 762-1710
www.reelefx.com

**Jack Rubin & Sons, Inc.**
523 Flower Street
Burbank, CA 91502
Phone: (818) 562-5100; Fax: (818) 562-5101
www.wirerope.net

**The Shotmaker® Co.**
10909 Van Owen
North Hollywood, CA 91605
Phone: (818) 623-1700; Fax: (818) 623-1710
www.shotmaker.com

**Staton Jimmy Jibs**
2223 E. Rose Gardenloop
Phoenix, AZ 85204
Phone: (602) 493-9505; Fax: (602) 493-2468
www.jimmyjibs.com

**ShowRig**
15823 S. Main Street
Los Angeles, CA 90245
Phone: (310) 538-4175; Fax: (310) 538-4180
www.sgps.net

**SpaceCam Systems, Inc.**
31111 Via Colinas, Suite 201
Westlake Village, CA 91362
Phone: (818) 889-6060; Fax: (818) 889-6062
www.spacecam.com

**Timco**
10314 Farralone Avenue
Chatsworth, CA 91311
Phone: (818) 700-9005
timco@aol.com

**Trovatocine Trovato Manufacturing, Inc.**
66 North Main Street
Fairport, NY 14450
Phone: (585) 377-8070; Fax: (585) 377-3811
www.trovatocine.com

**Tyler Camera System**
14218 Aetna Street
Van Nuys, CA 91401
Phone: (818) 989-4420, (800) 390-6070; Fax: (818) 989-0423
www.tylermount.com

**VER Sales, Inc.**
2509 N. Naomi Street
Burbank, CA 91504
Phone: (818) 567-3000; Fax: (818) 567-3018
www.versales.com

**Weaver Steadman**
1646 20th Street
Santa Monica, CA 90404
Phone: (310) 829-3296

**Wescam**
7150 Hayvenhurst Avenue
Van Nuys, CA 91406
Phone: (818) 785-9282, (800) 876-5583; Fax: (818) 785-9787
www.wescam.com

**Z-Jib (Zero-gravity boom arm) K-Hill, Inc.**
Ft. Worth, TX
Phone: (817) 831-3011
www.khill.com

## Letter from the Author

Hi, and thank you in advance for buying my book. I am trying with this book to accomplish two things that I learned from the author Zig Zigler: "If you help enough people get what they want, you'll get what you want." I want to help as many folks who want to get into the film industry as I can. I absolutely love my jobs. Yes, I did say jobs. Because of my career in the film business as a grip, I have been able to explore my other passions as well. I love to write, and I love to train students at my seminars. In this newly revised grip handbook, I have added more need-to-know information about basic grip equipment. I have learned from my many students and other folks whom I've met that I should also include some basics about tools. As you thumb through the new and improved *The Grip Book*, I'm sure that you will come across some things that you already know. Good for you! But, there will also be many other readers out there for whom this material is entirely new and whom will benefit from the "need-to-know" material provided in the text. So, sit down, peruse the book, and learn!

Thanks again,
Michael G. Uva

## About the Author

Michael Uva is a highly motivated self-starter. He created one of Hollywood's largest privately owned fleets of rental trucks for grip equipment in just a few years and then sold it. He learned his business strictly through on-the-job experience and never attended any formal motion picture or cinema-related schools or classes. When Michael began his career as a grip, no specialty books regarding his craft were available. After several years of learning his craft from other key grips and grips, Michael wrote the first edition of this book to share the knowledge he had gained. That edition proved very useful to new and experienced grips alike, so Michael wrote a second edition. He also teaches at the University of California at Los Angeles on occasion. Michael's goal in writing this third edition of *The Grip Book* is to help new students, other grips, and production members by providing a firsthand, fingertip reference guide to the grip equipment used in the industry.

## Acknowledgments

I would like to take a few moments of your time to share with you the names of people I want to thank. The only reason you should read this section is because, if and when you do make it to Hollywood, these are the types of people you want to work with. These people are some of the best grips and other personnel still working in the business, and they have helped me on a relatively routine basis.

First and foremost is Doug Wood, key grip, I.A., Local 80. Doug gave me that first proverbial break in the business of making movies. Not only was this guy a giant of a man in stature (his nickname was "King Kong"), but he was also probably one of the best, if not *the* best, dolly-grips you would ever see. In fact, I looked up the word "smooth" in the dictionary, and next to it was his picture. All kidding aside, he was one of the best. I loved him like a brother. (Doug is now with the Lord.)

Next on my list is Gary Welsh, key grip, I.A., Local 80. Doug Wood taught me the trade of the business, but Gary taught me the business of the business. I have nothing but respect and admiration for this guy.

Then there is John Stabile, key grip, I.A., Local 80. This kid, as I call him, is one of Hollywood's youngest and hottest key grips around. This guy looks 18 years old but has the knowledge and experience of a 48-year-old. My humble hat is off to you, John.

These guys are only a few of what I consider to be the greats of the business. Look them up yourself when you hit Hollywood.

I have worked with so many good grips, but if I listed them all this book would be really boring and the only people who would read it would be those listed here. (There is no shortage of ego in this industry . . . perhaps that is why there are so many greats!)

Before I get on with the show, I really must say a special thanks to someone who has been my sidekick and is a cofounder of Uva's Grip Truck Service, Mr. José A. Santiago. I met José over 25 years ago when I was just breaking into the industry. He was sweeping floors at the place where I was working part-time. He had come to the continental United States from the Virgin Islands only three years earlier. At that time, José only spoke broken English, but he had, and still has, flair. He swept the floor with a smile, cleaned toilets, whatever was required of his job. He showed me then, as he continues to do so now, that he could do any job assigned to him. You just need to show him how to do the job, dirty or glamorous, and give him the chance to prove himself. After only eight years in this country, he was driving a DeLorean auto, had bought his second home with a pool, and was helping his mother back in the Virgin Islands where she still lives. José is now one of Hollywood's most sought-after key grips. Just another success story, I guess, but one we are both living.

Good luck to all of you who venture down this road. I would love to hear from readers who have gotten the breaks and are making the big bucks.

## A Bit of Encouragement

I have included the illustration below to encourage my readers. These words were discovered cast in stone (okay, cement) in Hollywood at the Kodak Theater, located next to the world famous Mann's Chinese Theater. They are part of an artistic statement designed by Erica Rothenberg and entitled "The Road to Hollywood." This concrete "red carpet" includes many quotes from directors, producers, actors, and now, of course, a key grip. Who knew? If you turn back to the acknowledgments section of this book, you will learn that this key grip is my good friend José Santiago. Besides being very, very proud of José, I am telling you about him to let you know that *you can also make it here*! (P.S. Look Mom . . . I have arrived!)

# *Introduction*

## What This Book Is About

This book is designed to teach you about the equipment you will need and use on a daily basis. I will also lightly touch on some stage terms, tricks of the trade, and procedures. With this book, perseverance (and I mean *lots* of perseverance), and just plain old hard work, you can become a successful grip. I challenge you to do it. But, let me get off my soapbox (later changed to an apple box . . . you'll see) and get back to teaching you how to become a grip. I am writing this book based on my experience and the experiences of other grips with whom I have worked. There is a saying among grips that there are ten ways to do the very same job—and usually they all work. This book will help you to learn the names of basic grip equipment and ways to use it (every so often I will also throw in the nickname of a piece of equipment).

### *About the Equipment*

In this book I have selected a cross-section of only the most professional equipment. I have not by any means listed all the super equipment available. First off, such a book would be too costly to produce, and second, I just want you to get a feel for what tools are available. I recommend that you go to any and all technical trade shows concerning the film/television industry. You are no doubt aware of the industry's widespread and growing use of computers, with each new application being better, faster, and more readily available. There are several fantastic remote control film and television heads (fluid, remote, and geared heads), as well as many new cranes and dollies, new and improved grip equipment, and redefined methods of gripping. I will try to cover a little of each of these aspects to let you, the reader, know what is available out there. I will be providing the knowledge for you to go out there and make your own decisions. I am not just going to tell you what equipment to get; instead, I am going to help you figure out for yourself what equipment to get based on your needs and the situation. The goal is to make sure you realize that such a discussion is more than a catalog of parts!

If I don't show you a picture of a piece of equipment, I have probably explained it either somewhere else in the book or in the glossary. Once again, this book is not the end-all of grip books, but it is a leap in the forward direction. If you learn one thing and use it to improve your skills, others will notice, and it might just get you called back, which is one of the many things I have aimed for in this book.

### *Tricks of the Trade (T.O.T.)*

I will use the acronym T.O.T. for all the tricks of the trade I will be passing along to you. T.O.T. is an appropriate acronym because, I like to think, a child (you know, a tot) could remember most of these little tricks. You may have heard that old saying, "It's the little things that mean a lot." Well, that certainly holds true in this business. Besides, these tricks will separate the men from the boys and the women from the girls. You will find T.O.T.s sprinkled throughout this book.

> **T.O.T.**
> Your attitude is of major importance in this business. I have hired one person over another even if the person I hired was a little less qualified. Why? Attitude! I need, and the film industry needs, people who can work hard and sometimes long hours, under really tough conditions. I am not saying you have to be a saint, but if you don't like it when it gets tough, let somebody else do it for you—and they will reap the rewards for their hard labor.

## Getting Started

So you want to get into the movies. Well, so did I. Now I am in, and you can get in, too. It doesn't take a college education (but it helps) and not even a high school diploma (but who the heck wants to walk around without one—not any grip I know). If you are halfway intelligent and can count to at least seven two out of three times, I believe you can learn about the basic tools of gripping.

Let me begin by promising you the same thing I promise all of my students: Nothing. You don't need someone to tell you that you will get rich, be famous, and live happily ever after if you buy this book. But, if you like traveling and working with a group of highly skilled technicians, actors and actresses, directors, and producers, then this is the job you should try to pursue. I don't want to say it is the greatest job, but, to give you an idea of how good it can be, I started writing the first edition of this book while I was on location for the movie *The Big Easy* in New Orleans—sitting in a room on the 15th floor of a luxury hotel overlooking the Mississippi River.

When people ask what my job is like, my answer is very unconventional: It's almost pure freedom, like a singer singing a song. Singers must know all the words, but they put their own style and twist to it. For example, I must sometimes mount a $500,000 camera setup on a $200,000 car, and how I do that is a challenge. As a grip, you are kind of like an on-set designer, engineer, and administrator/worker, all rolled into one person. You are needed! You are one major support system. It is a great job. Give your all to whatever you do, and the future will develop itself. Trust me on this.

First and foremost, start by figuring out just what job you *think* you may want to do in the film industry. I use the word *think* because you may find that, after you have reached that coveted position, it is not as fulfilling as you thought it might be, would be, or should have been—but that's another story. For now, let's assume you are absolutely, positively sure beyond a shadow of a doubt that you have made the right career decision. Good, let's get started.

Because gripping is the subject you have chosen to study, let me tell you what a grip is. A grip is the person who, as we grips like to think, solves other people's problems. A cameraperson might turn to a grip and say, "I'd like to rig a camera on top of a car . . . or on top of a mountain . . . or off the side of a building." As grips, we are the guys and gals who have to figure out how to rig it safely and as quickly as possible because of the tight shooting schedules we usually have to work with.

Grips come in assorted sizes and colors. There are a lot of big, macho-type grips. You can recognize them right off. They are the guys with the heavy moustaches who usually walk like small apes, myself included. Grips can also come in the form of women. Gripping does not really take a lot of body strength, although it does require a lot of mental strength to outsmart the object you are working on.

Let me illustrate. When I am asked (as I often am), "What *is* a grip?," I like to tell this story. First, imagine that you're in your home, say, in the early 1960s, at Christmas time. Uncle Milton suddenly runs into the room as the family is about to open the gifts, which have been lovingly placed around the tree by Mom. Well, good old Uncle Milty does not want to miss a single moment, so out comes the new 8-mm camera. He wants to save this special moment for all posterity. He flips on the switch, and a huge blinding light from the twin lamps on the camera is now burning the retinas out of everyone's eyeballs. Everyone in the room, almost in unison, raises a hand to cover what's left of their vision. Tight-lipped smiles quickly emerge (which say, "You're blinding me with that stupid light!"), and everyone gives a quick wave (which says, "Okay! Enough already. Film the next person!"). The twins, seeing this great fun, jump to their feet and dance a jig for their now most favorite uncle. Yes, they are on film. Their overlit, bright faces smile joyfully, while their harsh, heavy, dark shadows dance like huge monsters on the rear wall, aping their every move. Aunt May (Milty's wife of 30 years) fans herself to relieve the tremendous heat from the camera lamps. Ah! The joys of home movies.

We have all seen this type of home film. Professional movie making could be very much the same; even though it costs a whole lot more, it could be just as boring. Now enters the grip department. We are the folks who place different materials in front of those huge light sources to make them a bit more flattering, or softer, or even colder looking. We have a million different tricks up our sleeve (okay, not really a million but a bunch).

Grips usually do not decide what material to put in front of a light; that is usually the job of the cameraperson, along with the gaffer (you will learn what a gaffer does in a minute). On many occasions, though, we can suggest something that will work for the shot. (Believe me, folks, it *is* a team effort.) Besides the soft materials in front of the lamp, we may also use a flag and cutter (I will explain later) or maybe a net to change the texture or the intensity of the lamp.

A grip is like an expert handyman—kind of a jack-of-all-trades and, we like to think, a master of all, as well. Most grips usually find they can do just about anything, but after a few years in the business you will find that you begin to specialize. For example, you may become a *dolly grip* (I'll teach you more about dollies later). The dolly grip does all the pushing and wheeling. Then there's the *rigging grip*, who mounts cameras and lights anywhere they are needed, which is my *forte*. I like this aspect best. And then there's just the everyday grip, who does, you guessed it, just about everything. In this book, we are going to be focusing on the basic tools of gripping.

As a grip, you will be working with the *gaffer*. This is the person who is in charge of the lighting. You will also work with the *director of photography*, usually called the DP. The DP is the person who may tell us what light goes where or who just tells the gaffer what sort of light mood he or she would like to see—for example, a night scene, a day scene, rain, and so forth. Basically, the DP tells the gaffer what he or she wants, and then the gaffer has the *electricians* who work with him or her go out and set up the lights where needed. You will also work with a host of other technicians, sound people, makeup artists, and so forth, and you'll learn something about their specialties as you go along.

To be a grip, you must believe in yourself and be prepared to work long hours and sometimes under not-so-Hollywood-glamorous conditions. It is not an easy task to become a film technician. You must have determination and you must learn the equipment. If you know what a piece of equipment looks like by name and can be fast to retrieve it when called for, then you're well on your way to being a good grip.

## A Little Grip History

Before I tell you more about what a grip is, let me tell you how the word *grip* came to be. Legend (and there are many of them in this industry) has it that in the heyday (another word for the beginning) of film, the basic film crews consisted of a director, a cameraperson, a few assistants, and workers. The workers set up all the equipment, lights, cable, stands, and so forth, so they were like the handymen on the set. The worker/handyman carried his tools in all sorts of containers, such as a tool tray, a box, or a carpet bag (sort of like a doctor's bag, only larger). The bag that contained the tools of the handyman's trade was called a *grip bag*. (Starting to get the picture?) Over time, these workers developed special talents. Some developed skills in building or rigging things. The originally unspecialized workers eventually separated into specialty groups: electricians did all the wiring and lighting, and workers with the tools grabbed their tools or grip bags and built or rigged whatever was needed.

The modern-day grip is still the physical backbone of the industry. Trust me—all the other departments bust their butts, too, but it always seems like the grips are lifting or carrying something. They're sort of handy people to have around. The standing joke among grips is, "We fix other people's problems."

A cameraman I sometimes work for has given me what I consider the best description of a grip: *an intelligent muscle.* This does not mean you have to be over six feet tall, weigh 280 pounds, and be built like a football player to do the job. What it does mean is that you are smart enough to move a mountain, if need be, because you know who to call to get the job done, quickly and safely.

## The Grip Department

The grip department has the following positions:

* Key grip (boss)
* Best boy grip (could also be a best girl grip)
* Grips

### Key Grip

The key grip is the head guy, the big cheese, the main man, the *bwana*, the keeper of the keys, the master who knows it all (and that's just what he thinks of himself; you should see what the rest of the crew thinks of him). The job of a key grip is to gather a crew consisting of a best boy (second grip) and as many grips as needed to get the job done. If there are any preproduction meetings before the scheduled shooting day, the key grip will attend these. During location scout meetings, the key grip will also have to determine what additional special support equipment (extra dollies, cranes, mounts, etc.) will be needed, if any. After the location scout, the key grip will determine the production needs and whether or not any additional special support equipment (a second four-wheel-drive truck, a couple of snowmobiles, boats, etc.) is needed for the particular terrain in order to get the company's film equipment to a certain spot. Once on location, the key grip works with the gaffer (head electrician) and starts directing what grip equipment goes where. While all this work is in progress, the key grip will begin to plan what will be needed for the next series of shots, based on his or her years of experience and what has been derived from meetings with the producer, director, and cinematographer during preproduction meetings.

### Best Boy Grip

The best boy is an extremely important position in the grip department. He (or she) is the direct link between the key grip and the other grips. The best boy is like a foreman on any job. The key grip tells the best boy grip what she or he wants and where and why. The best boy grip directs the grips, giving each an assigned task to complete and instructions on when to report back upon completion of the task. The best boy grip is also in charge of all the grip equipment and expendables (tape, gels, nails, etc.) on the grip truck. He inventories the equipment when it leaves the truck and when it returns, ensuring that the company does not run out of expend-ables in the middle of a shoot. The best boy grip also gives a status report to the key grip on the works in progress, along with an honest estimate of how long each job will take to complete. He must be accurate within 3 to 5 minutes, as time is money in this industry.

## Grips

Grips are the workhorses of the industry. This is not to imply that the rest of the technicians do not work hard; they do. It is just that grips tend to do the dirty work, along with their electrical brothers and sisters. Grips usually do most of the rigging of light support equipment (securing the lights in place). They mount the cameras in every imaginable place under the sun (and moon), and they are respon-sible for the safety of all the equipment they rig. When a stunt coordinator asks the grip department to help build a ramp or a safety stop (we're talking about a person's life or limbs here), the stunt department, as well as the film industry, is placing its trust in the grips' ability to do it right.

## A Typical Day for a Grip

For a grip, a typical day on a film or television set goes sort of like this.

### Call Time

A lot of folks have feelings about the time one should be ready to work on a movie set. Some say that, if the call time is set at 7:00 a.m., for example, then this is the time you begin your work. I fully agree with this statement! If the call time is, in fact, 7:00 a.m., this means to me that you have arrived at the set's loca-tion, parked your car (if necessary), put your tool belt on your hip, and are ready to swing your hammer at 7:00 a.m. This is my personal philosophy. I will tell you the same thing that I have told *newbies* (new personnel just starting out) for years: "If you arrive early, you're on time; if you arrive on time, you're late; if you're late, you're fired!" I know in this politically correct world this won't happen, but recog-nize this: I do not have to call you back for the next job. I am not trying to be a hard-nosed, intolerant, key position person with a huge ego. I am just hoping that you get my thoughts on the matter. There are many, many people who would give their eyeteeth for a chance to be in this business. I want you to stay. (I really would not fire you.)

So, getting back to this time-of-day stuff, you are supposed to be ready to start work on the set at the call time; the call time is *not* the time to show up. Most pro-duction companies usually have a self-serve sort of breakfast, maybe hot or maybe just donuts ("grip steaks") and coffee. This meal is usually served a half hour prior to call time. Remember, call time means you have had breakfast and are ready to work.

The key personnel for each department will usually have done their home-work, which means they have already discussed what will (should) be accomplished that day. The key grip will gather his or her personnel and explain what the day's work will be, then each grip will be assigned his task. Be ready to work, with both your tool belt and your radio on.

**T.O.T.**

*Never* enter a stage if there is a RED light flashing. This means they are rolling film.

### Setting up a Shoot

Your first time on a stage will be something like this, or close enough for you to look like you know your way around. A makeshift movie set has been built by the construction set-building crew in a studio or sound stage. When you walk in, you will notice that above the set is a series of walkways that are built close to the ceiling. There will be a set or two of stairs mounted on the side walls of the stage leading up to these raised walkways. These walkways are permanently built into the stage, so they are called *perms* (short for permanent walkways or cat-walks). The perms usually range from around 25 to 100 feet above the ground, and they are spread about 25 to 35 feet from each other, crisscrossing the entire stage. The perms are used to mount lights, which are hung from the system of rafters and trusses that support the roof of most stages. From these perms we will also mount items such as rags and set walls, which are usually supported by rope or sometimes cable.

The grips will now build a second set of catwalks or portable walkways that hang by chains underneath the perms and over the newly erected set. These tempo-rary walkways are called *green beds* because they are usually painted green. They hang above the set wall height and along the entire edge of the set. This portable scaffolding usually consists of walkways that are about 3 feet wide and about 10 feet long, although these can be longer or shorter, as well as narrower (about 2 feet wide). The green beds also have cross catwalks.

All the walkways are guarded by safety rails. Between the walkways are a series of heavy-duty lumber boards ranging from 2 × 8 feet and 2 × 12 feet to 4 × 4 feet and 4 × 8 feet. The space between the walkways is referred to as the "ozone." You never, no matter what the old salts may say, climb onto boards in the ozone area without wearing a full body harness and fall protection strap. The reason why you might have to climb over the safety rail and balance-walk the lumber in the ozone would be to install a "stick," or cross, from which to hang a lamp or set wall. This is one part of the grip job where you do not try to fake it until you make it. Be honest, and above all, be safe.

**T.O.T.**
*Never* walk in the ozone without a full body harness and fall protection strap.
Above all, be safe.

The *greens* (as we call the green beds for short) are also used for lighting, as
well as special effects or whatever items needs to be "flown," or hung, just above
the set. Because they are sometimes just about a foot above the set walls, they offer
a great vantage area for lighting or effects. The greens are sometimes braced to the
top of the set wall as well as from the perms. They are usually accessed from a ladder
mounted from the floor to the beds, and they are also accessed from the perms.

Sometimes a *backing* will be flown or hung from the beds. These scenes are
placed behind the set so it looks as though the movie is really being filmed at a given
location. These backings, which are also called *drops* and *translights* (translights are
huge slides, as for a projector), are also sometimes flown from the perms. They may
even be flown or hung from sailboats (long adjustable poles, raised like a mast on
a sailboat, that are welded to a very heavy base on wheels). These drops, backings,
or translights will be seen through the windows or doors of an interior set or behind
the edge of a building on an exterior set. They will add depth and dimension to the
film.

After all the green beds are built and the backings are hung, the lighting crew
will start to add lights. Grips work with the electricians and put up any hardware
(grip equipment, such as baby plates, set wall brackets, or whatever) that is needed
to support the lights. After the lights are secure, safe, tied, and pinpointed in the
proper direction, the grips will add the necessary gels (diffusion or color). The gobos
(flags, nets, silks, etc. for definition (see p. 56)) will also now be placed by the grips.
This process contributes to creating a feeling of reality that can be captured on film
or video.

## Call Sheet

In this section I will refer to an example of an empty call sheet (Figures 1.1
and 1.2). A call sheet, as the illustration shows, has all the information that the technicians and actors will need for the next day's work. I have numbered each item on
the call sheet that I feel should be explained. This sheet of paper is a very important item in the everyday life of a grip. When you learn to read it, you will see how
it aids you in preparing for your job.

### Front Side of Call Sheet

1. *Day of shooting:* For example, day 1 of 50 days
2. *Picture:* Name of the film or commercial
3. *Production no.:* Identification number for a film or commercial

**Front Side**

## UVA'S
## CALL SHEET

*1* DAY OF SHOOTING      W/A _5_

PICTURE _2_      PROD. No. _3_    DIRECTOR _4_

CREW CALL: _6_    SHOOTING CALL: _7_    DATE _8_ _8_

| SET DESCRIPTION: | SCENE NO: | CAST NO: | D/N: | PAGES: | LOCATION  – | PHONE NO: |
|---|---|---|---|---|---|---|
| _9_ | _10_ | _11_ | _12_ | _13_ | _14_ | |

| CAST AND BITS: | CHARACTER: | P/U ● | RPT TO ● | ON SET |
|---|---|---|---|---|
| _15_ | _16_ | _17_ | _18_ | _19_ |

| ATMOSPHERE AND STAND-INS: | COMMENTS | REPORT TO | ON SET |
|---|---|---|---|
| _20_ | _21_ | _22_ | _23_ |

| ADVANCE SCHEDULE: | SPECIAL INSTRUCTIONS: |
|---|---|
| _24_ | _25_. |

| _26_ | _27_ | _28_ |
|---|---|---|
| ASSISTANT DIRECTOR | UNIT MANAGER | APPROVED |

4. *Director:* Name of the director
5. Extra line for additional information
6. *Crew call:* The "call" or "call time" is the time to report to work; "set" describes whatever or wherever you are shooting (a stage or even a forest can be called a set—after all, it has been said that "all the world is a stage")
7. *Shooting call:* When the lights, camera, and actors should be ready to shoot
8. *Date*
9. *Set description:* Explanation of the shot (day or night, interior or exterior) and a brief summary of what action is to take place

## Back Side

W/A _____

PICTURES   PRODUCTION REQUIREMENTS  — PICTURE _____

DIRECTOR _____1____  PROD. No. _2_  CALL TIME _3_  DATE _4_

**Column headers:** CAMERA | Time | No. | MAKEUP | Time | No. | RESTAURANT | Time

### CAMERA (A)
- Camera Pkg.
- Other Cam. Pkg. (B)
- Cameraman
- Operator
- Extra Operator
- 1st Asst. Cam.
- Xtr 1st Asst. Cam.
- 2nd Asst. Cam.
- Xtr 2nd Asst. Cam.

### SPECIAL PHOTOGRAPHIC
- Cameraman - Process
- Matte Supervisor
- Port. Proj.
- Moviola
- 1/2/3 Head Proj.
- Projectionist
- Stereo Mach./Proj.

### TECHNICAL
- Key Grip
- Best Boy
- Dolly Grip
- Comp. Grip
- Dolly
- Greensman
- C.S.E.
- Painter
- Plumber
- Propmaker Constr.
- Special Effects Foreman
- Effects
- Single Dr. Rm.
- Mltple. Dr. Rm. No.
- Makeup Tables
- Wardrobe Racks for: No.
- Schoolroom for No.
- Tables & Benches for No.
- Heat Stage No.
- Heaters

### ELECTRICAL
- Chief Light Technician
- Best Boy
- Lamp Opers.
- Gen. Operator
- Wind Mach.
- Wind Mach. Oper.
- Local No. 40
- Batteries
- Camera Mechanic
- Air Conditioning
- Booster Lights
- Work Lights

### MAKEUP
- Makeup Artist
- Extra MU
- Extra MU
- Body MU
- Hairstylist
- Extra Hair
- Extra Hair

### WARDROBE
- Costumer
- Mens Wardrobe
- Ladies Wardrobe
- Extra Wardrobe

### SOUND
- Mixer
- Mikeman
- Cableman
- System
- Playback Mach./Oper.
- Batteries/Hookup
- Radio/Mic.
- Walkie Talkie
- Electric Megaphone
- Wigwag/Phone

### STILL
- Still Man/Still Equip.

### EDITORIAL
- Film Editor

### PROPERTY
- Property Master
- Asst. Prop Man
- Lead Man
- Swing Gang
- Draper
- AHA Representative
- Animal Handler
- Wranglers
- Live Stock/Animals

### PRODUCTION
- 1st Asst. Dir.
- 2nd Asst. Dir.
- 2nd 2nd Asst. Dir.
- Addit. 2nd A.D.
- D.G.A. Trainee
- Script Supervisor
- Prod. Coord.

### RESTAURANT
- From Commissary
- From Caterer
- Breakfast for:
- Lunches for:
- Dinners for:
- Gals. Coffee
- Doz. Donuts
- Tables & Chairs

### POLICE
- Flagmen
- Set Watchman
- Night Watchman
- Uniformed Police
- Studio Firemen

### HOSPITAL
- 1st Aid Man

### MUSIC
- Piano/Player
- Sync Man
- Sideline Musicians

### LOCATION
- Location Manager
- Police
- Fireman
- Permits

### TRANSPORTATION
- Trans. Coord.
- Trans. Capt.
- Sedan
- Station Wagon
- Mini Van
- Crew Cab
- Buses
- Pick-up Truck
- Picture Cars
- Prod. Van
- Honey Wagon
- Grip Trk/Trlr
- Prop Trk/Trlr
- Ward Trk/Trlr
- Sound Trk
- Elec. Trk/Trlr
- Generator Trk/Trlr
- Crane & Oper.
- Water Wagon
- Make Up Trlr.
- Greens Trk/Trlr
- Insert Car/Lights/Gen.
- Construction
- Special Effects
- Motor Homes
- Camera Truck

10. *Scene:* Numbered scene from the script (you can turn to this scene number in your script and know exactly the dialog and the action that should take place)
11. *Cast numbers:* Numbers assigned to cast members, from the lead person (usually #1) to whatever bit (smaller part) player is in the shoot, which allow everyone to see which character (actor/actress) is playing (acting) with another player (actor/actress)
12. *D/N:* Day or night

13. *Pages:* How many pages or eighths of a page will be shot for a certain scene (a script page is usually broken down into eighths of a page)
14. *Location and phone:* The street address and phone number of the place (location) where a film or part of a film will be shot
15. *Cast and bits:* The actors' and actresses' real names (and assigned numbers, as mentioned above); bits are bit parts of a usually small scene
16. *Character:* Character name from the script
17. *P/U or pickup:* The time at which an actor or actress is to be picked up from his or her hotel, if on location, or from his or her home if necessary (actors and actresses usually have very busy schedules and may need those extra few minutes while being driven to the set to study their parts)
18. *Report to MU (report to makeup):* Scheduled to allow the extra time it sometimes takes for makeup to be applied to an actor or actress.
19. *On set:* The time the actor/actress is to report to the set in costume, with makeup on, knowing their lines, ready to rehearse and then shoot
20. *Atmosphere and stand-ins:* Actors' doubles who will stand in for lighting the scene; extras or background people are the atmosphere
21. *Comments:* Pertains to transportation (what vehicles are due where at what time)
22. *Report to:* Where to go
23. *On set:* When to report to the set
24. *Advance schedule:* Tells the crew what to be prepared for on the next day's shoot
25. *Special instructions:* Alerts crew if special rigs, rain gags, mounts, and so on will be needed
26. *Assistant director:* Names of assistant directors
27. *Unit manager:* Name of unit manager
28. *Approved:* Signed by the unit production manager (UPM) or first assistant director (AD)

### Back Side of Call Sheet

1. Director
2. Producer
3. Call time
4. Date

Each department is categorized by a number (column marked "A") and time (column marked "B"). The number ("A") column is used to list the number of camera packages required, the camera operators required, and so on for that one day of shooting (for example, there might be an action stunt requiring as many as six cameras, camera operators, grips, etc.). The time ("B") column indicates the time the crew is to report to the set. This column may show the time when only one person is due on the set or when many people are due at the set at the same time or at different times. For example, a camera package due time may be 7:00 a.m., and the first assistant camera operator due time may also be 7:00 a.m., but the rest of the crew may not be needed for half an hour so the grip department due time may be 7:30 a.m. Get the picture?

## Warehouse Stages

With the rental cost of stages on the rise, a lot of productions are turning to warehouses as stages. This is a very economical way to make a film, yet keep the cost down. This is also where you, as a grip, really have to put in an extra effort. The warehouse stage will probably not have a high enough or strong enough ceiling to support a catwalk or perm system for lighting from above, so you will usually have to build and suspend a pipe grid system from the roof. You must be aware of the strength rating (sometimes referred to as the *snow load* in cold climates) for the truss supporting the roof. If you suspend too much weight from the rafters, you can and will cause damage.

Problems also arise in the area of tying off ropes, such as for hanging a light. You will have to find a place to nail a wall cleat. Look for wood vertical support beams or wall rings. If there is no place to nail into, you may have to use a large pipe face C-clamp and bite onto a metal vertical support pole. I recommend using a pipe face and cranking (tightening) it down, as you do not want anything falling due to slippage. I will usually use two pipe face C-clamps per pole in order to create a safety. If no tie-off is available, you can use a huge number of sandbags. Use enough sandbags to ensure that the weight on the other end of the rope will not move. If it is not 100% safe, don't do it.

> **T.O.T.**
> If you have to decide whether something is safe or not, it is *not* safe. There should NEVER be any doubt about safety. I cannot emphasize this enough.

## How It Goes on the Set

The day has now begun. The lights are all set, and the flags, nets, or silks have been adjusted or tweaked. The actors will now come to the set and rehearse, first for themselves, as well as for the director and the director of photography. At that point, a director may not like what he or she has seen and may order a complete change of script, a new mood for the scene, and different lighting. What I am trying to emphasize here is that things change.

When things change, and they often do, you may even hear some crew members grumble and say, "Why do we have to move everything again?" The reason is very simple: It's our job! As I always say, "Hey, it's their football, so we play by their rules." Translation: Film making is a work in progress. That's what makes it an art form. There are many ways to achieve the end goal, and we are hired to help do that. We collaborate with others to make this happen.

Okay, now let's assume that nothing really has to be moved, and just a little more tweaking is necessary. There, we are set. The grips will once again come into play during a film take (filming the action). A highly skilled dolly grip will move the camera at the exact times necessary during the filming on a camera dolly (a smart cart of sorts that travels fore, aft, and sideways as well as in a circular motion). All the pushing power is supplied by the dolly grip. The dolly grip must also anticipate the actors' moves and know the film's dialogue. These cues will prompt certain actions, such as arming (lifting of the center post with hydraulic air pressure) as the cameraperson and camera raise up to a high-angle shot while pushing the dolly so it will end up in the right spot at a given time. (This is an art form in itself.) A huge team effort is now in play. Meanwhile, an entire additional group of grips and electricians might be prelighting another set (placing more equipment in place to expedite the next filming to be done), which may be used for shooting later in the day or the next day.

> **T.O.T.**
> 1. All direction references are made from the perspective of what the camera sees.
> 2. *Camera right is* to the camera's right side as if you are looking through the eyepiece.
> 3. *Camera left* is to the camera's left side as if you are looking through the eyepiece.

When you're working on a set for the first time, you will hear many terms that you may not know. I will clue you in to some of these throughout this book. Even though they do not directly pertain to the grip department, these terms do pertain to the project or film that you are working on. When you hear these terms, you will know what to do. For example, when the camera assistant calls out "Hair in the gate!" that means the grip department should not move anything. The phrase "hair in the gate" means that there was a small chip of film or debris caught in the corner of the camera gate (also called the pressure plate, which holds the film flat as it moves through the camera), possibly causing a small scratch. (We have all watched old movies with white lines or little wiggly things passing through.) A "hair in the gate" means we have to reshoot the last take.

If you are working on a set and the director of photography (DP) says, "Drop a double into that lamp," quickly look both ways for an electrician. If one is not close by, drop it in, then tell the gaffer or the first electrician that a double has been dropped into the light. This will inform the gaffer that the light value has been reduced and ensure that they get another light reading before shooting begins.

### What to Expect

A lot of times you are in a hurry to get a piece of equipment the boss has called for. You race from the set and run smack dab into several people who seem to be just standing around. You may find it difficult to get to the equipment with a lot of people in the way and to return to the set as quickly as you want. Let me tell you right now that this will happen a lot; just roll with it. If you find this sort of situation to be a big problem, though, you have a couple of choices. The first one is to work your way through the throng by channeling Bugs Bunny and repeating "Excuse me, pardon me, excuse me" and then on the return trip politely urging the crowd to "watch your eyes" (as if that were possible). I personally say "knee caps and ankles!" when I am carrying C-stands so people will look down. The second alternative is not to take up this line of work.

Other obstacles you will find in your way include:

* People standing in the only doorway
* People sitting on stairs blocking your access
* People sitting on the ice chest full of cold drinks on a hot day

What I'm trying to convey is don't get mad, and don't get even. Be polite—and get the *callback!*

### Pace on the Set

You will also notice that it seems to take a little more time to do things at the beginning of a workday, but as the daylight starts to drop off you work like crazy. As one director I work for said, "It's like shooting *Gone with the Wind* in the morning and the TV series *Happy Days* in the afternoon."

### What Key Grips Like

I have spoken to several other key grips to research this grip handbook, and almost all of them stated that they wanted a newbie to be a person who is seen and not heard unless spoken to or there is a safety issue. A lot of key grips will readily take the suggestions of a newbie, and they may even ask for suggestions, but be sure your timing is good and that you know what you're talking about. Sometimes you may just have to stay quiet until you get your chance to speak up. No one likes to be upstaged, including you. I'm not saying you should not suggest anything, but try to phrase it correctly. You might try something like, "Hey, boss (key grips love to be called boss), do you think it would work this way?" Every person loves the help now and then, but few like a know-it-all, especially if you are new. (It's sort of like driving a different car and you have to get the feel of the gas pedal.) Like most things in life, practice, practice, practice. Trust me, when you're the new person on anything, you will probably be asked to follow and fetch. I know it sounds cold, but this is the reality. After all, they don't let a brand new doctor, just out of school, do brain surgery. (Thank goodness gripping isn't brain surgery.)

**T.O.T.**
Looking good in this business is almost as important as being good. I am not saying you have to dress like a model in *GQ*, but I am saying you must be neat and clean (without any holes in your clothes) if you want to get a start. Who would you give a break to first, if the choice were between two people you didn't know? A clean-clothed, intelligent-looking person or a slob? You choose! You don't have to have a short G.I. haircut or spit-shined shoes, but give yourself a chance. You need every advantage over the next person applying for the job. Get in, get the job, and prove yourself—then let your hair grow.

Now, back to other ways of getting that job. Check to see if any motion picture and television studio equipment rental companies are in your area. You see, all the equipment used by a movie studio or television company may not be owned by them. They sometimes rent their equipment from different vendors. So check it out. Another way to learn how to be a grip is to check out the television stations in your area. They do not always call their workers grips; they usually call them *stage hands* or *stage managers*. Then there are the local playhouses that might need an intern. Remember, folks, you have got to learn how to walk the walk and talk the talk. Get around the entertainment industry and get a feel for it. You will know when you know. It's sort of like that first day at a new job or when you move to a new place. At first it is all so strange; then, slowly, quietly, it somehow changes and you are the old salt. This business is just the same.

Now, this last bit of advice is only for the really, really, really determined people who will do just about anything to get into this business. *All others may skip this advice!* Say that there is not a film commission in the area where you live. Does Hollywood know your city as well as you do? Possibly not. So, start your own film commission for your area. Sure, you should check with the city fathers and mothers. Get any necessary permits. Then call your state film commission and tell them who you are and what you are doing and how they can get in touch with you. As I have been trying to tell you, if it were easy anyone could do it.

All the same, I truly wish you the best of luck. (You will find that the harder you work, the luckier you will be. It just seems to happen that way.)

## Warning/Disclaimer

This book was written to provide pictorial information only on the subject matter that is covered. It has not been written or is to be sold to give legal or professional service. If you need a legal expert for assistance, then one should be sought. Also, before you try to grip, find an experienced grip who is well qualified to train you properly. *This book is a great aid, but it is in no way the final word on this subject.*

This book does not reprint all the information that is available to the publisher and author. It has been written to complement and/or supplement other texts. This book is intended as a guide to help the reader identify a piece of equipment by sight and by the manufacturer's proper name. It was written to be as complete as possible in that regard, without attempting to train the reader to do this sort of work. I take responsibility for any mistakes, whether they are typographical or substantive.

This book is intended to be used as a pictorial reference only. The authors and the publisher will not accept any liability for damage caused by this book. It is *highly recommended* that the reader work with a *highly skilled, highly trained* motion picture film technician *first*. The sole purpose of this book is to entertain and educate. As they say on television: "Kids, don't try this at home." Buying this book will not make you a grip. It merely shows you the tools of the trade, not how to use them. Work only with a trained professional.

Remember, safety first and foremost.

Safety is the number one concern of all persons who work on a movie set.

Take it personal!

Make it personal!

Thanks! And, once again, *good luck.*

# The Big Break
# (Strictly for the Brand New Grip!)

## by Ron Dexter

MIKE'S NOTE: Ron Dexter has been a camera operator/DP/Director since 1962. He is a member of the National Association of Broadcast Employees and Technicians Election Board, a union negotiator, a director of television commercials (since 1972), a member of the Directors Guild of America, and the owner of a television commercial production company (since 1977). He is also an equipment designer, mechanic, and teacher. His short commercials have aired in 20 foreign countries and 35 U.S. states. Ron inherited his business philosophy from his dad: "He said to give people more than they bargained for, and they will be so relieved about not being robbed that they will gladly pay the bill and not question it the next time." I have had the pleasure of working for this acclaimed director–cameraman since the very start of my career. Consider this master's words of advice to be almost gospel. He truly knows the complete ins and outs of the commercial studio business. It gives me great pleasure to pass on some of his knowledge. Let me introduce director Ron Dexter, a cameraman, inventor, and real Yoda of knowledge: *"May his force be with you."*

Most people prepare and wait for the chance to move up the ladder. Often that next chance is just a trial step to see whether you are ready. That chance usually is given when the opportunity-giver believes you are almost ready, not when *you* think that you are ready. In the following pages, I will offer a little advice on how to be a professional on the job. This should serve to help you get ready to move up the ladder in your field.

Your talk about moving up may be taken as normal ambition or a swelled head. Once you've been given a chance, don't assume too soon that you have made it. You may have to step back down to your old job for a little longer because you are not quite ready or just because there is no need for you in that new position at the moment. Breaks are often given on less demanding jobs so you will have a better chance of succeeding.

Too often a break goes to one's head. You cannot become an old pro in just a few weeks. Knowing the mechanical skills of a job is only part of the job. Every advancement requires additional communication skills. This is where people often have trouble when they advance to the next level. Sometimes both the mechanical and personal skills suffer for a while. Running a crew is a skill that takes time to learn. How you give orders is very important. The following pages will offer advice on how to be a good boss when you have advanced to a leadership position.

It is wise to take on smaller challenges first before tackling the big ones. Getting the best help is also wise, as is asking for help from a more seasoned crew. Often the opportunity for the next step up the ladder comes not from the boss for whom you have tried to make a good showing but from a coworker who has noticed your honest effort and hard work. A recommendation from a coworker who has credibility is worth more than the observations of bosses who do not have time to notice much about the working situation.

The following sections cover set etiquette, good and bad bosses, equipment, and health on the set, and also offer some professional advice, reflection, and sources of further information.

## Set Etiquette

Most people in the entertainment business at one time or another have a problem with set etiquette. For a newcomer on a set it is like being dumped in a foreign country. The language alone is a struggle. People moving up the ladder experience problems, and even old-timers can lose their bearings. The rules are often different than from those in the real world, and the glamour factor can distort one's views.

The following is a compilation of issues raised by various professionals in the industry. These are not elaborate theories but observations and opinions gleaned from many years of working in the business. Things are done differently on different sizes and types of shoots. Without a carefully defined structure, a large shoot would be absolute chaos. On small shoots, departmental lines can become blurred, but certain rules of etiquette still apply. Newcomers should keep all the rules in mind until they are sure which ones apply. Here are a dozen universal rules for any set:

1. Show up a bit early for the call.
2. Be polite. Say "please" and "thanks."
3. Let people do their job.
4. Be humble.
5. Ask questions about assignments if in doubt.
6. Watch what's going on in *your* department.
7. Make your superior look good.
8. Don't embarrass anyone.
9. Don't be a "hero."
10. Listen very carefully before you leap.
11. Learn and use coworkers' names.
12. Work hard and willingly.

The following elaborates on some of these areas in more detail.

### Call Time

*Call time* means the time to go to work or be ready to travel. It is not the time to pour a cup of coffee and catch up on the gossip. If you want to socialize, come a bit early and enjoy the coffee and donuts that are usually there.

### New On the Set

If you are new on a job or production, it is best to let your knowledge be discovered *slowly as you work with people.* They will be more impressed if you do not try to show them everything you know right away. Some outspoken people really do know a lot, but it is the big mouths that make the truly knowledgeable ones suspect. For every outspoken knowledgeable worker, there are ten who are full of baloney.

### Offering Expert Advice

If you have experience in a special skill, offering advice can be tricky, especially if you are new on a set. Humbly offer your advice to your immediate superior and let him offer it to the group so it will more likely be heeded. If he gives you credit, good. If he takes the credit, he will remember that you made him look good. Try (*very softly*), "I worked construction for a few years and, well, you know, it might work here."

### Offering a Hand

When should you offer to give workers outside your department a hand? When it does not threaten their job and your helping will not do more damage than good. Helping someone carry equipment cases is often allowed *if permission is given.* Spilling or dropping things is *not* help that is appreciated nor, usually, is setting a flag for a grip. A camera assistant who builds a good relationship with the grips may be allowed to adjust a flag as the sun moves *if* the grips know the camera assistant is not trying to make them look bad or eliminate their jobs and *if* the assistant knows what he or she is doing. Getting a feel for what is appreciated and what is not is the key. Do not assume that people want help, and respect their refusal when they don't. Maybe they just do not have the time to explain how to do it right just then.

### Can We Help?

Our business is not an exact science, and there are often many ways to do things. A wise boss will listen, but some bosses (especially directors) are not secure enough to solicit help when they should. They are afraid to look dumb and can blunder ahead trying to be "the director." Crews have to be careful how they offer help. Asking "What are you trying to do and can we help?" sometimes breaks the ice and opens up a dialogue when things have stalled, but sometimes even that is taken as doubting the director's ability.

### Don't Be a Hero

For every mistake a "hero" discovers there is someone who made that mistake. Don't let that person be blamed publicly. If you see something that appears to you to be a mistake, say something quietly and humbly to your immediate superior. "This may sound stupid, but is the word 'stupid' on that sign spelled wrong?" Let your boss go to her boss so she can quietly say something to the next person up the ladder. The sign might be out of frame or be so small that it won't make any difference, or it may have already been decided that it is really okay. If you run out and yell something, trying to be a "hero," you are taking a big risk. The person at fault will remember for a long time the public embarrassment created by the young "hero" on the set. The worst thing would be to go over your immediate boss' head to the director, assistant director (AD), or a different department. You won't hear, "Who is that smart kid?"

### Titles

People are often very concerned about their job titles. A title is an objective measure of success. Respect people's titles. People who are the most secure with what they are doing usually couldn't care less about their titles. For others who may be less secure, it costs you nothing to call a prop person a prop master, if that's what that person prefers. Take a cue from what people call themselves. You may give coworkers a boost by using a title when introducing them, even if they don't seem to care about their title. Here are some examples:

| Rather Than | Use |
|---|---|
| Cameraperson | Cinematographer |
| Prop person | Prop master |
| Gaffer | Lighting director |
| Script clerk | Script supervisor |
| Wardrobe | Stylist |
| Someone's friend | Associate producer |

### Always Out of Line for Crews

- Inappropriate sexual jokes and talk around women; political, religious, or racial jokes and slurs
- Having such a good time at night on location that safety and performance are compromised the next day
- Alcohol or drug abuse

- Negative criticism of anything or anybody within the hearing of clients, producers, visitors, cast, and locals (keep your opinions to yourself)
- Bad mouthing other production companies, equipment houses, and crews
- Loud talking on the set
- Radical wardrobe on location (make your personal statements in your own neighborhood)
- Accepting conflicting jobs in the hope that you will somehow work it out
- Replacing yourself on a job without warning
- Not saying anything when you see a dangerous situation evolving

Even if people are dumb enough to take unnecessary risks, if you see danger evolving, you are morally obligated to say something. People often rely on others as a measure of how safe something is. Your concern may make people think twice. In our business, there are many ways to make things look exciting that are not as dangerous.

### Wrap Time

Wrap time means just what it says. Wrap it up. It is not time to break out the beer and slow down. Although beer is a nice touch, alcohol or drug use invalidates most company insurance policies on the set and on the way home.

---

## Being a Professional Crew Member
### An Eager Attitude

Acting eager to work not only is a sign that someone is fresh out of film school but also says that work is a two-way deal. Eagerness shows that one is willing to make an effort for a good day's pay. Sometimes old-timers think it's not cool to look eager, but it really makes a difference when a crew seems eager: "What can we do for you?" "Yes sir!" "We're on it!" "You got it!" Eagerness is a key factor in getting a call-back from a production company. The following two sections give you more tips on what to do to get hired again—and what not to do.

### How to Get Hired Again

- Show up early for the call and ready to work.
- Give 110% effort.
- Be honest and straightforward.
- Assume that people are honest and good until they prove otherwise to you. (You may have heard only one side of derogatory gossip.)
- Cheerfully help others if asked.
- Cover your immediate superior's interests.

### *How Not to Get Hired Again*

- Demanding Hertz rental rates for your 10-year-old car
- Demanding full equipment rental rates for your sideline rentals (negotiate and ask "what's fair")
- Putting more on your time card than the rest of the crew without approval
- Increasing your rate after you are booked (don't say, "By the way, my new rate is . . ." during the job)
- Obviously having just come off another job at call time
- Spending too much time on the phone
- Not observing what's going on in your department
- Talking too loudly
- Fraternizing above or out of your category

### *Personality Problems*

We are never the cause of unpleasant events on the job. It is always the other guy who has "personality problems." In most disagreements, both parties are usually right to some extent. Usually the "rightness" or "wrongness" has little to do with the job and a lot to do with our egos.

Winning an argument can lead to losing the war. If two people who do not get along have to be kept separate, one or both will lose work. If one of them has anything to do with hiring, it can be a disaster for the other.

Don't risk your future over making a personal statement. Tempers cool off when a job is over and pressures are gone. Then it is wise to be humble and apologize even if you are sure that you were right. Sometimes two people will fall all over each other claiming who was more at fault.

Good friends will not blindly support everything that we do. They should whisper in our ear that maybe, possibly, we are out of line. Advice on the spot in the heat of anger is sure to be rejected. If you see a coworker who is losing perspective, think about it a bit and even write down what you think. Making it clear on paper may make it more understandable. Even if you do not show your coworker the paper, look at it at after the job to see if you still agree with your observation. If it still seems appropriate, you may show it to the other person or talk about it.

Approach any discussion about behavior with caution. *Listen first.* You will be much more able to tailor your questions or comments to what the person already feels. Often, just that person's telling you about something, with a few questions from you, will help them understand a problem.

Sometimes we all have personal problems that are difficult to leave at home. Both production and fellow crew members should take this into consideration. There is an intimate relationship between work and personal life. If someone is unhappy on the job it is difficult not to take it home and *vice versa*.

### Résumés

Unfortunately, some people exaggerate their experience on their résumés. That makes all résumés suspect. Personally, I throw most of them away. Most of my hiring is based on personal recommendations. It is much easier to bring in a person known by at least part of the crew. Most of my crews are hired by the department keys and the rest by the AD, producer, or coordinator.

### Peer Evaluation

Many jobs come from recommendations from established crew members. They know when someone is ready to move up. They also know when a certain project is over someone's head and when someone else with a bit more experience is needed.

### The Answering Machine

People often do not want callers to know whom they have reached on an answering machine, and a cryptic or incomplete message greets the caller. For friends who recognize the voice, it can be entertaining. But, for the stranger who wants to leave an important message, it creates distress. Is that the person I'm trying to reach? Was that the right number? Should I look for another number? Is he or she in town? Will he or she show up on the set at call time? Is that a nickname? Is that his or her child, spouse, or dog? Try this instead: "You have reached 123–4567. This is William, known as Will. I will return your call if you leave your name and number. If you need me immediately, page me at 234–5678. Please leave your phone number after the machine beeps. Thank you!" (Or, "I am out of town for work until the 16th. Call 456–7890 for my availability. Thanks.")

### Company Vehicles

Being professional also includes how you treat production vehicles (by the way, these hints apply to any vehicle, even your own):

- Don't abuse a company or rental vehicle just because it is not yours.
- If you hear strange sounds, find out what they are. Occasionally, turn the radio down so you can listen for knocks and grinds.
- Don't drive a vehicle until it dies. If you suspect a problem, tell someone in production or transportation so things can be fixed. If you are on the road, stop and get it checked. Call production immediately.
- When you get gas, check the oil and radiator fluid (engines die for the lack of either one). Check the tires for proper inflation.
- If the radiator requires a lot of water, check the antifreeze mixture (engines rust up with too little antifreeze). Let someone know.
- Watch the gauges and warning lights.

- If a vehicle steers strangely and shimmies, drive below the shimmy speed and tell production or transportation about it.
- Don't trash a good vehicle with props and equipment. Protect the floor, roof, and upholstery.
- If a vehicle just clicks when you try to start it, check or have someone else check the battery cables. Push or jump start only if you know what you are doing.
- Lock up the vehicle when you are not in it.
- Remove props, tools, and equipment from the vehicle at night if your driveway, street, or parking garage is not perfectly safe. Stolen articles can mean disaster at the next day's shoot.

### Examples of Bad Bosses

- Starts making improvements in someone's work as soon as she starts reading it.
- Their improvements will ensure that they take credit for saving the project.
- Their contributions must look good in the eyes of their superiors no matter what the effect on the project was.
- Any mistakes have to be covered up to avoid embarrassment, even if the results hurt a project.
- They don't give examples of what they want, and they avoid commitments by saying they will know when it is right when they see it.
- They never show up on time to a meeting of subordinates. They must always appear to be busy to justify their position.
- They schedule extra inconvenient meetings to make their staffs work harder.
- They are never available to approve works in progress that might save people some work.
- They never inform others about possible problems.
- They save problems as ammunition for criticizing their crews.
- They never blame outsiders for problems. By saying, "You should know better," they keep the blame at home.
- They never give praise, raises, or titles, for doing so would build too much confidence.
- They use the threat of firing to keep people in line.

### My, My, My

A "my crew," "my set," "my shoot" attitude by a production manager or production coordinator rubs most people the wrong way. Along with the "my crew" attitude is often an attitude that future jobs are dependent on making that production person happy: "Do things *my* way, treat *me* right, and I will see that you work in this town again." First of all, people are very uncomfortable working under such conditions. Directors, producers, directors of photography (DPs), key grips, and gaffers, can call their crews "my crew," but not the assistant director (AD) or production coordinator who only puts out the work calls. The crew is usually selected by the director, DP, and others. The coordinator is just making the calls.

Often accompanying this me–my–I attitude is never admitting to a mistake. A scapegoat for any mistake must be found and admonished—often with a job security threat: "If you want to work for me, you must make me look good in the boss's eyes." On the other hand, DPs or department heads may talk affectionately about "my crew." They are saying, "You had better take care of them," "Don't abuse them," and "Talk to me before you try to take advantage of them."

If people congratulate you for doing a good job, give your crew credit for making it possible. Credit every good idea and effort so people hear it. It costs nothing.

## Being a Good Communicator

Let's say a director has very carefully researched and planned how to do something mechanical. Instead of telling the crew exactly what to do, he might start with, "I'm sure that you have a better way of doing this, but I had to plan this before you were on the job," or "I didn't get a chance to ask you about this. Let's get through it and see if my idea will work at all." You can reduce their resistance to your offering expert information by being humble. Even if your way is best, a crew may be able to add shortcuts and ensure safety. Do listen and let them do their job.

Be sure to listen to and communicate clearly with runners and assistants as well. Confirm that they understand your instructions. Instruct them to call back if there are problems finding something or if things cost much more than expected. Sometimes limited availability will require finding substitutes, and often suppliers can offer better solutions. Tell runners and assistants to call in as things change. Take the time to explain what you want so the runner has some idea of whether something will work, but warn runners not to make major changes unless they call first. Giving a priority to items can help. Simple things may seem insignificant, but they could be crucial for the first shot. Ask for forgiveness if you have to repeat things or explain things that your crew or assistants may already know.

## Teachers and Students

This last point is worth elaborating. Like almost every seasoned person in the business, I am happy and feel obligated to pass on what I know to the younger generation. When there is time I like to explain not only how to do something but also the principles behind how it is done. Unfortunately, sometimes people are insulted when they are told something they already know. Perhaps I forgot that I told them the same thing before, or I have no way of knowing what they already know. My intent is to pass along useful information. Prefacing information with "You probably already know . . ." will help avoid any suggestion of insult. I start a job with a new crew with "Forgive me if I repeat myself or tell you things that you already know."

On the other hand, I never expect people to know more than what I know they should know. Asking me how to do something or how to approach a problem or situation only makes me, the teacher, feel better in passing along my infinite wisdom. I am never bothered by being asked again how to do something even if I have already explained it before. On the other hand, if someone does not ask the second time and does something wrong, I am perturbed. I know that people cannot absorb all the information that is thrown at them. When things are not understood, I give people the benefit of the doubt and assume that I was the one who failed to make myself clear.

There is so much to learn about our business that few on-the-job situations can teach us all that we have to know. One has to eat, sleep, and live the film business to keep ahead of the competition. The grip must learn mechanics; the electrician, the theory of light; the camera operator, photography—and they know how to operate all of the equipment besides. Our business always has someone waiting in the wings for us to falter if we do not keep up with the times. When we feel secure that we have it made is when the competition catches up.

## Being Professional When You're Boss
### The Morning of the Shoot

- Arrive *before* call time and assist the AD or transportation captain in placing the grips' electrical generator far enough from the location yet close enough not to impede a fast setup and departure.
- Bring a shot list and confer with the AD to check if there have been any last-minute changes.
- Inform the best boy what equipment will be needed first and any additional equipment that may be needed later. Try to get a jump on the next shot.
- Key grips should have their ears keenly tuned to at least three voices: the director, the director of photography, and the first assistant director. This minor eavesdropping will allow the key grip to keep abreast of this trio's desires and of changes as they occur during the course of the shoot.

### Always In Line for Production

- Uniform deals for the whole crew
- Paying per diems promptly
- Paying for a wrap dinner
- Prompt equipment rental checks
- Keeping crews informed about job scheduling

### Always Out of Line for Production

- Booking crews when a job is not yet firm
- Not sharing cancelation fees with canceled crews
- Holding checks or time cards

## Filling Out the Time Card

*"Don't ever hire Fred again!" "Why?" "He pads his time card."*

What really happened: The crew went into meal penalty by 420 minutes. The production manager went to three "almost staff" people and asked them to waive meal penalty. This means that the crew did not stop filming to eat on time. Usually, six hours after call time, they are paid a penalty for the time that they did not eat until the meal is called to break. With that concession the manager went to the rest of the crew with "everyone is waiving meal penalty" and got concessions from everybody but Fred, who was in the darkroom. Fred feels that rules are rules; he was the only one who put in for meal penalty, and he was blackballed for it.

Yes, this happens too often. If the rules of filling out time cards are being bent in any way, it has to be a group effort so no one has hours that are different from the rest. Production will use all kinds of reasons to keep the hours down. If the department works as a group, talk to the contact with the producer to reach a fair settlement. Fewer problems will arise.

Some producers have no idea how many extra hours camera assistants, prop persons, and production assistants (PAs) put in. (That's why PAs with no clout often have to work for a flat rate.) Warning your contact with production ahead of time that there will be extra hours on a given day will take the burden off your back. If you do not clear putting in extra hours, it might be wise to "eat" some of those extra hours.

For example, let's say you find out that a turnaround is necessary to complete a job for tomorrow's shoot. You had best get permission to do so. Production may decide that putting on another person to finish the job might also solve the problem. You should have some idea of how long it should take to do a job.

Turnaround is not a device to pad your time card; instead, it is a device to prevent producers from working people so long that it becomes dangerous. You need your sleep. It is your responsibility to get enough rest and to plan your work to avoid too many hours.

## Crew Issues to Address

The following is a list of things to think about on a film set for the crew members:

- Film students and relatives on the set—always ask first
- Renting every new toy to try it out—don't
- Old pros who ration their own efforts, teaching younger people not to hustle and thus making everyone look bad (there is a balance between abuse by management and featherbedding by crews)
- Who is responsible for safety? (Everybody)
- Turnaround, meal penalty, overtime, kit rentals, travel pay
- Flat rates
- Key grips picking seconds (best boys), including producers, coordinators, PAs (be sure they are qualified)

- Loyalty ("You paid me peanuts when you didn't have money. Now that you have a big budget you are hiring all expensive professionals.")
- Crews who test new directors and DPs
- Crews who always want more help
- Unqualified assistants hired by production
- Seeing that the director or DP could do things differently to make it easier
- Crew invited to dailies
- Knowing the time and place for appropriate conversations (such as a PA who is asked about his aspirations by a director whom he is driving home one night and is ignored the rest of the shoot; he or she may harbor ill feelings) and remembering that loose lips sink ships—maybe yours
- Definitions of terms such as call time, wrap, kit rental, booking a job, replacing yourself, flat rate, union, P and W, OT, turnaround, and meal penalty (a new person on the set needs to know these terms; see the Glossary)
- "All producers care about is money."
- "We'll take care of you next time."

### From Other Departments

Check with all departments that may appear to need support from the grip department.

---

### Location Etiquette—Getting Along with Locals

Whether you are the leader of a crew or working on the crew, do not think that just because you are in the television or movie business you are something special. To a local person, you may be a once-in-a-lifetime opportunity for fame or an emissary from hell. Your success on a location—and the success of future crews on that location—depends on your behavior. Everywhere you go you are treading on someone's turf. Tread lightly. The locals' opinions of you will determine how cooperative they will be. The first impression is often the most important.

The first contact should be made by the crew member who is the most diplomatic person and who has the most in common with the people who live in the area. Say, "Hello, how are you? You might be able to help us. We are trying to find out who owns . . ." Don't say, "We're here from Hollywood and we're going to . . ." They may see Hollywood, television, movies, and big cities as the reasons why their children are tempted by drugs and sin. Or, you might be the first convenient person to vent anger upon about something that you have nothing to do with. To a shop-keeper, you could be either a potential customer or a shoplifter. Clothes appropriate to the area make you stand out less.

Start any conversation with a perturbed local with, "I'm sorry, let me get these people out of your way." Don't say, "We'll be a minute . . ." Being there legally or having permission from a higher authority may not carry a lot of weight locally. The local residents may have a battle going on with that same higher authority.

Drivers should park out of people's driveways and parking spaces. Get permission. Do not block traffic. When it is time to leave, get directions to the next location, get oriented, and be ready to roll.

Treat motels and lodgings with respect. Use heating, cooling, and lights as needed. Do not take towels for your own or company needs. Close the door and turn off the lights when you leave. Be quiet, especially early and late. Park in stalls. Keep a low profile with the camera gear. Word gets around a small town about your behavior.

An obvious effort to protect people's property will soften the blow when the unavoidable damage does occur. Make a vocal effort to remind your crew to be careful. Cover floors, and ask people whose homes or businesses you are using to put away their valuables. Your crew is probably very honest, but bystanders may not be.

## Some Thoughts on Equipment
### Crews and Their Own Equipment

Buying equipment to supplement your income can be wise, but do not assume that it will help you get work. Would your employers be glad to rent from you *and* would you then become competition to your own regular suppliers? If a camera assistant buys filters and batteries to rent, she is cutting into one of the moneymakers for the camera rental house. Rental houses lose money on camera body rentals but make it up on accessories such as batteries and filters. You might jeopardize your own standing with the rental houses.

It is tough deciding how to charge for equipment that you happen to bring along to the job. If something is requested, a rental price should be agreed upon. If you happened to bring along something that saved the day, be careful about how to collect for it. Some producers are fair and some are not, no matter how much time and money you might have just saved them. Sometimes your future job may be at risk. It could be assumed that because you are not in the rental equipment business, what you bring along might be regular tools of the trade.

Asking for a little something is better than demanding it. First save the day, then humbly ask for compensation. Try, "What's fair?" I know, production rarely scrimps on their own comforts. But, it is your job to make a good film and their job to save money. In collecting for your equipment, don't "nickel and dime." Let people feel they are getting a bargain: "Give me regular rates for X and Y and I will throw in Z." "As used" deals (where an employee gets paid for equipment only if it is used) are generally welcome, if you can live with them.

Remember that your garage operation is in competition with the established businesses that have more overhead to support (insurance, rent, employees, etc.). In short, be cautious with your sideline business. Do not let it interfere with your job, which is your major source of income. It is better to give something away than to lose work. If your toys make you a better technician, they are worth the cost even if you do not make a lot on them.

Your job performance should in no way be compromised by your equipment rentals. You should deliver your equipment as any other rental house would do and not get paid to deliver it. You cannot spend all your time on the set just watching out for your equipment. It is there just like anyone else's stuff. Everyone's equipment should be taken care of. If you show concern for everyone's equipment, then others are more likely to respect yours, too.

Do not bother a company about equipment checks. Many rental companies have to wait for money, as do producers of commercials.

## The Professional Look

There is a good reason to use professional-looking tools and equipment—to protect yourself if things go wrong. If you have the accepted standard equipment, you can always blame the equipment. If your equipment looks homemade, problems can become your fault for not ordering the right thing. Although saving the day with a tool jury-rigged on the set can be heroic, bringing those same tools to the set can look unprofessional. I have watched crews with chrome-plated tools in fancy cases make expensive mistakes and then charge the client an arm and a leg with a smile. I have also seen some bare-bones riggers do wonders with surplus junk for peanuts and then watched them have to argue over a few real extra dollars after saving the client thousands. Yes, the impression is important. A coat of paint and some painted boxes might be a good compromise. Your knowing how to make your rigs work will cover for some lack of flash, but do consider the impression. People are impressed by fancy-looking equipment even if it does not work very well.

## Health on the Set

To survive in a world full of germs and viruses we have to build an immunity to them. If we were raised in a sterile environment, we would die from contact with the first germ. Less sanitized societies have a stronger resistance to germs. Our over-purified food and water may even increase our susceptibility to sickness. We are a society obsessed by cleanliness, but with the spread of new powerful diseases people's concerns about their health should be everyone's concern. Cleanliness on the set should be maintained at a level at which even the most fastidious will feel comfortable.

### Soft Drinks

All actors should have their own bottles for soft drink casting. During the shoot with the *hero* bottle or glass (the bottle or glass to be filmed), each actor's bottle or glass should be refilled or washed in a sanitary washing system. Restaurant supply houses sell disinfectant washes.

### Coffee

Steaming coffee is always a problem. Liquid hot enough to steam is too hot to drink. A–B smoke (simulated smoke made with two chemicals by a special effects team) is pretty strong to sniff. One solution is to add steam to the film or video in postproduction, which is not difficult nowadays.

### Kissing

How do you cast and shoot a close-up toothpaste commercial? Check with SAG (the Screen Actors Guild) for rules about kissing, and do not push actors to do something they are not comfortable with.

### Cold and Flu

Infecting fellow crew members is somewhere between careless and criminal. In Japan, people wear masks when they have a cold. It is a badge of concern for even a stranger's health. We have magic medicines to hide cold symptoms, but we are no less infectious. Keep your distance if you have a bug or think you might be getting one. Some say that colds are more infectious when you first get them. Many people find that vitamin C helps prevent colds but does not do much after you have one. Do keep warm.

### Smoke Masks

There is much debate about created fog or special-effect smoke. If masks are used, everyone should be provided one if they so request. Problems arise when one grip has a Darth Vader-type, industrial-strength mask and makes a big deal about health risks. It looks like everyone else is less well protected. We have been told so much about health safety problems by production that it is difficult to draw a clear line on what smoke is safe and how much. Some crew members are more fatalistic about their safety and ignore the concerns of the more sensitive.

### Spray Paints

The smell of spray paints is strong, and efforts should be taken to protect cast and crew from having to breathe it. Outside, with a little breeze, an actor can simply hold her breath if only a little dulling is necessary. *Ask* whether the spray paint is okay. Do not *tell* the actor or actress that it is okay.

### Camera Eyepiece

We can catch infections through the eyes. Some people have very sensitive eyes. Assistants should be protective of the camera operator or DP who says he has such a problem. A separate cup or cover should be standard procedure if requested. Eye problems can put people out of work.

### Hot Weather

People often do not drink enough water. Sipping quite cold water may not be good for us, but lots of slightly cool or air-temperature water should always be available. Personal plastic jugs with the names of the crew members written on them is wise on hot shoots. Everyone should be encouraged to drink water.

### Cold Weather

Any day can turn cold and wet. It is smart to bring clothes for a wet, cold day (or even a hot day). Get in the habit of carrying a bag with rain gear and a change of clothes.

### Bee Stings

Many people are allergic to bee venom. Parks, where the food table can attract bees and wasps, are particularly bad. Be sure to cover the meat, especially. A can of stinky cat food some distance from the shoot may lure bees away.

### Makeup and Hair Products

The Directors Guild of America and Screen Actors Guild have rules covering many of the makeup and hair products with regard to any pyrotechnical procedures.

## Last Thoughts and Parting Advice
### *"Juices"*

We talk about creative juices in our business. Here are some (very unscientific) thoughts on the matter.

The best juice is adrenaline. It flows into our systems when we sky dive, bungee jump, downhill ski, or finish a great shoot day. It flows when we see good dailies or—the ultimate—a great cut.

Adrenaline keeps us young, with an upturned mouth and a continual smile. Every smile releases a little adrenaline, a laugh even more, and keeps us well. Have you heard about laugh therapy? It works. We only become ill after a hard shoot when our adrenaline releases are down.

Adrenaline accelerates the creative process and helps the mind to think clearly and see things that we normally wouldn't. It puts us on a roll. We pump more adrenaline on shoot days. Our efficiency is three times that of a prep day. At the end of a shoot day, it takes a couple of hours to come down from the adrenaline pumped up. At dinner, we can fall asleep over the soup. At the end of a shoot, it takes a few days to rebuild our stores. Relaxing too much is dangerous. Without a cut to see or a new job to start, we relax and don't pump adrenaline. This is when we succumb to the cold that we suppressed during the shoot. We can also get addicted to adrenaline. We need to do something exciting or creative. Is that why we become workaholics?

The worst juice is bile. We pump it when no one listens. A good idea dies just because it was not someone else's. Bile flows when last-minute changes arrive or the rig doesn't work. When we have bile in our systems our brain grinds to a halt. Solutions do not pop up like they did with adrenaline. All we want to do is get it over with. We give up: "If you insist on garbage, I'll give you garbage." Bile turns our mouth down and makes us old.

How about other juices? It is said that not many creative juices flow during a $200 lunch. True, but we can discover that others can be reasonable about baseball, babies, movies, and food. Maybe after lunch we can also be reasonable about a storyboard and each other's ideas. The juices needed to digest lunch may also buffer the ego juices, and the delivery of ideas may be less charged with emotion or the need to defend one's precious ideas may be a bit dulled. For more of this kind of thinking, try reading Kurt Vonnegut.

### Success and the Ego

Success in the entertainment business can be rocket propelled, but DPs and directors often do not know how to handle success any better than a rock star, a politician, or a whiz kid. Making big bucks and having everyone desiring one's services can go to one's head. Ghandi kept himself humble by doing humble things every day. We often do not have the time or inclination to practice being humble. It is human nature—power corrupts. A formerly humble worker can become a tyrant in a new job that has a little power. One of the casualties of the demise of the studio training system was gradual advancement through the ranks. Now people can move too fast, sometimes from the bottom to the top in one or two steps. Be humble. Do not be a threat to people. Let them feel worthwhile. Let them succeed. Give them plenty of credit for their efforts.

### Financial Responsibility

One measure of success is the ability to buy things that we could not afford on the way up. All the goodies out there to buy sometimes strap the technician, camera assistant, or budding director with payments that can be a chain around the neck when the real break arrives. One often has to work for a lot less money— or none at all—when taking the next big step up the ladder. Lots of vans, boats, and even houses are lost for nonpayment when the economy slows. Losing hard-earned possessions is a blow to one's self-esteem. You can blame the economy, some union out on strike, or changes in the business, but how far one extends oneself financially is one's own decision.

## Ron Dexter's Suggested Book and Source List
### Sources

Birns and Sawyer, (213) 466–8211, carries a good stock of motion picture and television technical books. Still camera stores, such as Sammy's, (323) 938–2420 and (800) 321–4726, carry many books on still photography, but the stock varies. Opamp Technical Books, (323) 464–4322 and (800) 468–4322, orders and ships anything in print with a credit card order, as does Book Soup, (310) 659–3110. For used books, try Book City, (818) 848–4417, and Larry Edmunds, (323) 463–3273. Samuel French, (323) 876–0570, on Sunset Boulevard in Hollywood also has used books. SuperCrown and Bookstar offer special-order services and discounts. Try Barnes and Noble, as well as Amazon.com on the Internet.

### Publishers

Focal Press, (800) 366–2665, has a very informative collection of books on photography, film, and video. The books are quite well edited, focused on particular subjects, and aimed at specific levels of readers. They contain gold mines of material. Amphoto publishes a very good line of books on still photography, many of which have sections and techniques applicable to television and motion picture work.

MIKE'S NOTE: The above lists suggest just some of the many sources out there in the world. If you want to learn, start asking questions. Go to your local library. Call bookstores. Visit bookstores, ask colleges, and just keep trying to find what you're looking for until you are satisfied.

# Essential Equipment

## Apple Boxes

An apple box is a wooden box. Why it is called an apple box, I can only guess, but legend has it that the forerunner to this modern-day box was, in fact, a box used to carry apples. Grips would just flip the open side down and stand on it. An apple box has multiple purposes. It can be used for sitting, standing, prop elevation, and leveling off uneven heights. Apple boxes come in four common sizes, as illustrated in Figure 2.1:

- Full apple boxes are 12 in. × 20 in. × 8 in.
- Half apple boxes are 12 in. × 20 in. × 4 in.
- Quarter apple boxes are 12 in. × 20 in. × 2 in.
- Eight-apple boxes are 12 in. × 20 in. × 1 in.

The eight-apple box is also called a *pancake*. The nickname for the apple box is the *man-maker* (kind of an inside joke, as it will make a man taller). Apple boxes are usually made of a strong wood that is glued or nailed together. In the center of the better built boxes is a stiffener or center support that enables the boxes to withstand a heavy load.

### T.O.T.
You can use an apple box for a quick flag for a light on a beaver board or skid plate.

### T.O.T.
In rainy conditions, elevate electric connectors on an apple box, wrap them in Visqueen (plastic material) or a piece of a plastic bag, and tape the wrapping closed.

## Baby Plates

Baby plates are used for holding down small fixtures or grip heads (Figure 2.2). They can be nailed to the top of set walls or to practically any surface into

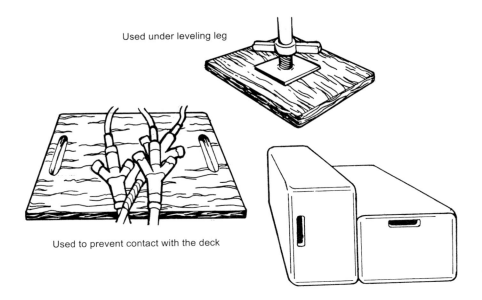

Used under leveling leg

Used to prevent contact with the deck

**Figure 2.1** Apple boxes.

which a nail can be driven, such as a tree or apple box. Baby plates are available in three sizes:

- 3 in.
- 6 to 12 in.
- Right angle

The pin size is 5/8 in. (make a note of this size). The 5/8-in. pin has a small hole through it, near the end, for a safety pin or wire to go through. Something should be slipped through this hole and secured to prevent a light from falling off in an underslung or inverted position. The pin has a recessed area near the end in which the lamp's locking pin/knuckle rides. This allows the lamp to rotate on the pin without falling off when the light is being panned.

*Note*: Always check the weld between the pin and the plate before use.

**T.O.T.**
You can use a baby plate in a high-roller head if the need arises.

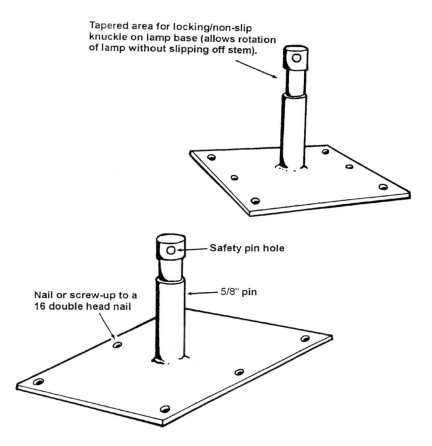

Tapered area for locking/non-slip knuckle on lamp base (allows rotation of lamp without slipping off stem).

Safety pin hole

5/8" pin

Nail or screw-up to a 16 double head nail

**Figure 2.2** Baby plates.

### T.O.T.

Never mount a baby plate to just a set wall unless it is to a stud. If you must mount a baby plate, have another grip hold up two pieces of cribbing stacked to protect his or her hands and to serve as a back plate to screw into; otherwise, the screw will pull out of the thin lauan (which is only about 1/16 to 1/8 in. thick). Always put a short safety line on the baby plate. Trust me on this . . . I have seen baby plates pull out of the wall and crash on the ground.

## Bar Clamp Adapter Pin

This pin is a mounting accessory that was initially intended to slide onto the bar of a furniture clamp in order to affix small lighting fixtures or grip equipment.

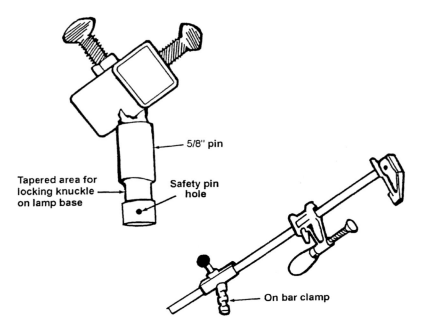

**Figure 2.3** Bar clamp adapter pin.

Another application of the bar clamp adapter is to insert the 5/8-in. pin into a grip head and employ the locking shaft opening to secure a particular device (Figure 2.3).

1. The 5/8-in. pin is about 3 in. long.
2. The pin slides on a bar clamp (also known as a furniture clamp).

   *Note*: The pin works great on a gobo arm (C-stand arm).

## Basso Block

The basso block works like a smaller version of an apple box (Figure 2.4). It is very handy and stores easily. Basso blocks come in several sizes: full, half, and quarter. A full basso block is equal to a half apple box, and a half basso block is equal to a quarter apple box.

## Bazooka

A bazooka (Figure 2.5) is a device for mounting lighting fixtures onto studio catwalks (see next T.O.T.). Along the floor of a catwalk, spaced roughly every

**Figure 2.4** Basso blocks.

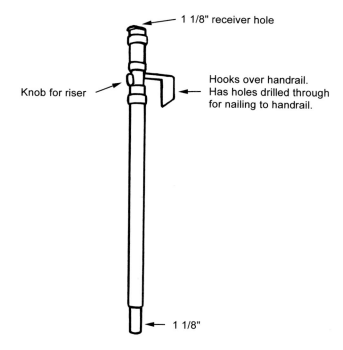

**Figure 2.5** Bazooka for perms and green beds.

18 in. apart, is a series of holes measuring 1-1/8 in. in diameter into which lighting fixtures or grip accessories may be inserted.

1. A bazooka has a 1-1/8 in. receiver on one end, which is called the *junior receiver end.*
2. At the other end is a 1-1/8 in. pin that fits into the deck of the catwalk or perm.
3. A 90-degree plate, which is attached to the bazooka, hooks over the perm handrail. The plate has several holes drilled through it for nailing or screwing it to the handrail, as a safety.

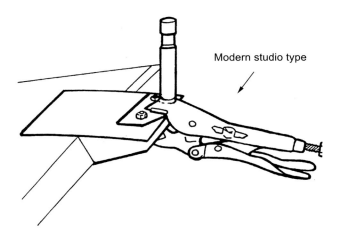

Modern studio type

**Figure 2.6** Bead board holder.

4. The bazooka has a knob for one riser on it. This is used to make minor adjustments to raise a light just high enough to allow its beam of light to focus through the perms.

*Note*: Always safety the light separately to the safety rail.

## Bead Board Holder

1. The bead board holder is a vise grip with two large plates attached to the grippers (Figure 2.6).
2. The plates provide a larger surface area that allows the bead board to bite tightly without breaking the material.

Other names for the bead board holder are *onkie-bonk* and *platypus* or even *duckbill*.

## Big Ben Clamp

One end of this clamp will accept any junior receiver. The other end will fit onto a pipe or tube with a diameter of 1-3/4 to 3-1/4 in. (Figure 2.7).

## Branch Holder

The branch holder is used by sliding a limb of a small branch into the receiving mechanism. It employs a clamping action to tighten the knob, which can be

**Figure 2.7** Big Ben clamp.

**Figure 2.8** Branch holder.

adjusted to smaller branches. The two types of branch holders are the C-clamp type and the tree type.

### C-Clamp Branch Holder

1. The C-clamp branch holder has a 4-in. to 6-ft. iron plate welded at a 90-degree angle to one face of the C-clamp (Figure 2.8).
2. This type of C-clamp has a small 2-in. angled plate welded to its opposite face, which makes it more versatile and gives it a better biting action on the tree branch.

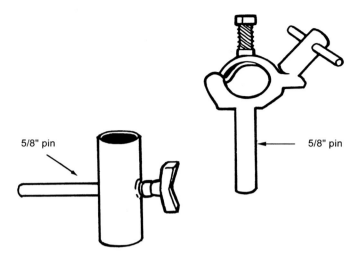

5/8" pin

5/8" pin

**Figure 2.9** Branch holder, tree.

3. The bottom of the C-clamp has a spade welded onto it, which allows the clamp to fit into a high roller.

### Tree Branch Holder

1. The tree branch holder is no more than a tube, either 2 in. or 3 in. in diameter, into which the branch slides.
2. A 5/8-in. pin is welded to the outer case, and the branch is locked into place by a small knuckle.
3. The small branch holder has a 1-3/8 in. inner diameter (ID) that is fitted with a 5/8-in. pin, and the large branch holder has a 2-3/4 in. ID fitted with a forked receiver for the 4-1/2 in. grip head (Figure 2.9).

Although the tree branch holder is not as versatile a branch holder as the C-clamp, this handy device may be used to conveniently position a multitude of items.

## Cable Crossovers

Cable crossovers are necessary on any shoot in which a car may have to drive over electrical cables. A crossover has a hinged heavy-duty polyurethane cover that opens to expose four to five valleys for cables (Figure 2.10). These covers make it safe for cars to drive over the cables and also for people to walk over them without tripping. Be sure that either the grip or the electrical department has cable crossovers on their trucks. They come in several sizes, ranging from two channels (or valleys) to five channels. They are also called *yellow jackets*.

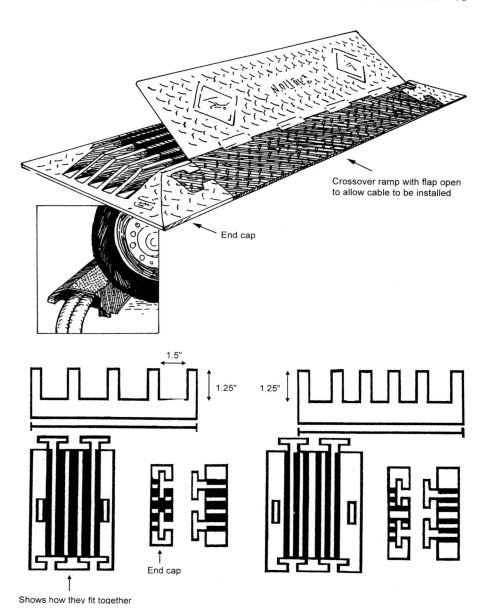

Crossover ramp with flap open to allow cable to be installed

End cap

1.5"

1.25"

1.25"

End cap

Shows how they fit together

**Figure 2.10**  Cable crossovers.

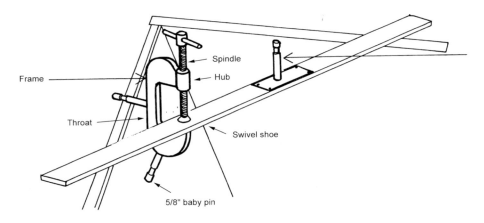

**Figure 2.11** C-clamp with a baby pin and a baby-pin plate.

## C-Clamps

C-clamps are used when an extremely secure quick mount is demanded. C-clamps for motion picture use come fitted with two 5/8-in. pins.

1. They come in many sizes. We use them as small as 1 in. and all the way up to 12 in. The type we use in the film industry has either (a) a pipe face, or (b) a flat face.
2. The pipe face has a small 1- to 2-in. piece of iron or channel iron welded to the flat face at a 90-degree angle. This gives the clamp a better clamping action when it is attached to a pole or pipe.
3. Most of the C-clamps that grips use have either a 5/8-in. baby pin or a 1-1/8 in. junior receiver mounted vertically or horizontally (Figure 2.11). Both clamps come in either pipe face or flat face.

*Note*: Never use a pipe face C-clamp on a wood surface; the edges of the face will create indentations on the wood surface. If no flat face clamps are available, you can use a pipe face with two pieces of cribbing sandwiched between the surface you are working on and the clamp.

---

**T.O.T.**

Rebar covers are the red, orange, or yellow plastic covers seen at construction sites, where they are used to cover the ends of metal rods. On location, use rebar covers on rebar (steel) rods. They can also be used as safety tips on any protruding objects, such as C-stand arms. (You can also make another type of protective cover by cutting a slice into a tennis ball and placing it on the object.)

**Figure 2.12** Camera wedges.

## Camera Wedge

A camera wedge is the same as a regular wedge, except that it is smaller and fits into tighter places (Figure 2.12). It is about 4 in. long and tapers from 1/2 in. to 1/16 in. wide.

**T.O.T.**
If you have a need for a camera wedge and none is available, you can sometimes use a clothespin. Just remove the spring, and (*voilà*) you have two small wedges.

## Cardellini Clamp

This clamp is excellent. It is quick, lightweight, fast, and has many designs (Figure 2.13).

## Chain Vise Grips

1. The chain vise grip can be used on any pipe with a diameter of 6 in. or less.
   a. The back of the chain vise grip has a 5/8-in. pin welded onto it (Figure 2.14).
   b. The tightening knob also has a 5/8-in. pin welded onto it. If need be, several chain vise grips can be "locked" together.
2. After the chain vise grip has been locked into place, it is a good practice to wrap a piece of gaffer tape around both handles to secure them together. This prevents the locking action from "popping" or accidentally unlatching.

## Clipboard

1. Clipboards are lightweight, wooden devices that are designed to be clipped to the barn doors (light shapers attached to a light fixture) of a light in order to

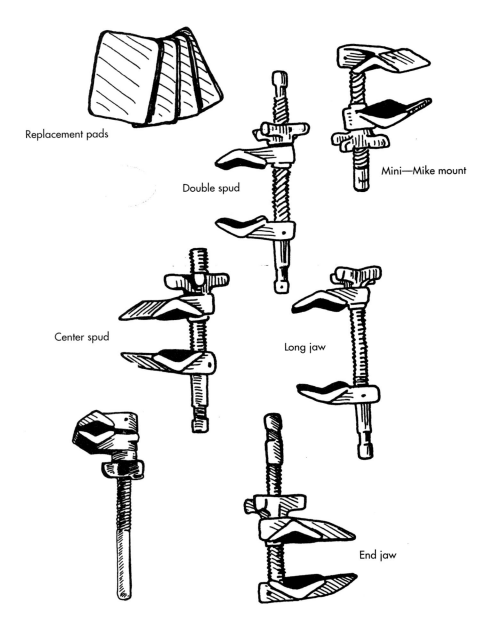

Replacement pads

Double spud

Mini—Mike mount

Center spud

Long jaw

End jaw

**Figure 2.13** Cardellini clamps.

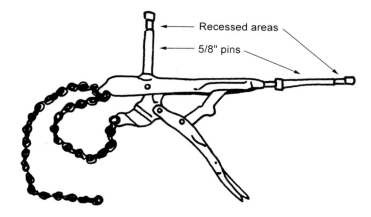

Recessed areas

5/8" pins

**Figure 2.14** Chain vise grip.

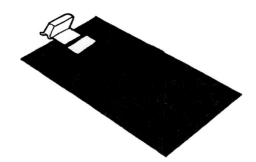

**Figure 2.15** Clipboard.

provide an additional plane or degree of control (Figure 2.15). This sometimes eliminates the need to set a flag.

2. Clipboards come in three sizes:
   a. Baby
   b. Junior
   c. Senior
3. The clip rotates on the board tightly so you can use it in several directions.

## Condor Bracket

These brackets (Figure 2.16) are designed for use in a condor (cherry picker). They fasten directly to the front or the edge of the condor basket or bucket and leave room for an operator. (*Remember*: Never exceed the weight restriction of the basket.)

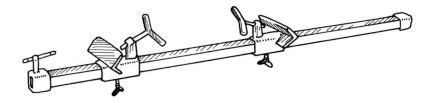

**Figure 2.16a**   Condor bracket, modern type.

**Figure 2.16b**   Condor bracket, mount-rail type (shown in stored position).

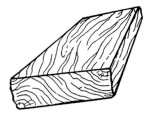

**Figure 2.17**   Cribbing, 2 in. × 4 in.

---

**T.O.T.**

The grips will usually rig the condor (cherry picker/lift) with the mounts (candlestick or condor rail mount), and the electricians will rig the lights into the mounts. They work together to ensure safety.

---

## Cribbing

1. Cribbing are short boards used to elevate, level, or block a wheel or chair or other pieces of equipment (Figure 2.17).
2. Cribbing is made from 1 in. × 3 in. × 10 in. or 2 in. × 4 in. × 10 in. lumber.
   a. Usually, the edges are rounded to prevent splintering.

*Note*: Cribbing can be any length, but 10 in. fits into a legal milk crate perfectly. (A legal milk crate is one that is either rented or bought.)

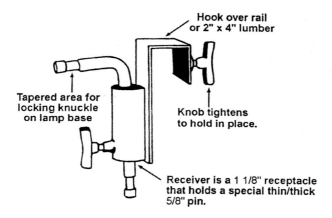

Hook over rail
or 2" x 4" lumber

Tapered area for
locking knuckle
on lamp base

Knob tightens
to hold in place.

Receiver is a 1 1/8" receptacle
that holds a special thin/thick
5/8" pin.

**Figure 2.18**  Crowder hanger.

## Crowder Hanger

1. The crowder hanger (Figure 2.18) is similar in design to a set wall bracket.
2. The crowder hanger mounts onto a 2 in. × 4 in. or 2 in. × 6 in. piece of lumber without nailing.
3. It will accommodate a stand adapter, or it can work as a 1-1/8 in. receptacle only.

## Cucoloris

1. The cucoloris is used to create a shadow pattern on a backdrop or on any subject (Figure 2.19).
2. When it is positioned in front of a light source, the cucoloris breaks up an evenly or flatly lit area into interesting pools of light and shadows. For example, this broken lighting effect can represent sunlight that has filtered down through tree branches.
3. The cucoloris is made from wood or wire mesh.
   a. The wood cucoloris is opaque with open pattern areas.
   b. The wire mesh or celo cucoloris is more like a mesh scrim with open-patterned areas burned into it. The celo type is more durable due to the strength of its wire mesh material. It also creates a more subtle pattern because of its wire mesh construction, which reduces the light output rather than completely blocking it.
   c. The closer a cucoloris is to the light source, the more diffused the resulting pattern will be on the subject.
   d. The closer a cucoloris is to the subject, the sharper the shadow patterns will be.

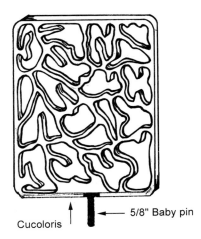

Cucoloris       ◄——— 5/8" Baby pin

**Figure 2.19** Cucoloris.

    e. The nickname for the cucoloris is a *cuke* or *cookie*.
    f. Both wood and celo cucolorises come in the following sizes:
- 18 in. × 24 in.
- 24 in. × 36 in.
- 4 ft. × 4 ft.

    *Note*: A tree limb supported in a branch holder can also be called a cucoloris or "branchaloris."

## Cup Blocks

1. Cup blocks are made of wood and designed to be placed under wheeled objects, such as light stands or parallels, to prevent them from rolling (Figure 2.20).
2. They are also used as an apple box would be (e.g., to elevate a table, desk, or chair).
3. The average size is 5-1/2 in. square and 1-1/2 in. thick, with a dished-out center (about 1/2 in. deep).

## Dots and Fingers

    Dots and fingers function along the same lines as scrims or flags—with one functional difference! Whereas scrims and nets are generally used to reshape a beam of light, dots and fingers are employed to alter or correct an isolated, internal segment of light without affecting the overall pattern (Figure 2.21).

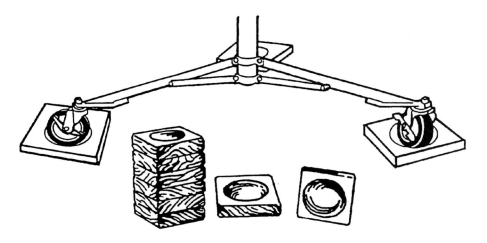

**Figure 2.20**   Cup blocks.

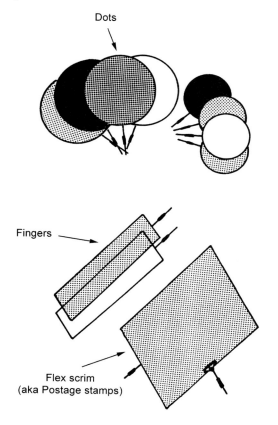

**Figure 2.21**   Dots and fingers.

1. For example, suppose a man's bald head is giving off an unwanted highlight. A dot strategically placed would hold down that small portion of light hitting the bald spot without affecting the lighting for the remainder of the scene.
2. Both dots and fingers have long handles to facilitate their placement and angle.
   a. They may be secured with grip heads or articulated arms (flexarms).
   b. Due to the thin wire constructions of the outer frame, no frame shadows are cast on the subject matter.
3. Basically, dots and fingers are shaped like little nets and flag, or like a little cutter or a dot.
4. Dot sizes are 3 in., 6 in., and 10 in.
5. Finger sizes are 2 in. × 12 in. and 4 in. × 14 in.
   a. Both dots and fingers are available in various thicknesses and materials:
      • Single
      • Double
      • Silk
      • Solid
      • Lavender

*Note*: Remember that, as you move the dot or finger closer to the light, the shadow will grow larger but will also become softer.

## Drop Ceiling Scissor Clamp/Cable Holder

1. This is one of the greatest inventions you will ever find for working in an office with false, or drop, ceilings.
2. As its name suggests, the drop ceiling mount is designed to scissor open and close over the conventional T-bar drop ceiling frames (Figure 2.22).
3. The clamp or holder is fitted with a standard 5/8-in. pin.
4. The drop ceiling cable holder works in conjunction with the scissor clamp to provide a neat, efficient way to run cable to the fixtures.

*Note*: This mount is used for smaller lighting fixtures only, so care should be taken not to hang too much weight from any drop ceiling.

## Drop Down, 45-Degree Angle

As the name implies, take a look (Figure 2.23). This is used in applications that require a reflector or lighting fixture to be positioned lower than the top of the combo stand with a 1-1/8 in. receiver.

1. The 45-degree drop down allows the unit to be mounted on an inverted plane.

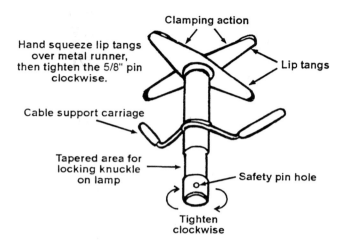

Clamping action

Hand squeeze lip tangs
over metal runner,
then tighten the 5/8" pin
clockwise.

Lip tangs

Cable support carriage

Tapered area for
locking knuckle
on lamp

Safety pin hole

Tighten
clockwise

**Figure 2.22**   Drop ceiling clip.

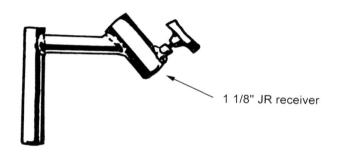

1 1/8" JR receiver

**Figure 2.23**   Drop-down (45-degree angle).

2. The angle allows the unit to be swung or tilted without interference from the stand.
3. The mounting pin and receiver accommodate 1-1/8-in. equipment.

## Empty Frames

Empty frames are great (Figure 2.24). You can cover them with whatever expendable material you may need, and they will hold it in place perfectly. The most common empty frame standard sizes are:

- 18 in. × 24 in.
- 24 in. × 36 in.
- 4 ft. × 4 ft.

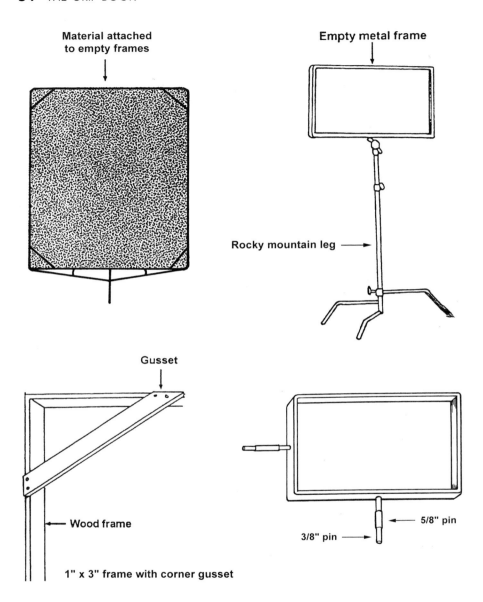

Material attached to empty frames

Empty metal frame

Rocky mountain leg ⟶

Gusset

Wood frame

1" x 3" frame with corner gusset

5/8" pin

3/8" pin ⟶

**Figure 2.24** Empty frames.

Of course, if these frames are not large enough, build your own. Normally we use 1 in. × 3 in. lumber to build a larger frame—say, to make a 10 ft. × 10 ft. or a 6 ft. × 9 ft. odd size. When building your own uncovered frame out of wood, be sure to put a gusset (wood corner brace) in each corner to add strength to the frame and keep it from distorting when moved. A frame built out of wood can also have a baby plate attached to each side of it so it can be held in place by a C-stand.

To fly (hang) a frame that you have built, drill a small hole in it (if time permits) to tie ropes through it. You can also tie ropes to the gussets if the gussets are securely fastened.

To apply a gel to the frame, you can spray an adhesive or use automatic tape gun (ATG) tape, then just lay the gel on, and *voilà*, it's ready! If you're in a hurry to gel a frame, use four grip clips. Another thing to remember when you apply gel to a wood frame that you have built is always to use a tab of tape (1/2 in. × 1/2 in. long) on the gel, then staple through the tape to the wood frame. This tab of tape will help keep the gel from tearing. (Without the tape, it is almost guaranteed that the gel will rip.)

Here is some advice that can help you identify a frame that someone has requested—for example, a "4 × 4CTO" (CTO stands for "color temperature orange"). (Gel colors are very close—1/8, 1/4, 1/2, full—and it can be difficult to tell the difference.) First, check the edge of the frame. Often, there will be a piece of tape, attached by a pin, that is marked to identify which gel is on the frame. If the frame has no such tape, pull out the frame and check for a magic marker description on the gel itself, usually in the corner. If there is no marking, check along the edge of the gel—the information will sometimes be printed along the entire edge of a new roll. If that fails, resort to a swatch book of gels. Hold the sample and the gelled frame up to a light source. After a few tries of making a match, you will get the hang of it. Always be sure to tell the boss of any problems you encounter.

---

**T.O.T.**

When you skin an empty frame (install gel or filters), be sure to clean up your mess when you (and anyone else) are done. We do not want to be blamed for any gel scraps or a messy work area.

---

**T.O.T.**

To make a fast rain hat for the camera and lights, use a gelled frame, which is usually available. Make sure you angle the rain hat so the water runs to the rear and side. Never let the rain hit the glass of the lamps. When using a gel as a temporary rain hat, aim the gel side up and the frame side down; this way it will not fill with water and cause the gel to separate from the frame.

**T.O.T.**

Noise problems can arise when the wind starts blowing a gel that has been put into a frame and placed in front of a light on an exterior location. If the gel will make a noise during a sound take (filming), there are ways to prevent this:

1. Hold the gel by hand.
2. Use clear cellophane tape X'd over the gel.
3. Use a C-stand arm offset just enough to apply pressure to the gel at its center to hold the gel in place. This only works on a large light source, due to the shadow the C-stand might cast when using a small light.

**T.O.T.**

Identify a gel on a frame by marking the gel name and type with a magic marker in the corner of the gel. This labeling will not show when light is projected through it.

## Flag Box/Scrim Box

1. The scrim box is a box with dividers in it (Figure 2.25).
2. The 18 in. × 24 in. flags fit perfectly in front, with just the handles exposed. This protects the scrim flags when not in use, such as during transportation to and from the job.
3. The box has two handles, one on each side, and a detachable wheel frame with cantered wheels.
4. The 24 in. × 36 in. flags and scrims fit in the rear slot.

## Flags and Cutters

Flags and cutters are opaque instruments designed to prevent light from reaching areas where light is not desired (Figure 2.26). They are also called *gobos*. A gobo is defined in dictionaries as a strip of material used to block light from a camera.

**T.O.T.**

Before setting a flag, first use your hand at the proper angle to make a shadow; it will save you time.

**T.O.T.**

The angle of a flag should match the angle of light.

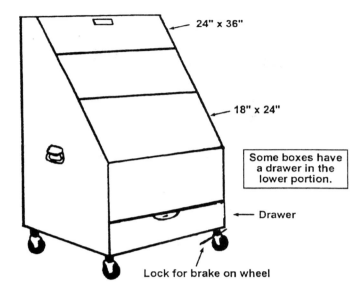

24" x 36"

18" x 24"

Some boxes have
a drawer in the
lower portion.

← Drawer

Lock for brake on wheel

**Figure 2.25** Flag/scrim box.

**T.O.T.**

If you need to use a net, flag, or diffuser next to a window, you can sometimes just tape it to the window with paper tape.

**T.O.T.**

When called for, the grips sometimes call a flag a *solid* instead of a flag, but it means the same thing.

1. Essentially, flags and cutters are very similar. The main difference is that flags are usually closer to being square in shape and cutters are longer and narrower.
2. Flags and cutters are made of black, fire-resistant cloth, which is sewn onto a closed metal frame.
3. Their handles are usually painted black.
4. They come in various sizes, but the three most common sizes are:
   a. 18 in. × 24 in.
   b. 24 in. × 36 in.
   c. 4 ft. × 4 ft. (also called *floppies* due to the fact that the 4 ft. × 4 ft. piece of material "flops" down)

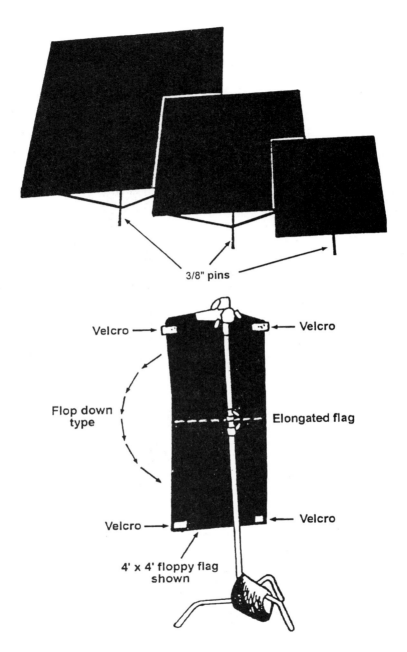

**Figure 2.26** Flags and cutters.

**T.O.T.**

Charlie bars are long wooden sticks usually 3 to 4 ft. long with different widths, ranging from 1 in. wide to approximately 6 in. wide. They are made from lauan (thin plywood) or 1/8-in. to 1/4-in.-thick plywood. A 3/8-in. pin is attached for mounting them in a C-stand. Charlie bars work great as gobos, flags, or shadow-makers to make soft shadows, such as that cast by a window pane or whatever other effect is needed. They are also known as *sticks*.

**T.O.T.**

Use a 1 in. × 3 in. × 4 ft. piece of lumber on floppies (flags) with grip clips, or use a 40-in. gobo (C-stand) head and arm to prevent the floppy part (the flop) from blowing in the wind. Clip one end of the flag with a grip clip, wrap the board or the arm on the opposite side of the center of the stand with the flag, then clip or use the head of the C-stand arm to bite the floppy part of the flag. This will prevent the flop from blowing up in the wind. When using the gobo head and arm, just open the plates on the head and sandwich the corner of the flop's edge in it. Do the same with the gobo arm plates as close to the other side as you can.

**T.O.T.**

Place a flag far enough away from a light to prevent burning, or use black wrap (black foil) on the flag.

**T.O.T.**

The closer you get to the subject, the harder the shadow. Try this: Hold your hand between a light and a wall, close to the wall. Notice how dark the shadow is on the wall; this is called a *hard shadow*. Now, pull your hand back in the direction of the light and watch what happens to the shadow. It weakens or softens, becoming a *soft shadow*.

### Cutters

The cutter is usually used for a larger lighting unit, when you have to get farther away from a light, or when light would leak or spill off the end if a smaller flag were used. Cutters usually come in various sizes, the most common being:

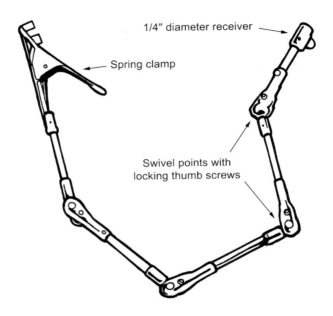

1/4" diameter receiver

Spring clamp

Swivel points with
locking thumb screws

**Figure 2.27** Flexarms.

- 10 in. × 42 in.
- 2 in. × 36 in.
- 18 in. × 48 in.
- 24 in. × 60 in.
- 24 in. × 72 in.

## Flexarms

1. Flexarms (Figure 2.27) are also referred to as *articulating arms*.
2. They are designed primarily to hold fingers, dots, and flex scrims.
   a. The joints of flexarms use a thumb-screw locking in order to support more weight.
   b. The flexarm terminates in a spring clamp at one end and a 1/4-in.-diameter locking receiver at the other.

## Furniture Clamp

1. As the name implies, the furniture clamp (Figure 2.28) is similar to the type of clamps used by the furniture industry. It is also called a *bar clamp*.
2. Furniture clamps are available in lengths of 6 in., 12 in., 18 in., 24 in., and 36 in.

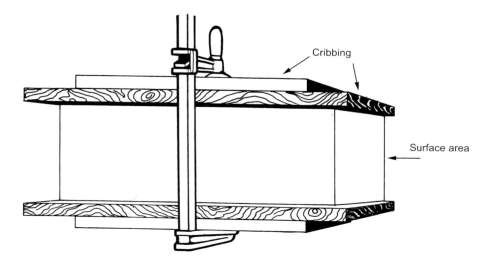

**Figure 2.28a** Furniture clamp with cribbing.

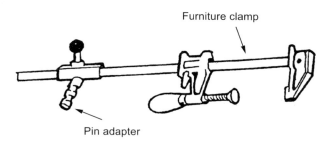

**Figure 2.28b** Furniture clamp.

3. Furniture clamps are adjusted by moving a spring release over a serrated bar, which locks into any notch on the bar.
   a. Fine adjustments of the clamp are made with a worm-screw handle.
4. The furniture clamp usually works with a bar clamp adapter on it.
   a. When using a furniture clamp on any surface, always try to use two pieces of 1 in. × 3 in. cribbing. The reason for this is that, when the clamp is tightened to the surface, the foot covers only a very small surface area.
   b. If too much pressure or weight is applied too far out on the arm of the bar, the foot could punch a hole through a wall or dent the surface, leaving a mar or causing the light to shift, or fall off. A couple of 1 in. × 3 in. cribbing pieces are thin enough not to take up too much room, but they will provide greater surface area for the pressure being applied, thus helping the clamp have a better grip on the surface.
   c. Another reason for using cribbing is a common grip concern: not to damage any area or structure on which this clamp is being rigged. If you

**Figure 2.29** Furniture pads.

take extra precautions and display consideration for someone else's belongings, it shows a lot of professionalism.

*Note*: Never install a light on a clamp without a rope or wire safety. Trust me on this. It will never be just "one quick shot" as grips are so often told. Just make it "one quick safety."

## Furniture Pad

Furniture pads, also called *sound blankets*, are heavy-duty quilts that are used for a multitude of applications (Figure 2.29):

1. Sound technicians use furniture pads for acoustic deadening and isolation.
2. Camera operators use them as a pad to sit or lie down on when shooting low angles.
3. Grips use furniture pads to protect furniture, walls, floors, etc.

> **T.O.T.**
> Some furniture pads have large grommets (eyelets like those in your tennis shoes), so they can be hung.

## Gaffer Grip

1. The gaffer grip (Figure 2.30) is a multi-use device that is unique in that it comes with two 5/8-in. pins. One pin is on the handle and one is on the jaws.
2. Adjustable jaw openings provide normal expanded mounting capabilities.

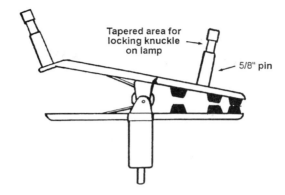

**Figure 2.30** Gaffer grip.

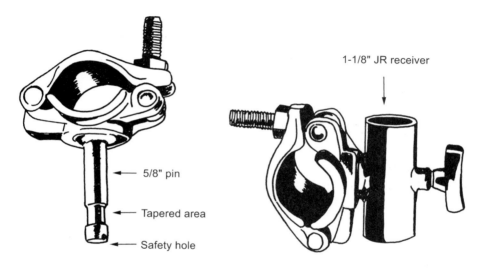

**Figure 2.31a** Grid clamp with baby pin.

**Figure 2.31b** Grip clamp with junior receiver.

3. Gaffer grips are normally used for quick-mounting small light fixtures to virtually anything, such as a door, pipe, furniture, or light stands.
4. One of their many applications is as a means of securing foam core.
5. They are also called *gator grips* due to the style of the rubber teeth in the jaw.

## Grid Clamp

1. Baby grid clamps (Figure 2.31a) are designed to provide maximum hold. The baby grid clamp fits pipes 1-1/4 to 2-1/2 in. in diameter.

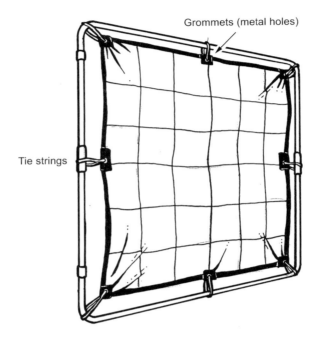

Grommets (metal holes)

Tie strings

**Figure 2.32a** Grifflon.

 a. When the bottom nut has been securely fastened, the grid clamp is virtually unmovable.
 b. The clamp terminates in a 5/8-in. pin.
 2. Junior grid clamps (Figure 2.31b) are the same as baby grid clamps, except
 that they terminate in a 1-1/8 in. receiver.

## Grifflon

 Let me explain a grifflon to you. It is an extremely durable material made of
three-ply, high-density rubber (Figure 2.32). It looks like cloth with webbing woven
through it to prevent it from ripping. A grifflon takes a direct light and bounces it
back onto the subject. If the sun were backlighting the subject, for example, it would
bounce the sun back onto the subject's face. The most common sizes of grifflons
are:

- 6 ft. × 6 ft.
- 8 ft. × 8 ft.
- 12 ft. × 12 ft.
- 20 ft. × 20 ft.

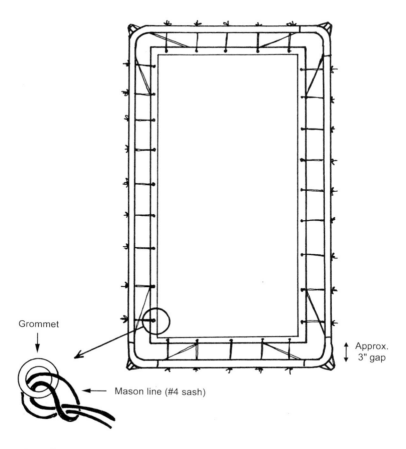

Grommet

Approx.
3" gap

Mason line (#4 sash)

**Figure 2.32b** Grifflon.

*Note*: If the grifflon should tear, a grifflon material tape is available specifically to repair it. Apply the tape, which is made of the same material as the grifflon,
directly to the tear, and (*voilà*) the hole is fixed.

## Grip Clip

"Grip clip" is the most common name for these devices (Figure 2.33). Other
names that are used quite frequently are:

- Hargrave #1, #2, #3, or #4
- Handy clamp
- Spring clamp

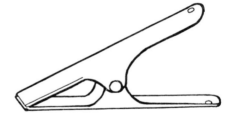

**Figure 2.33** Grip clip.

- Pony clamp
- Brinks and cotton

When a grip clip is called for, it is usually asked for by size. The number comes from the manufacturer (for example, Hargrave #1):

- #1, smallest
- #2, most common
- #3, large
- #4, extremely large (hardly ever used)

**T.O.T.**
The grip clips are nothing but large reusable metal clothes pins. They seem to be used on almost every shoot. You'll see.

**T.O.T.**
Use a #1 grip on your tool belt to hold your gloves.

## Grip/Electrical Stage Box

1. The grip/electrical stage box or grip box, as it is usually called, is nothing more than an extra-heavy-duty chest of drawers (Figure 2.34).
2. It has a metal wheel frame that is detachable.
3. This box is loaded with common hardware—from bolts, nuts, wire, and nails to power tools.

**Figure 2.34** Grip/electrical stage box.

## Grip Helper

The grip helper is another special bracket (Figure 2.35). It allows a flag or scrim to fasten securely to a heavy-duty stand. The grip helper has a 1-1/8 in. pin on the bottom and a 1-1/8 in. receiver on the top. The pin drops into a 1-1/8 in. receiver on the stand. The light then slips into the top end of the receiver, remaining perfectly in the center. The arm extends from 3 ft. to 6 ft. and will rotate 360 degrees. It is fixed at a 45-degree down angle. The grip helper's other end has a 4-1/2 in. grip head mounted on it. A 40-in. single extension arm mounts into the 4-1/2 in. head. This extension arm has a 2-1/2 in. grip head on it that will hold the flag, frame, or net.

## Grounding Rod/Spike

1. Grounding rods or spikes (Figure 2.37) are used for electrical ground hookups or for securing guide wires or ropes.
2. They are all steel rods (usually hardened).
3. The spikes are about 2 to 3-1/2 ft. long.
4. Their nicknames are:
   a. Ford axle (at one time old automobile axles were used to make them).
   b. Bull pr–ck (use your imagination).

**Figure 2.35** Grip helper.

**Figure 2.36** Ground rod/tent peg.

## Hand Truck

A picture is all you need to explain this tool (Figure 2.37).

## Ladder

The three basic types of ladders (Figure 2.38) are:

1. Ladders made of wood or fiberglass
2. Ladders made of aluminum

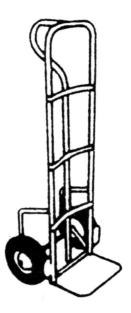

**Figure 2.37** Hand truck.

3. Rolling A-frame ladder, which has a center ladder that can be raised or lowered as needed

*Note*: Never use an aluminum ladder when working with anything electrical. This could be the fastest way to a short career. It can ground out and cause injury or death. And, remember, do not use the top step; get a taller ladder instead.

·

**T.O.T.**
Almost every ladder built today has a level or height that should not be exceeded; for example, a six-step or 6-ft. ladder has five steps and a top platform, but this top platform is *not* a step. Nevertheless, people get careless and use it anyway. Do *not* use the top step; get a taller ladder instead.

**T.O.T.**
The proper angle of an extension ladder is 4 to 1.

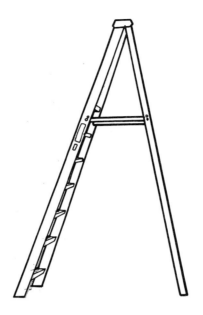

**Figure 2.38a** Ladder.

**Figure 2.38b** Rolling A-frame ladder.

## Lamppost System (by Backstage Equipment)

These lamppost systems (Figure 2.39) are excellent for any pre-rigs or last-minute changes. They are perfect for those swing sets (moving walls) that we squeeze into tight corners of our sets. They are held in place with just four screws.

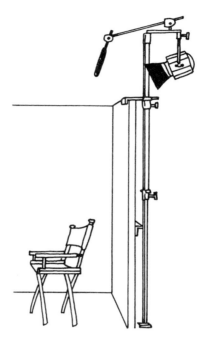

**Figure 2.39a**   Lamppost system.

**Figure 2.39b**   Lamppost system with offset.

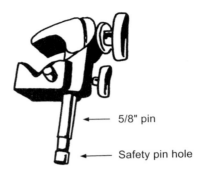

5/8" pin

Safety pin hole

**Figure 2.40**  Mafer clamp.

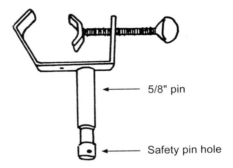

5/8" pin

Safety pin hole

**Figure 2.41**  Matt pipe adapter.

## Mafer Clamp

1. The mafer clamp (Figure 2.40) is a great little clamp. It looks like a C-clamp that has a 5/8-in. pin on it.
2. The clamp has a rubber tip that will attach to most pipes and flat surfaces.

## Matt Pipe Adapter Baby

1. The matt pipe adapter baby (Figure 2.41) is a simple yet effective means of securing a light or grip equipment to a pipe or tubing.
2. It terminates in a 5/8-in. pin.

## Matt Poles—Polecats

1. Polecats (Figure 2.42) are adjustable poles that will support lightweight lighting and grip equipment.

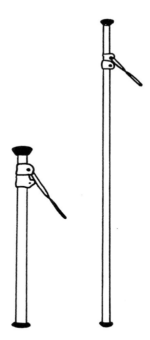

**Figure 2.42** Matt poles.

2. They can be used vertically or horizontally.
3. A unique cam-action lock exerts pressure to securely wedge the suction-cup-affixed ends into place.

   *Note*: Only use a mafer clamp or a light-action clamp device on this tool. The reason is that the walls of the tube are thin and designed to support only light equipment hanging from it.

## Meat Ax

1. The meat ax is a grip-arm-like accessory (Figure 2.43).
2. The meat ax is designed to clamp onto the handrail of a studio overhead catwalk or any other suitable surface on which you can put a clamp.
3. The long extension arm is adjustable to pivot in all directions around the clamp.
4. The end of the arm is equipped with a gobo head.
5. A small handle is affixed at the opposite end to facilitate adjustment and positioning.
6. The meat ax comes with two clamp styles, one for the 2 in. × 4 in. handrail and the other for a pipe clamp.

Plate with slot
for tilting

Gobo head

**Figure 2.43** Meat ax.

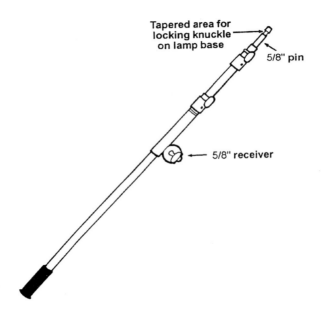

Tapered area for
locking knuckle
on lamp base

5/8" pin

5/8" receiver

**Figure 2.44** Miniboom.

## Miniboom

1. As the name implies, the miniboom is a miniature boom arm designed to support lighting fixtures (Figure 2.44).
2. The arm is designed for when a limited amount of extension is required.
3. The unit is lightweight, yet provides stability through the use of counterbalance weights.

**Figure 2.45** Muscle truck (also known as a sandbag/cable cart).

**Figure 2.46** No-nail hanger.

## Muscle Truck (by Backstage Equipment)

The muscle truck, as its name suggests, is a heavy-duty cart (Figure 2.45). It is used to transport sandbags, cable, or any heavy object that will fit in its well.

## No-Nail Hanger

This bracket (Figure 2.46) easily fits over a 2 in. × 4 in. or 2 in. × 6 in. piece of wood. It will also fit over a door. It has a 1-1/8 in. receiver and will easily convert to a baby pin with a C-stand adapter pin.

## Offset Arms

An offset arm (Figure 2.47) offsets the light—for example, when you need to hide the stand outside the room and have only the light itself inside the room.

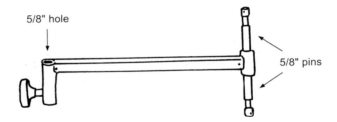

5/8" hole

5/8" pins

**Figure 2.47a** Baby offset.

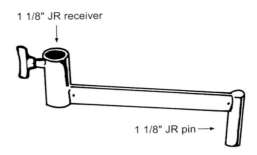

1 1/8" JR receiver

1 1/8" JR pin →

**Figure 2.47b** Junior offset.

1. Offset arms are similar to side arms.
2. These are arms that have a receptacle that will fit on a stand that is 5/8 in.
3. A junior offset is the same thing, but with a 1-1/8 in. receptacle at one end and a 1-1/8 in. pin on the other.

## Parallels

1. Parallels, when totally assembled, are portable scaffolding designed for use as elevated platforms for camera or lighting equipment (Figure 2.48).
2. All elements are constructed of lightweight steel tubing and are designed to fold for easy storage and transportation.
3. The upper platforms are two sections that may be removed to facilitate the hoisting or lowering of equipment.
4. Parallels can also be supported on screw jacks for leveling on feet or wheels.
5. You can stack one set of parallels on another.

*Note*: I do not recommend stacking more than three sets of parallels (18 ft. high) when they are built on wheels. You can build towers without wheels higher, but it is not recommended. If you must build towers higher than three sets, be sure you tie-off the tower at every other level (four-point tie-off) and brace it as much as possible. Remember, be safe!

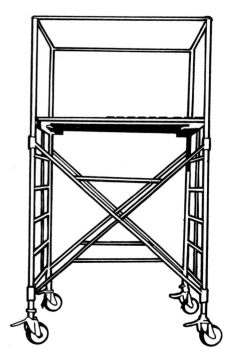

**Figure 2.48a**  Parallels.

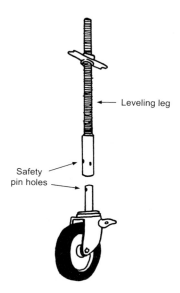

**Figure 2.48b**  Parallel screw jack.

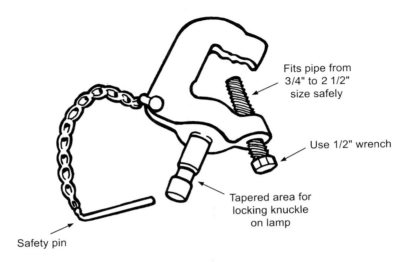

Fits pipe from
3/4" to 2 1/2"
size safely

Use 1/2" wrench

Tapered area for
locking knuckle
on lamp

Safety pin

**Figure 2.49** Baby pipe clamp.

**T.O.T.**
When putting a camera on a set of parallels, always screw down a 4 ft. × 4 ft.
× 3/4 in. sheet of plywood as a base on the top platform for stability.

## Pipe Clamp, Baby

1. Pipe clamp babies (Figure 2.49) are designed and strengthened to allow fixtures to hang on a pipe without the danger of slipping off the pipe while the clamp is loose.
2. These are designed to hang from either theatrical or other heavy steel pipes.
3. They are not recommended for use on lightweight or thin-walled pipe or tubing, because as soon as you tighten up the bolt you will probably break right through a tube that is too thin.
4. The lock-off bolt can be tightened to hold the pipe clamp in any desired position with ease. It terminates in a 5/8-in. pin.

## Pipe Clamp, Junior

1. The junior pipe clamp (Figure 2.50) terminates in a 1-1/8 in. receptacle.
2. You can also use a stand adapter pin (also known as a *spud adapter*) with a 5/8-in. pin on one end. The other end has a 1-1/8 in. pin.

**Figure 2.50** Junior pipe clamp.

**Figure 2.51** Pony pipe clamp.

## Pony Pipe Clamp

The pony pipe clamp (Figure 2.51) is a heavy-duty clamp that has an adapter with a 5/8-in. pin attached to it. This is an ultra-heavy-duty type of furniture clamp. The clamp consists of a 1-in. outer diameter (OD) tube or pipe that can be changed in length as needed.

## Poultry Bracket (Matthews)

The poultry bracket (Figure 2.52) can be used on a tree, pole, or other items. It has a 1-1/8 in. junior receiver on the top of its arm, and on the bottom of its arm is a 5/8-in. baby pin.

**Figure 2.52** Poultry bracket.

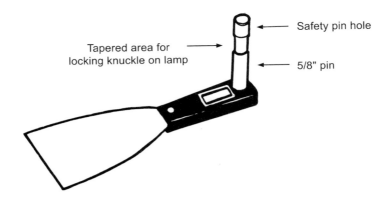

**Figure 2.53** Putty knife.

## Putty Knife

1. The putty knife (Figure 2.53) is designed to place a 5/8-in. pin where it is nearly impossible to put any other mounting brackets.
2. It is wedged into an area, such as a door frame or window sill.

## Reflector

A reflector (Figure 2.54) is designed to redirect or bounce natural or artificial light. The reflector has two sides to it:

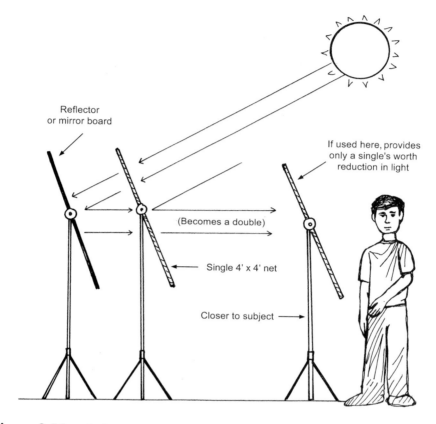

Reflector
or mirror board

If used here, provides
only a single's worth
reduction in light

(Becomes a double)

← Single 4' x 4' net

Closer to subject ——→

**Figure 2.54a** Reflectors.

← 5/8" receiver

**Figure 2.54b** Hand reflector board.

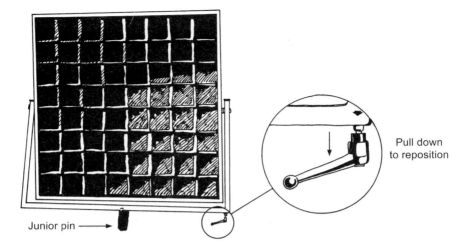

Junior pin ⟶

Pull down
to reposition

**Figure 2.54c** 4 ft. × 4 ft. reflector with soft side shown.

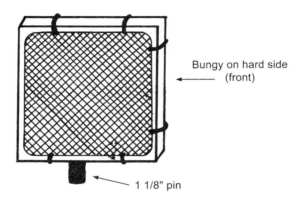

Bungy on hard side
(front)

1 1/8" pin

**Figure 2.54d** Attaching slip-ons.

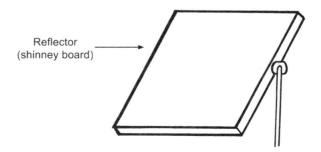

Reflector
(shinney board)

**Figure 2.54e** Reflector (shinney board).

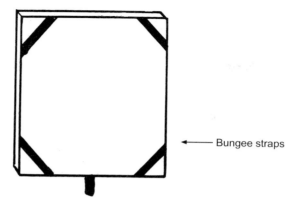

Bungee straps

**Figure 2.54f** Reflector (back side shown).

1. On one side, it is a very smooth surface. This is called the *hard side*. It gives you a very hard or bright light. It is identical to the practice of using a mirror in the sun to redirect light. It is sometimes called the *lead side*.
2. The other side is called the *soft side*. The soft side of the board gives the subject a diffused pattern of light. A good comparison is a sheet of aluminum foil. When it is fresh from the roll, it is like a mirror, giving a hard side bounce. After crumpling and then uncrumpling the foil, however, it reflects light less strongly and clearly; because of all the wrinkles in the foil, the light is not all bouncing in the same direction, so less light reaches the subject.

At the present time, reflectors usually come in silver, but gold is becoming very popular:

1. Gold boards are used a lot with African-American actors and actresses, because it gives the dark skin a nice tone.
2. Gold boards are also used on plants to give them a warmer amber color, much like the color of the "magic hour"—the warm, golden-yellow-orange color of sunset.

**T.O.T.**
If a reflector is too shiny, we can put on what is called a *scrim* in front of it. This will reduce the intensity of the reflected light from hard to soft, without changing the pattern. Usually, this is accomplished by simply moving the reflector back a few feet. If we cannot move a reflector back, then we use scrims. Scrim sizes are 42 in. × 42 in., and they clip onto the board by means of an elastic bungee cord.

---

**T.O.T.**
When carrying a combo stand with a reflector on it, use a sandbag as a shoulder pad. This way you have your bag right there when you have set your stand.

---

## Reflector Slip-Ons (Scrims)

1. Reflectors can also use a 42 in. × 42 in. slip-on single or double net (used to reduce light) that is held in place by means of an elastic strap (Figure 2.54).
2. They can only be used on the hard/lead side.
3. If reflector slip-ons are used on the soft side, they will remove all the leaf that is lightly attached to the board.
4. If a single or double width slip-on is required in front of a soft side, place the single or double net on an uncovered, closed-end, 4 ft. × 4 ft. empty frame, then put it in place after the sun has struck the board. The reflected light is reduced, as it passes through the slip-on only once. The reason it is done this way is that it is easier to control the reflected light and because the soft side is not damaged.

## Sandbags

1. Sandbags are made from canvas or heavy vinyl bags filled with sand or shot (lead pellets) (Figure 2.55).
2. The bags are placed on all light and grip stands once the stand has been set.
   a. They usually just lay over one leg, but they are sometimes hung by their strap-handle on a low knuckle on the stand.
3. The bags can come in several sizes. The most common are 15 lb. and 35 lb.
4. Their nickname is *silent grips*, because they will quietly hold a stand in place (unlike a grip).
5. The 35-lb. bags are often called *ball busters*.

---

**T.O.T.**
If you are on location and a sprinkler system comes on, quickly put sandbags on the heads closest to where you are shooting.

---

## Scrims—Grip

Scrims are also referred to as *nets*, which are nonelectrical dimmers. They provide a simple, versatile, yet extremely controllable means of reducing light output without affecting color, temperature, or generating electrical interference. They may

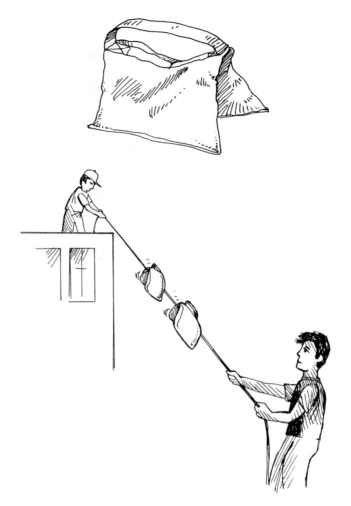

**Figures 2.55a and 55b**  Sandbags.

be used to reduce the entire beam of light or just a portion of it to creatively control highlights and shadows. Open-end scrims are constructed of spring steel frames to provide constant tension on the net material. The open end facilitates feathering or blending of the edge of the light beam without causing a harsh visual line. Scrims come in three basic configurations—single, double, and lavender—as well as silk.

### Single Net

1. The single net will reduce about 30% of the light that shines through it.
2. Its handle is usually painted white or green.

3. On newer equipment, the outer edge of the net that connects to the frame has a white or green cloth covering for ease in identification.
4. The single is one layer of material only. It looks like the material you might make a veil out of, but it has no design in it.

---

**T.O.T.**

To use a single or double net to reduce more light, wing (turn) the open end of the net away from its parallel position, laying it at an angle of almost 45 to 90 degrees from the light.

---

### Double Net

1. The double net will reduce the light shining through it by 50%.
2. It is constructed almost exactly the same as the single net, but the major difference is that this one, as the name implies, has two layers of net material. The handle and outside cloth cover of the double net are red.

---

**T.O.T.**

If the need arises, a grip can put a metal scrim in a C-stand and set it in front of the light, as opposed to installing the metal scrim in the light itself.

---

### Lavender Net

1. This is a very delicate net that will reduce the light by only about 15%.
2. The handle and edge of the cloth covering are painted blue or purple, hence the name.

---

**T.O.T.**

Because the material used in a lavender net is so fragile, I usually cut a piece of show card and fold it in half to make a sleeve to protect it.

---

### Silk

1. The silk net provides diffusion in addition to cutting (reducing) the light. It also softens the light source.
2. The silk net has a gold handle and cloth edge.

The actual extent of light reduction for scrims will vary according to the placement of the scrim relative to the light and the subject. Scrims come in various sizes, but the most common sizes called for are:

- 18 in. × 24 in.
- 24 in. × 36 in.
- 48 in. × 48 in.

**T.O.T.**
Sometimes the gaffers or DPs just call for an open end. They don't say the size, and like magic you are supposed to just know what they want. This is what *should* be said: "Hey, Joe, please get me a 24 in. × 36 in. open-end double," or "Get me an 18 in. × 24 in. single."

Remember! Always bring what is called for in the size wanted plus the *other* scrim not requested; for example, if a single is wanted, bring a double along with it. It will save you many a return trip when the DP or gaffer sees the single in place and realizes that not be enough light is being reduced. Conversely, if a double is called for, too much light may be reduced, thus requiring a single.

**T.O.T.**
Do not stack large or small nets together; if they fall over, the pin might punch a hole through them.

## Scrims, Butterfly Kits

Okay, now let's discuss butterfly kits. We have both butterfly kits and overhead kits:

1. Butterfly kits are usually smaller in size (usually about 5 ft. × 5 ft. or 6 ft. × 6 ft.), and they can be supported by a single stand (although this is not a good practice).
2. Overhead kits are larger, about 12 ft. × 12 ft. or 20 ft. × 20 ft.
3. Butterfly and overhead frames are portable.
4. Both use lightweight tubes.
5. They both can support any lighting control material, such as a:
   a. Silk (which diffuses light)
   b. Net (which reduces light)

    c. Solid black (which cuts light)

    d. Grifflon (which reflects light)

  6. Setup time is usually under 5 to 10 minutes.

*Note*: These textile materials are color coded for easy identification:

- White, a single scrim
- Red, a double scrim
- Black, a black solid
- Gold/yellow, a silk

### T.O.T.

When using 12 ft. × 12 ft. or 6 ft. × 6 ft. silk, place it with the seam up; otherwise, the seam's shadow may show on the actors or product.

### T.O.T.

Always put a minimum of four ropes on a 12 ft. × 12 ft. butterfly or larger frame, one in each corner, to tie off the frame when it is in place.

### T.O.T.

Blackouts (drops) (6 ft. × 6 ft., 12 ft. × 12 ft., 20 ft. × 20 ft., or larger) will be destroyed by the chlorine in pools. I have been told that something in the fire-retardant added to blackouts reacts to the chlorine.

### T.O.T.

All scrims, silks, grifflons, and muslins are usually made smaller than the frame; for example, for a 12 ft. × 12 ft. frame, the rag (silk, scrim, etc.) will measure approximately 11-1/2 ft. × 11-1/2 ft. This undersize allows for tightening scrims or silks tightly into place using their drawstrings (also known as *mason lines*).

### T.O.T.

To prevent a tarp from blowing up and down or lifting (flexing in the wind), I always add additional ropes every 10 feet when the tarp or solid is dead hanging (vertical), or I use an X-shaped pattern of ropes across the top and the bottom when the solid (rag) is flown in a horizontal position. A 1/4-in. hemp rope is fine to use.

**T.O.T.**

When trying to differentiate between bleached and unbleached muslin by eye, the bleached muslin appears very white, like a sheet, and the unbleached muslin has almost a light beige color.

Each kit (butterfly or overhead) will usually include a

- Frame
- Single
- Double
- Silk
- Solid
- Grifflon (sometimes, but you'd better check when you order—never assume)

**T.O.T.**

A word of caution. An overhead kit that is 20 ft. × 20 ft. presents 400 square feet of surface area to the wind. This much sail can move a boat 15 knots or better, so do not underestimate the forces that are at play here. Grips have a saying: "Seems like every time you set up a 20 ft. × 20 ft. overhead kit, the wind will come up." So, every time you set one up, make sure you have ropes on all four corners; usually 3/8-in. hemp is sufficient. You *must* tie down a 20 ft. × 20 ft. or a 12 ft. × 12 ft. kit when you fly it; otherwise, you may be flying to the next county to pick it up.

That makes up a butterfly kit. A grifflon is a separate unit. I will explain what each one does as we go along. Remember when I told you in the scrims section that the material is made out of a veil-like material? You have your single, which is one layer of material, and your double, which is basically two layers of the same material. Butterfly kits are the same as the scrims described earlier, only in larger sizes.

**T.O.T.**

It seems that everybody is still just asking for a butterfly kit, even when they want a 20 ft. × 20 ft. or a 12 ft. × 12 ft. kit, which is technically an overhead kit. They assume that a 6 ft. × 6 ft. or a 5 ft. × 5 ft. kit—a real butterfly kit—is the same thing. Oh, well; we'll just have to live with it.

> **T.O.T.**
> If too many nets are layered, they will broadcast a design on the subject. This is referred to as a *moiré pattern*. It is similar to looking through a screen door.

> **T.O.T.**
> When flying a rag in a frame or just hanging it, face the ribbon (the color canvas edge that supports the grommets) of the single, double, or silk away from the camera.

### Silks

We use two types of "silk":

1. Taffeta
2. Chinese silk

The silk that we use most often is taffeta, which is not actually made of silk but is a silk-like material. It is more durable than real silk. The other is a Chinese silk, which is a very fine, actual silk.

*Note*: Chinese silk is very expensive, and it rips or snags very easily, so we shy away from using it.

*Note*: Always wrap a silk (Chinese or taffeta) into a ball. Never fold it. The reason for this is that the material may develop creases that will cast shadows on the subject. Also, always use a silk (if possible) with the seams facing up or away from the subject. The seam may also cast a shadow on the subject if it is too close.

### Scrims, Flex

1. Flex scrims (Figure 2.56) are lightweight, smaller versions of regular scrims.
2. They are designed to be used in conjunction with articulating arms (flexarms).
3. Their usage is similar to that of fingers and dots.
4. Their size is usually 10 in. × 12 in.
5. They come as:
   a. Open-end singles
   b. Open-end doubles
   c. Open-end silks
   d. Closed end
6. They are used where a larger flag will not work.

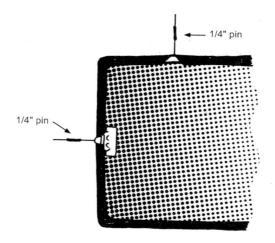

**Figure 2.56** Flex scrim (also known as a postage stamp).

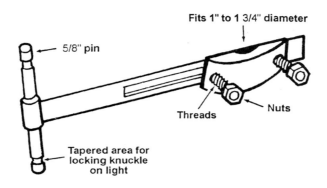

**Figure 2.57** Side arm.

## Side Arms

Side arms, which are adjustable in length, are designed to clamp onto a round surface 1 in. to 1-3/4 in. in diameter (Figure 2.57).

1. They provide a mounting platform for lighting or grip equipment.
2. Common applications include attaching them to lighting stands for low-angle placement.
3. Another common use is hanging the arm from overhead pipe grids.
4. The baby side arm terminates in a double-ended 5/8-in. pin.
5. The junior side arm has a 1-1/8 in. receiver.

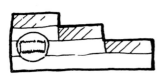

2" x 4" step blocks

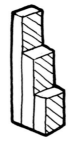

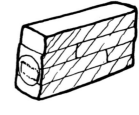

Step blocks in stored position

**Figure 2.58** Stair blocks.

## Stair Blocks

1. Stair blocks (Figure 2.58) are small wooden blocks attached together like a set of miniature steps, offering a variety of elevations.
2. They are commonly used for elevating a table, couch, and other items.
3. Each step is approximately 2 in. higher than the last, with approximately 4 in. between steps.

**T.O.T.**

Legal milk crate = not stolen

## Stand Adapter Pin

1. The stand adapter pin (Figure 2.59) is a pin with a 1-1/8 in. base and a 5/8-in. pin on top.
2. This pin will go into a combo stand or high roller with a receptacle, if an adapter is needed.
3. A nickname for the stand adapter pin is *spud*.
4. It is also sometimes called a *butt plug*.

## Stands

Okay, you have made it this far. Good for you! Now, we are going to learn about stands. One stand is used the most, by far (as you may have gathered by how often we have already mentioned it)—the C-stand.

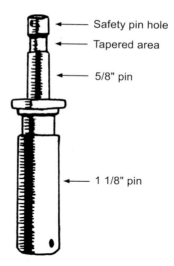

Safety pin hole

Tapered area

5/8" pin

1 1/8" pin

**Figure 2.59**   Stand adapter pin.

### C-Stand

1. The C-stand (Figure 2.60) (short for century stand) gets its name (legend has it) from how long it will take you to master using it.
2. It is also called a *gobo stand* or *grip stand*.
   a. The dictionary describes a gobo as an object used to block light from a subject, so it is only reasonable that a stand that holds a gobo is a gobo stand. The C-stand is considered to be the workhorse of the industry.
3. The century or gobo stand is designed as a multipurpose support for flags, lighting fixtures, prop stands, and other items that must be held in place on the set.
4. The legs are staggered in height, allowing them to fit in, around, and under furniture, props, and other lighting stands.
5. A "sliding leg" (also called a *rocky mountain*) is available on some stands. This feature permits one leg to be raised so it can rest on an elevated surface, such as a stair, counter, sink top, and so on.

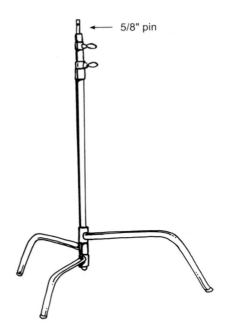

5/8" pin

**Figure 2.60a**  C-stand without a head or arm.

**Figure 2.60b**  C-stand head and arm.

**Figure 2.60c**   Full C-stand.

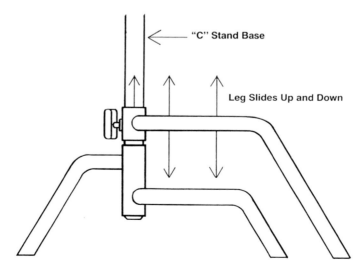

**Figure 2.60d**   Rocky mountain leg.

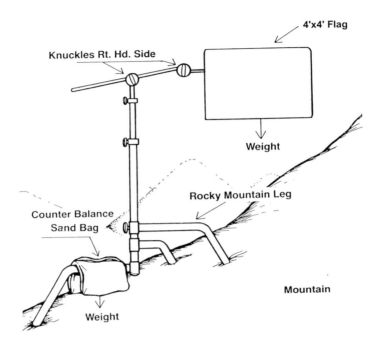

**Figure 2.60e**  Stand setup for mountain locations.

6. The standard 40-in., double-raised stand can reach approximately 13 ft., 8 in. or so.
7. A century stand weighs about 11 pounds.
8. All stands are constructed of durable lightweight alloys.
9. Each of the stand's risers is a tube inside a larger tube which will telescope about 38 in.
10. The C-stand is used with a head on it called a *grip* or *gobo head*.
    a. This bites onto a 40-in. tube or extension arm with another head on it (the gobo arm).
    b. The grip head sits on the century stand by means of a 5/8-in. diameter pin or rod, which, by the way, is the standard size for most lighting units under 2000 watts.

> **T.O.T.**
> When you hand off a C-stand to an awaiting hand, make sure you have grasped around the C-stand main post and the long gobo C-stand arm. If your fingers are wrapped only around the center post, they will get crushed as if they were in a nutcracker.

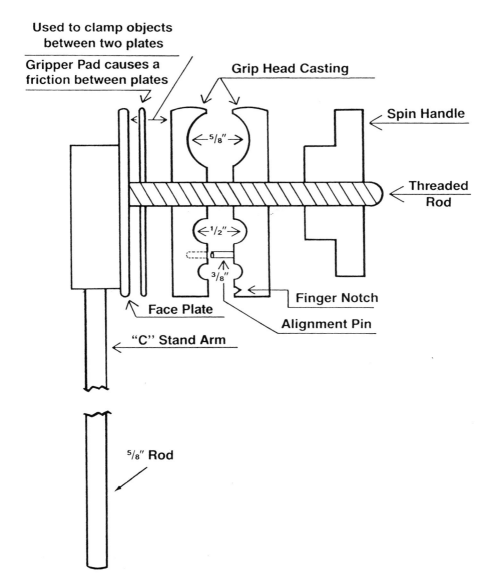

**Figure 2.60f** C-stand head.

### C-Stand Operation

1. Most 2-1/2 in. grip heads and gobo heads are designed to receive 5/8-in., 1/2-in., or 3/8-in. round accessories.
2. They will also accept an object of irregular shape, if not in the holes then between the flat plates, as shown in Figure 2.60f.

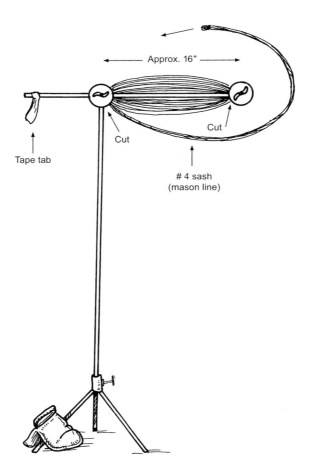

**Figure 2.60g** How to cut several lines the same length.

3. The head consists of a knob or knuckle, with outside and inside plates that butt up to a flat portion of the head.
4. The holes of the plates are kept aligned by inserting an alignment pin between the outer and inner plates, which are attached to one plate, while the other plate has a hole for free floating.
5. C-stands should always be used with the knuckles on the right. The quickest way to show the rest of the crew that you are inexperienced is to forget this Golden Rule. The reason the knuckles are on the right is that any time a flag (which is a weight) is put in the head, gravity will pull it downward. The knuckle or knob is tightened clockwise. The weight of the flag will cause the head to bite by pulling down (clockwise), causing a friction action and locking it in place.

6. The C-stand should be placed with the knuckles on the right with a leg placed in a forward position. This will help support the weight of an object such as a flag and keep it from falling over forward.
7. To help prevent the C-stand from falling over, a sandbag is placed on the rear-most leg to act as a counterbalance.
8. By the way, just a side note: Always place a sandbag on a C-stand, whatever configuration it is in. All you have to do is forget just once, and you've caused an accident.

**T.O.T.**
Tape the feet of stands that do not have plastic feet from the factory.

**T.O.T.**
In wind, use the thickest risers possible.

**T.O.T.**
Use a gobo arm to stop gel from blowing. Press the gobo arm lightly against the center of the gel, applying enough pressure to keep the gel from flexing in the wind and creating unwanted sound problems.

**T.O.T.**
Here is a normal rule of thumb: One riser up = 1 sandbag, 2 risers up = 2 sand-bags, and so on.

**T.O.T.**
Always try to place the bag on the leg opposite the weight, but, if the weight is down the center (such as a light sitting on the middle of a stand), any leg will do.

**T.O.T.**
When you see a light being carried to a set, you should anticipate that it will need a flag. Get a flag just the size of the unit or larger, plus a C-stand and a sandbag. It is better to have it close and look like you are doing your job than to be told, "Run and get me a flag." (Remember, always bring a C-stand and bag in addition to the flag.)

**T.O.T.**

If you have to grab a head and arm off of a C-stand, always pull from the back of the pile.

**T.O.T.**

When you break down a setup, always realign the knuckles on the stand, so they are ready to go back into action.

**T.O.T.**

Tennis balls make excellent safety tips on stands or any protruding object onto which a ball will fit after it has been punctured.

**T.O.T.**

If you have to put a large object in a C-stand head, such as piece of 1 in. × 3 in. lumber, always remember to install a wedge in the bottom of the head on the other side.

1. Let the head bite the 1 in. × 3 in. piece of lumber first, then slide the wedge in. Now tighten the knuckle or knob until they are both clamped in the head.
2. The wedge is used to prevent the threaded rod that holds the locked plates of the head from bending.
3. This trick also applies when using an overhead stand (high roller).

Okay, that wasn't so tough. As I said in the beginning of this book, I will tell you more about C-stands and how to use them after you remember what they look like. Now for the rest of the stands. They are used a lot but not as much as this last monster.

### Low-Boy Stand

1. A low-boy stand is nothing more than a combo/light stand—only lower (Figure 2.61).
2. It can be used as an umbrella stand, but it was designed specifically for when a combo/light stand cannot be used due its height.
3. The receiver is a 1-1/8 in. hole.

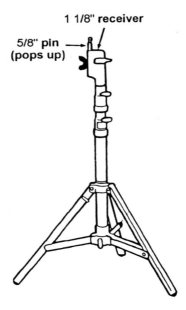

1 1/8" receiver

5/8" pin
(pops up)

**Figure 2.61** Low-boy stand.

### Reflector (Combo/Light) Stand

1. Combo reflector stands (Figure 2.62) are considered to be the standard type for use with reflectors.
2. The stand was originally designed for mobile or location production, back when studios were just beginning to get away from the backlot concept.
3. The combo stand features a three-leg base with a folding brace in each leg.
4. The stand is portable, yet it has enough heft to stand a moderate gust of wind blowing against the reflector surface.
5. The name "combo" is short for "combination," referring to the fact that the stands are used to support a variety of exterior lighting fixtures.
6. The combo/light stands are available with a rocky mountain leg (sometimes a sliding leg).
   a. One leg telescopes out of a tube inside a tube.
   b. The knob on this sliding leg is used to adjust the sliding leg into position to facilitate leveling on uneven terrain.
   c. The combo stand receptacle is 1-1/8 in.

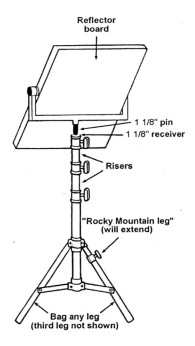

**Figure 2.62a** Reflector stand with rocky mountain leg.

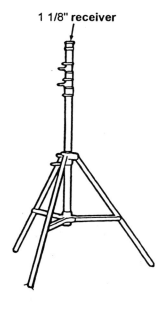

**Figure 2.62b** Reflector combo/light stand.

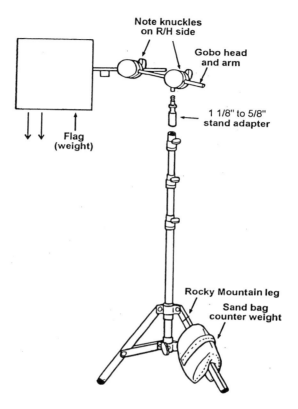

**Figure 2.62c** Reflector stand with gobo head and arm.

*Note*: You will find that most lights from 2000 kW to 12,000 kW have a 1-1/8 in. pin.

---

**T.O.T.**

A lollipop is a 4-1/2 in. gobo (large C-stand-style head) with a junior pin attached to the bottom of it; it is used for mounting into a 1-1/8 in. receiver.

---

### Overhead (High Roller) Stand

1. Although "overhead stand" is the proper name, we can just call it a *high roller* (Figure 2.63).
2. There are several sizes of high rollers, ranging from junior to high to high-high.

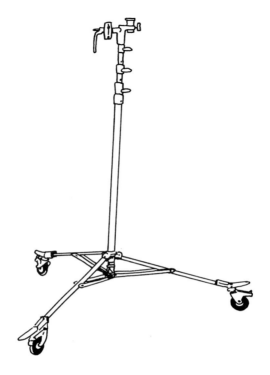

**Figure 2.63a** Overhead stand (also known as a high roller).

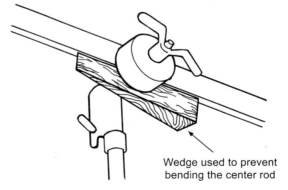

Wedge used to prevent
bending the center rod

**Figure 2.63b** Overhead stand with a wedge.

3. Depending on what job you are doing, you will have to determine which one you will need.
4. These are wide-based units designed for extra stability.
5. The legs slide up and down the center shaft to work in tighter environments.
6. The high roller stands are primarily for exterior work or on stages where you need a beefy stand.

7. Some of the high roller stands have a grip head, which is a 4-1/2 in. head that is almost identical to the C-stand's 2-1/2 in. head.
8. Most new high roller stands have grip heads with a receptacle on the backside that will receive a 1-1/8 in. diameter pin.

*Note*: Another standard size to remember is 1-1/8 in.

**T.O.T.**
Always unlock your high roller wheels before you fold the base up. This will allow the roller to fold correctly.

**T.O.T.**
A junior riser can sometimes be used in a high roller or mombo combo if the stand has a junior receiver on it. This means that you can make the stand taller. Make sure you bag it heavily.

**T.O.T.**
If you do not bag a lamp or stand, it might fall.

### Overhead Stand Usage

1. The overhead stand or high roller (Figure 2.64) is usually used to hold anything that has to go higher than a C-stand can hold it.
2. An overhead stand is also stronger, with a larger gobo head (but it does not have a gobo arm).
3. If need be, a gobo arm from a C-stand can be used by inserting it into the head of the overhead stand.
4. The high roller tubes, called *risers* or *stems*, are larger in diameter than a C-stand; for this reason, they are not as apt to bend in a high wind situation.

It is a good practice not to raise the first riser above 18 in. If the high roller is stemmed (raised) completely up, the top riser might bend in a strong wind, due to the reduced diameter of the tube.

*Note*: Remember, people, it is only a tube, so use your common sense.

### Stand Extensions (Riser)

1. The stand extension (Figure 2.65) will add extra height to various light and grip stands.
2. The extension attaches directly to a 5/8-in. pin or a 1-1/8 in. receiver, depending on the style of stand.

Ropes
(4 minimum)

**Figure 2.64a**  Overhead frame with silk.

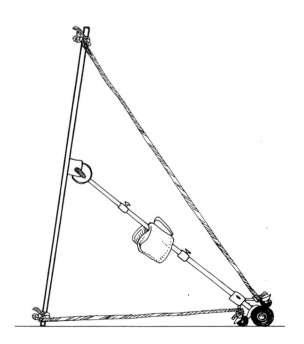

**Figure 2.64b**  12′ × 12′ overhead set for wind conditions.

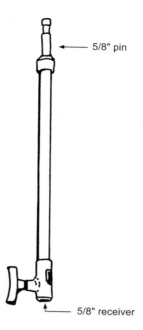

5/8" pin

5/8" receiver

**Figure 2.65** Stand extension pin.

3. The extension comes in various lengths.
4. If it is a 5/8-in. pin, it can be 3 in., 6 in., 9 in., or up to 18 in. long.
5. If it is a junior riser or junior stand extension, then it usually comes as a 36-in. rod that terminates in a 1-1/8 in. receiver.
6. The last 6 in. should be painted red, indicating that the end is about to pop out or is near.

## Studio Overhead Grip Arm

1. A studio overhead grip arm (Figure 2.66) is an overhead C-clamp that terminates in a century-stand-like grip head with an extension arm.
2. This unit can be clamped onto a pipe or a grid to hold flags, scrims, and other items.

## Taco Carts

The Grip Senior and Grip Junior (also known as *taco carts*) are made by Backstage Equipment. These grip carts are designed by Carrie Griffith, a key grip who knows just what grips need and is the owner of Backstage Equipment. The following carts (Figure 2.67) are used daily by several departments (grip, electrical, and

**Figure 2.66** Studio overhead grip arm on pipe clamp.

**Figure 2.67a** Grip Senior (also known as a taco cart).

**Figure 2.67b** Grip Junior.

**Figure 2.67c** Small cart.

**Figure 2.67d** Large cart.

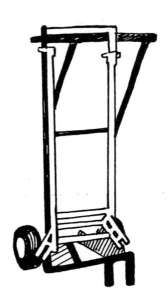

**Figure 2.67e** Century stand cart.

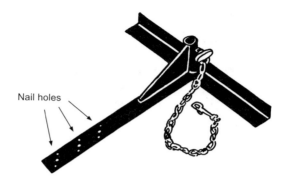

Nail holes

**Figure 2.68** T-bone.

props), just to name a few (remember that all the carts can be special ordered to your design as well):

- Grip Senior
- Grip Junior
- Large grip cart (modern style)
- Small grip cart (modern style)
- Century stand cart

### T-Bone

1. The T-bone (Figure 2.68) provides rigid support for the low positioning of Junior and Senior lighting instruments.
2. The T-bone may be nailed to the floor. (If it is not nailed, *always* bag it.)

### Telescoping Hanger—Stirrup

1. Telescoping hangers (Figure 2.69) are designed for hanging lighting fixtures from overhead grid pipes, extending these fixtures well down into a set.
2. The hangers can be adjusted for length and also permit pivoting around the vertical axis of the C-clamp.
3. The single hangers have a maximum length of 3 ft., and the double hangers telescope from 3 ft. to 6 ft.
   a. The hangers end in a 1/2-in. × 16 pitch female thread, into which a stirrup or other accessories can be bolted.

**Figure 2.69** Telescoping hangers.

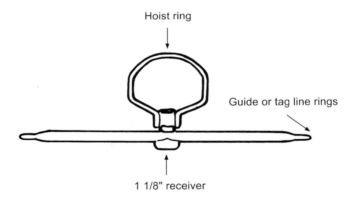

**Figure 2.70** Trapeze.

## Trapeze

1. As the name suggests, a trapeze (Figure 2.70) is designed to swing over a set where no overhead light is available, or where the grid is too high.
2. By attaching a chain to the center of the horseshoe, the trapeze can be dropped onto the set.
3. You can also use a rope on a trapeze.
4. The rings on either end receive ropes (tag lines) that are used to center the fixture.

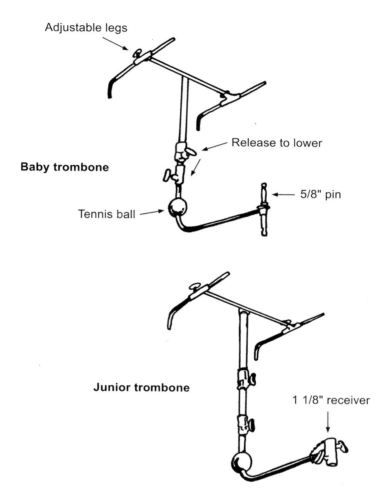

Adjustable legs

Release to lower

**Baby trombone**

5/8" pin

Tennis ball

**Junior trombone**

1 1/8" receiver

**Figure 2.71**  Trombones.

## Trombone

1. Trombones (Figure 2.71) are named for the way in which they bend or telescope.
2. They are designed to hang from a set wall and to adjust to the width of the wall.
3. A rubber ball on the telescoping shaft keeps the mount from marring the wall surface.
4. The only difference between the baby and the junior trombone is the mounting device: a 5/8-in. pin or a 1-1/8 in. receiver, respectively.

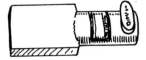

**Figure 2.72** Tube stretchers.

**Figure 2.73** Tubing hanger.

## Tube Stretcher

1. Tube stretchers (Figure 2.72) are made out of pipe instead of wood.
   a. Basically, they fit inside a wall spreader and do the same thing as a wall spreader (see the wall spreader section).
2. I strongly suggest not exceeding a 16-ft. spread.

## Tubing Hanger

1. A tubing hanger (Figure 2.73) is used to support overhead frames or other types of rigging.
2. One end fits into a 4-1/2 in. grip head.
3. The opposite end terminates in a clamp designed to hold pipe or tubing with a 1- to 2-in. outside diameter.

## Turtle

The turtle base stand is perfect to mount a large lamp very low. The one pictured in Figure 2.74 is equipped with wheels. They also make them without wheels.

**T.O.T.**
Turtle stands are low base stands used to mount lights low. If none is available, a skid plate with a junior receiver on it will also work.

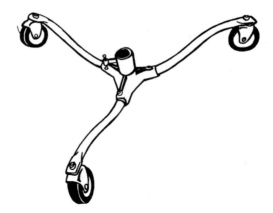

**Figure 2.74** Turtle base.

**Figure 2.75** Umbrella on low umbrella stand.

## Umbrella

Okay, here's a tough one. The umbrella is nothing more than a large picnic-like umbrella (Figure 2.75). And who usually gets it? The director or cameraperson. (Remember, these are the guys and gals who called you.)

## Wall Bracket (Set)

1. Similar in design to baby plates, wall brackets are fitted with 1-1/8 in. receivers (Figure 2.78).
2. The junior wall plate can be nailed in either a vertical or horizontal position.
3. The set wall bracket provides an extremely stable base for mounting a fixture on top of a set wall.

## Wall Plate—Junior

1. Junior wall plates (Figure 2.79) may also be called *set wall brackets*.
2. They are similar in design to a baby plate.
3. These products are fitted with a 1-1/8 in. receiver.
4. The junior wall plate can be nailed in either a vertical or horizontal position.
5. The set wall bracket provides an extremely stable base for mounting a fixture on top of a set, wall, and so on.

### T.O.T.

If you run out of baby plates, drop a spud adapter (stand adapter) in it, and then you have a beefy baby plate.

## Wall Sled

1. The wall sled (Figure 2.76) is a mounting device designed to support lighting equipment from a set wall without the necessity of nailing directly into the wall.
   a. The weight of the fixture exerts pressure to force the sled against the wall.
   b. The weight of the entire unit is supported by a chain or a rope that is secured to the top of the set.
2. The baby wall sled is equipped with dual 5/8-in. pins.
   a. While the first pin is holding a lighting fixture, the other may be utilized to hold a grip arm or head.

The junior and senior wall sled are the same in size. Both of them have 1-1/8 in. receptacles. Now, usually when we refer to "baby" we are talking about a 5/8-in. pin and when we refer to "junior" we are talking about 1-1/8 in.

## Wall Spreader

1. Wall spreaders (Figure 2.77) are used to suspend grip and lighting equipment wall-to-wall by inserting a precut 2 in. × 4 in. or 2 in. × 6 in. stick of lumber into the mounts, then wedging the complete unit between the walls.

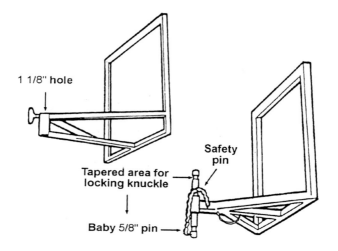

**Figure 2.76** Wall sled.

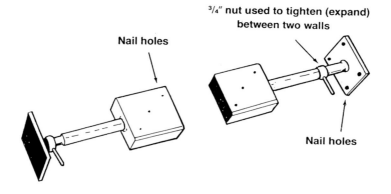

**Figure 2.77** Wall spreaders.

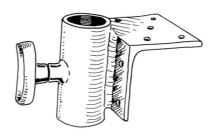

**Figure 2.78** Wall bracket (set).

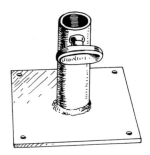

**Figure 2.79** Wall plate (junior).

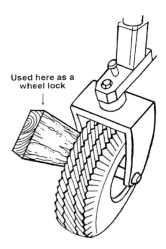

**Figure 2.80** Wedge, used here as a wheel lock.

2. Supporting pressure is extended by a screw device. Caution must be taken in not applying too much pressure.
3. It is also recommended that wall spreaders should be positioned in direct line with the wall studs.

## Wedges

1. This is exactly what you think it is—a wedge (Figure 2.80).
2. A wedge is usually 10 in. × 4 in. × 1/16 in. and tapers to 1 in. thick.
3. You will find it to be one of your most used pieces of equipment.

# Expendables

## Automatic Tape Gun (ATG) Tape

Automatic tape gun (ATG) tape is a clear, double-sided sticky tape. When using this tape, it is best to use only a short strip of it, approximately 1 to 2 in. long. (It's like that old commercial—"a little dab'll do ya.") This stuff works great. Use it on wood or glass or for putting up gels, but remember that it can make a gel unusable if the sticky tape touches the wrong spot.

Remove ATG tape from the old gel by simply pulling it off. Some tape will remain on the gel, but most of the tape will remain on the surface to which the gel was applied. To remove this remaining tape, use about a foot or so of gaffer tape. Stick it on the ATG double-face tape that was left behind, rub your finger on the back of the gaffer tape, and press firmly so it will stick to the ATG tape. Now simply pull the tab on the gaffer tape. When the gaffer tape is removed, the ATG tape should come with it. Actually, you will have to press the gaffer tape on the ATG tape several times to remove all the ATG tape. (Sort of like removing lint from your clothes.) By the way, grips always try to clean up their mess. That's what the real pros do!

### T.O.T.

Put a tiny tab (about an inch) of ATG tape on the baby plate back to help hold it in place while you put in the screw.

### T.O.T.

ATG tape is sometimes called snot tape.

*Note*: I recommend that you have the production company rent a package of expendable equipment (foam core, show cards, gels, and hardware) on an "as-used" basis. This way production will only pay for what has been used.

## Baby Powder

We use baby powder on a dolly track (steel and wood) to prevent the wheels from squeaking when rolling along the track.

## Bead Board

Bead board comes in 4 ft. × 8 ft. sheets of foam that are about 3/4 to 1 in. thick, although it does come in thinner or thicker sheets as well. It has a very porous surface that does not bounce all the light.

**T.O.T.**

Bead board can be used to insulate a wall or door if you have a sound recording problem.

**T.O.T.**

Tape foam core to the back of bead board to give it rigidity in a windy area. This will help prevent the bead board from breaking in half.

## Black Wrap

Black wrap is nothing more than aluminum foil with a heat-resistant, dull (matte) black coating on both sides. It has many uses. I use it as a heat shield to prevent a hot light from blistering wood or paint. Just tear off a sheet like you would aluminum foil and place it between the lamp and a wall. It will act as a heat sink and a reflector of the heat at the same time, and it will also cut light to prevent spill from the wall without bouncing back any light (as regular aluminum foil would). It can also be used on a flag that may be have to be too close to a light. This usually prevents the flag from burning.

**T.O.T.**

Never form-fit black wrap foil to a light, because it will destroy the light. Apply black wrap to a light loosely. If the light is wrapped too tightly, the globe will heat up and burn out.

## Bobinett

Bobinett is the mesh, veil-like material that we use to make our scrims (single or double nets). We order it by the yard. We also stretch it over a neon light to lower the light intensity a little. (*Note:* Neon lights cannot be fully dimmed.)

## Butcher Paper

Butcher paper comes in rolls of paper approximately 100 ft. × 3 ft. wide and is used to cover walks, floors, or painted surfaces. It is just a heavy, plain brown paper.

## Clothespins (C-47s)

The clothespins we use (also called C-47s) are wooden clothespins with metal springs. We use these to hold cut pieces of gels in place on the light doors or any other place where a clamp action is needed. I have been told that they have the nickname C-47 because the old major studios used to keep such clothespins in bin #C-47, but who knows for sure?

## Drywall Screws

Drywall screws are very sharp-pointed screws in different lengths that are used with battery-powered screw guns.

### T.O.T.
Let's say the screw is stuck in the wood. Here is a trick that sometimes works to loosen the screw. Put the hand-driven screwdriver tip squarely (90 degrees) in the slots on the head. Apply a counterclockwise pressure with one hand, and tap the top of the screwdriver handle with a hammer lightly with the other while you are turning it. If you cannot get enough counterclockwise pressure on the handle while trying to unscrew it, grab the shank (shaft) of the screwdriver with a pair of vise grips. This should give you more turning pressure. Keep tapping while applying counterclockwise pressure.

## Dulling Spray

Dulling spray, as its name implies, will dull a surface, such as chrome or a mirror, giving the surface a fogged look. It is often used to prevent reflections, such as a stage light bouncing off an object, or to mark or hide a camera's own reflection during filming. Next time you watch a movie, look at a mirror on a car or the contour of a car fender; chances are it will look like it has a morning dew on it (even if it is 97 degrees outside). Dulling spray wipes off with a clean cloth without leaving much more than a light wax-like surface residue. A warm, moist towel will usually remove all traces of dulling spray. If you run out of dulling spray and you need something, anything, to get rid of a "hard kick" (a reflection, usually from the sun or a lamp), you can be a genius, the hero of the hour, just by asking a makeup person for some hair spray. It does not work as well as dulling spray, but it works well enough to get the shot. A light coat or mist of Streaks 'n' Tips® will work, too.

## Duvatyne

Duvatyne is a tough, canvas-like black cloth. It has been saturated with a fire-retardant chemical at the factory. It is used to make the flags and cutters we use in the motion picture industry. We also carry a roll of Duvatyne when we go on location. The roll comes 48 in. wide by whatever length you order (it is usually sold by the yard). We use Duvatyne to black out a window and give the appearance of night-fall outside during a daytime shot. Sometimes we use Duvatyne as a shoulder pad or a scratch-proof cloth. It will be a very handy and often-used item in your inventory. By the way, it does not work as a spill wipe or a cleanup rag, due to its fire-retardant chemicals.

### T.O.T.
To make a Duvatyne poncho, peel off about 4 to 5 ft. of it, cut a hole approximately 18 in. from one end, and use it as a large black bib to eliminate reflections of the people behind the camera.

## Foam Core

Foam Core comes in a 4 ft. × 8 ft. sheet. It is a thin (3/16 in., approximately) piece of foam laminated on both sides with a strong paper that has a glossy white finish. It is used to bounce (redirect) light from the source onto an object. Foam core comes in two colors:

1. White-on-white (white on both sides)
2. Black-on-white (black on one side and white on the other)

The dull black side is often used as a teaser, or cutter, of light.

**T.O.T.**

To give the effect that cars or people are casting shadows on a subject, create a windmill that has a center-mounted pin. Now cut out 3 in. × 36 in. slots from a 4 ft. × 4 ft. piece of foam core, then spin it slowly in front of a movie lamp.

**T.O.T.**

Poor man's light process: Cut a 4 ft. × 8 ft. piece of foam core to 4 ft. × 4 ft. Cut different shaped holes in it. Put it on a gobo arm like a windmill. Shine a light through the holes as it spins on the C-stand (gobo) arm threads.

**T.O.T.**

Sometimes it is wise to cover a painted surface with foam core to deflect the direct heat from a lamp. Remember, a heat shield will reduce heat, but it is even better to be overprotective.

**T.O.T.**

Use florists' frogs (bases for flower arranging) with foam core and show cards. Frogs look like 20 #4 nails standing tip-up in a lead base. We use a range of sizes, from 1 to 4 in. They can be round, square, or rectangular, but it does not matter what the base shape is as long as they fit into the area needed. They are useful for holding foam core in place to bounce light onto the subject.

## Grip Chains

Grip chains are what most grips in the industry use to secure (tie down) almost everything, ranging from a large light stand to a chain that has to stay in place. Grip chains are a must on all shoots. They are also called *sash chains*.

**T.O.T.**

I highly recommend that you use a double-headed nail such as a #8 or #16 duplex, when using grip chain.

## Laminated Glass

Laminated glass is used to protect the lens of a camera if you cannot get or afford Lexan (see Lexan discussion, below). The laminated glass we use is usually a 24 in. × 24 in. piece of glass attached to a sheet of 1/2-in. plywood with a square hole cut through it (approximately 20 in. × 20 in.). If you attach the glass with cribbing, you can cut the cost down and do pretty much the same job. The reason we prefer to use Lexan is that it is lighter and faster to work with, and this is a business where safety and speed go hand in hand.

## Layout Board

Layout board is a thin (approximately 1/16 in.) piece of cardboard that comes in 4 ft. × 8 ft. sheets. It is used to cover floors and surfaces to keep them from being marred.

## Lexan

Lexan is clear plastic that we use in front of the camera to help protect the operator and camera from an explosion that is being filmed or from a gun shot near the camera. Lexan comes in 4 ft. × 8 ft. sheets of various thicknesses. I feel the safest when the Lexan is at least 1/2 in. thick. To cut Lexan, use a combination saw blade on a 7-1/4 in. circular saw. Use a carbide-tipped blade. Let the blade settle its way through the plastic, then make your normal cut through the plastic.

## Penny Nails (#8 and #16)

At about 2-1/2 in. long, #8 penny nails are smaller than #16 penny nails, which are about 3-1/2 in. long and have a little thicker shank and wider head. Both types of nails are common or duplex (double) head nails. (The word "penny" comes from the weight of the nail from days of yore.)

**T.O.T.**
If you hammer a nail tip before driving it into a piece of lumber, it aids in preventing the wood from splitting.

## Plywood

Always use at least 3/4-in. A/C plywood. It is strong enough to support the weight of a dolly. The reason we use A/C is that the A side of the plywood is very smooth and acts as a good tracking surface. The C side has knots or is rough, but that is okay. This side lies on the ground. Birch plywood that is 3/4 in. thick is super smooth and strong but twice the price.

**T.O.T.**
Always use A/C or A/D plywood for dolly tracks.

**T.O.T.**
When cutting a piece of wood with a skill or circular saw, raise the blade so only the tips of the blade protrude through the wood while cutting. This will help prevent the blade from binding in the wood.

**T.O.T.**
Carry wood or lumber with one end high and the other end low in order not to smack anyone.

## Pushpin

A pushpin is used a lot to put up gels on wooden window frames. Always put a small tab of tape on the gel where the pushpin is going to enter. This will prevent the gel from tearing where the pushpin has pierced it.

## Sash Cord #8

Sash cord #8 is a clothesline type of white cloth (not vinyl) cord that is used for many purposes. It is also called *cotton cord*.

**T.O.T.**
A quick safety tie-off is to tie a half hitch in a #8 sash cord, then put a drywall screw with a large area washer on it through the center of the knot. Now screw the screw into the set's 1 × 3 lumber for a good bite, then tie off the unit needing to be made safe.

**T.O.T.**

Estimate the length of a rope by using the span of your arms. Measure your span from fingertip to fingertip with arms spread wide. Now, grab the rope and loop it after each span count; for example, ten loops of a 6-ft. span is approximately 50 to 60 ft. Remember that this is only a ballpark measurement.

**T.O.T.**

It's up to you if you put a lanyard (short cord) on your tools in your pouch. Some folks make a small loop that goes over their wrist while working high in the perms, green beds, or from a tall ladder. There are two schools of thought on this issue:

1. If you drop the tool, it will not fall.
2. If you fall and the lanyard gets hung up, it could be a different problem.

## Show Card

Show card comes in 32 in. × 40 in. cards. Those that are dull black on one side and white on the other are most often used, although they come in a rainbow of different colors. Show card is made of a cardboard-like material that is a little thicker than a cereal box, about 1/16 in. It is used to bounce (redirect) a small quantity of light. Show card can easily be bent or curved to bounce light around both the side of an object and the front at the same time. It is sometimes laid in an actor's or actress's lap to create a fill light on their clothes or faces. It is a soft look. It is often also called *art card*.

**T.O.T.**

Clip the show card to a flag to create a support backing useful when setting the show card in a stand.

## Silicone Spray

Silicone spray is a dry type of lubricant. It is used where you cannot use an oil spray. I use it on steel dolly track in the dirt, because dirt will not stick to the track as easily as it does with spray oil, but this is only my personal preference.

### Spray Glue

Spray glue is a strong aerosol glue. It is fast and works great wherever you may need to glue something.

**T.O.T.**
Use Photo Mount™ spray to attach gels to windows. This is a great way to make a gel stay in place when gelling in a high-rise building.

### Spray Oil

Spray oil is an oil that is used to lubricate any moving part so that it will work properly. It also aids in preventing a squeak or noise during a sound take.

### Staples

Staples are used like pushpins to install gels. It is faster and easier to staple up a gel, but it is more difficult to save the gel when you remove it.

**T.O.T.**
When giving a staple gun to someone, always bring refills. If you don't, I promise you the stapler will run out every time. Shoot a long staple on an angle, which is the best way to get the staple back out.

### Stove Pipe Wire

Stove pipe wire is a black multipurpose wire that is sometimes called *baling wire* because it is the same as the wire used to bale hay.

### Streaks 'n' Tips®

This is actually a spray-on hair dye that comes in a multitude of colors. The spray washes right out with soap and water. We use it in the industry to tone down a bright object such as a white picket fence that may look too white for the camera. We just spray it on, like a spray paint mist. When it settles on the fence, the mist dries almost on contact, causing the fence to take on the tone of the color spray used. This is sometimes called "aging the fence" so it will look more real, used, or older to the camera. We can also apply the product in the color gray, for example, to an actor's hair at the temples to age the actor. Remember, it washes off with soap and water.

## Tapes

Use low-tack blue tape. It sticks great and is easy to remove without pulling the paint off. It comes in several widths. Most paint stores have it. It is sometimes called seven-day tape, because when it is peeled off after a week no sticky residue is left behind.

### T.O.T.
To make safety reflectors for rope, put tape tabs hanging down about 8 to 10 in. long, double them over, and tape them to themselves. This is so a person does not trip or get caught by the neck.

### Camera Tape

Camera tape is like gaffer or grip tape, except that it comes in 1-in.-wide rolls. Usually, we use black or white tape, although it comes in several colors. It is mostly used by the camera assistants to reseal film cans after they have been opened.

### T.O.T.
Tab your tape at the end of the roll so it is ready to peel off easily.

### T.O.T.
Remember! Tape will gather moisture, so remove it when you are finished with it.

### T.O.T.
Always mark damaged equipment with white tape. This is standard throughout the industry.

**T.O.T.**
Put gaffer tape over the thread on hard wheels and electric scissor lifts to prevent tire tracks on painted surfaces.

## Double-Faced Tape

This tape comes in two forms. One type is a sponge-like foam about 1/8 in. thick with a sticky surface on both sides. The other is a thin cellophane-like material with a sticky surface on both sides (sometimes called *carpet tack tape*). Double-faced tape of both types is used to tack something down, to hold it in place during and after a shot.

## Gaffer or Grip Tape

Gaffer or grip tape is a cloth-like tape that is 2 in. wide. It looks like the air conditioning duct tape most of us have seen. It comes in various colors, although usually gray is used. It is handy wherever a strong tape is needed.

**T.O.T.**
Always use a tab of tape to staple through a gel; otherwise, it will tear very easily.

## Paper Tape

Paper tape usually comes in 1- and 2-in. widths, although you can order it wider. It is much like masking tape, although we order it in black. It has a matte finish, which means that the surface seen by the camera will just appear as a dull dark area. Stray light will not bounce off the tape unless it is aimed directly at it.

**T.O.T.**
To reduce unwanted light from a fluorescent light tube, you can tape 1 to 2 in. of black tape right on the tube. This will act as a flag as well.

**T.O.T.**
*Black photo tape* is preferred over black masking tape for two reasons. The photo black tape will almost disappear on film due to its matte backing, whereas masking tape has a shiny back surface. Also, the glue on masking tape is white, and the glue on photo tape is black. Both are paper tapes.

**T.O.T.**

Always use paper tape on a painted wall or a surface where the paint or finish might pull off with a stronger tape such as gaffer or grip tape.

## Visqueen

Visqueen is plastic that comes in different thicknesses, widths, and lengths and in clear or black. We use .006 mil × 20 ft. × 100 ft. rolls.

**T.O.T.**

Order a box of crutch tips (so-called due to their use for things that lack a tip) as a quick repair for stand legs that might scratch a set floor. Such locations include set stages and locations such as houses, office buildings, or any other place you could damage the floor.

# Knots

Several types of knots can be tied, but in the film industry there are at least four knots that you will use on a daily basis:

1. Bowline
2. Clove hitch
3. Half hitch
4. Square knot

Each one of these knots is a must-know knot. Sure, it is great to know more types, but these are the most commonly used.

## Bowline Knot

This knot is used to hang anything that is a dead hang, or a straight pull-down. After you have read the instructions on how to tie this knot (Figure 4.1), practice it several items. Learn to tie it with your eyes closed. Practice until it becomes second nature.

*Note*: Never walk away from a knot if you are unsure of it. Call for help or ask someone's advice to check whether it is correct. Your life may depend on it. I recommend you get a book on knots—an old Boy Scout manual gave me a good start.

## Clove Hitch Knot

The clove hitch (Figure 4.2) is the knot most commonly used to tie-off a dead hanging object. Always put a half-hitch in your rope tail after you have secured the knot. This provides a little extra safety.

## Half Hitch Knot

The half hitch knot is nothing more than an extra little safety tie in your locking knot. You use a half hitch every time you tie your shoes.

1. The loop

2. Slip end through loop
from bottom

3. Wrap end around line

4. Slip end back down
through hole

5. Pull end up

Pull down tightening knot

**Figure 4.1**  How to tie a bowline.

1. Lay rope over pipe, attach a weight to end to keep taut during practice.

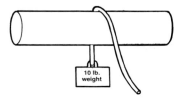

2. Wrap rope around pipe, then lay across the top of rope with weight.

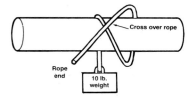

3. Lift the crossover rope and slide the rope end underneath the crossover rope.

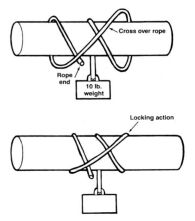

**Figure 4.2**  How to tie a clove hitch.

1. Lay black lace over white lace.

2. Start to tie a half hitch, wrapping the white lace around the black lace.

A half hitch

3. Now back loop the black lace around the white lace.

Back loop over white lace end.

4. Pull both black lace and white lace in opposite directions.

**Figure 4.3**  How to tie a square knot.

## Square Knot

The square knot (Figure 4.3) is the knot used most often to tie up a bundle of cable. First, you wrap the excess of the long tie around the loop of cable, then you tie a square knot. This knot is a strong locking knot but is very easy to untie quickly. This knot is also commonly used to secure bundles of tubes together, such as a 12 × 12 frame tube.

# Basic Tool Descriptions

## Standard Screwdriver (Common or Blade Type)

A standard screw driver, also known as a common or blade type, usually has a shank (shaft) ranging from 3 in. to about 12 in. long. Longer and shorter ones are available, as well. The tip, which is also called the *blade*, has a wide face and a thin blade. Some screwdrivers have a thin face and a wide blade.

## Phillips Screwdriver

The most common Phillips screwdriver (Figure 5.1a) is a number two tip (a 30-degree tip). If you use a number one (which has a smaller tip but still a 30-degree angle) in place of the required number two, you will strip the screw head and eventually the screwdriver tip itself. Always be sure that the tip is correct and is completely and squarely set in the screw's head. This position is called normal or 90 degrees to the surface. The screw's head is horizontal, and the screwdriver shank is vertical. This position should prevent skipping or stripping out of the screw's head. If you hear or feel a chatter or grinding sound when using a hand or power driver, stop and reset the blade or tip to the normal (90 degrees) position, then proceed.

## Reed and Prince Screwdriver

The Reed and Prince screwdriver tool (Figure 5.1b) looks very much like a Phillips screwdriver except that the Reed and Prince tip has a sharp point (a 45-degree angle tip). In contrast, the Phillips screwdriver has a blunt or flat tip. Be sure that you have the correct tool on your tool belt (Phillips number two). You will find very little use for the Reed and Prince—but I have one standing by in my hand-carry toolbox just in case.

## Files

I use a four-in-one file (Figure 5.2), which is quite handy. Keep one in your tool box. The four types of files you should know about are:

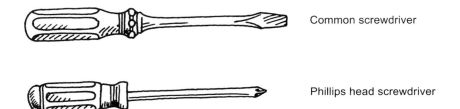

Common screwdriver

Phillips head screwdriver

**Figure 5.1a** Common and Phillips head screwdrivers.

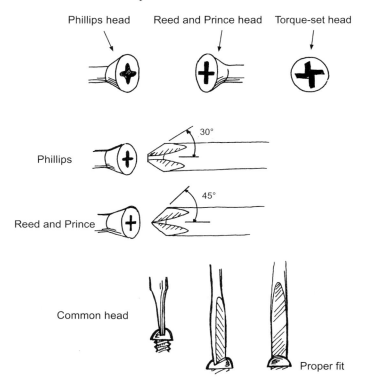

Phillips head    Reed and Prince head    Torque-set head

Phillips    30°

Reed and Prince    45°

Common head    Proper fit

**Figure 5.1b** Screwdrivers.

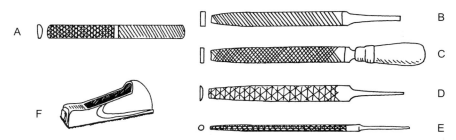

A    B

C

D

F    E

**Figure 5.2** Files. A. Four in one, Double/single (shown). Rasp/half—round (not shown). B. Single C. Double D. Half round double cross cut E. Rat tail F. Hand rasp.

1. Flat file (single cut), which is used for precise filing (See 5.2B)
2. Flat double-cut or cross file, which removes material faster than single cut (See 5.2C)
3. Round file (rat tail—when the file is round and has a slight taper to the end opposite the handle, it is usually referred to as a rat tail file) (See 5.2E)
4. Hand carriage rasp file (See 5.2F)

*Note*: Never use a file without a handle.

When you are filing, do not rush. Smooth, slow strokes will give you a better finish. Slightly angle the file to the material when you file. Slow strokes give the cut material a chance to fall from the teeth.

## Hacksaw

There are several types of blades and lengths. I carry a compact handle style. On the blades, the teeth style is called the *set*. The teeth are bent out wider than the blade so as to cut and allow the blade not to bind. When you look at the blade, the set has a wavy look. The pitch of the hacksaw blade is also important to know about. The number of teeth per inch is usually indicated—for example, 18, which means 18 teeth per 1 inch of blade. The more teeth per inch means a smoother cut. Remember, when you are cutting steel, aluminum, or PVC, it is recommended that you cut at the rate of 32 to 40 strokes per minute. Do not try to cut like you have a date in 5 minutes. All that does is heat up the blade and jam up the teeth. A nice, slow, even cut will keep the blade somewhat cold and allow the cuttings to fall from the teeth. The hacksaw is used to cut metal and/or plastic. The hacksaw blade is usually 10 to 12 in. long. The blade will fit on the saw with its teeth (cutting surface) facing down, up, or sideways. The teeth of the blade, when installed properly, will face forward (away from the handle).

## Lineman Pliers

Lineman pliers (Figure 5.3) are great for heavy-duty cutting or bending, or to grip an object. They are equipped with serrated jaws (teeth) as well as a cutting device for cutting light or thin metals or wire. They usually are about 9 in. long.

**Figure 5.3**  Lineman pliers.

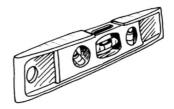

**Figure 5.4** Torpedo level.

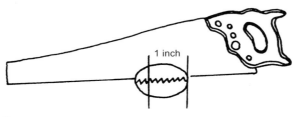

**Figure 5.5** Crosscut saw.

## Torpedo Level

Torpedo levels (Figure 5.4) are great levels. They are made from plastic or metal and fit easily into your tool belt. They are approximately 9 in. long.

## Crosscut Saw

The crosscut saw (Figure 5.5), or common all-purpose saw, is a must-have item. I carry a short version in my tool kit. Crosscut saws were designed to cut across the grain of the wood. They come in different sizes, from 20 in. to 26 in. I recommend an eight-point saw, which has eight points (valleys) with seven teeth (points or peaks) per inch of the saw blade. The eight-point saw is used most often for rough framing. If you must have a cleaner (smoother) finish, step up to a ten-point saw and cut more slowly.

## Circular Saw and Blades

There are several types of circular saw blades. I will only show you a few to get you started. The combination shown in Figure 5.6 is the blade that usually comes with the saw. I recommend that you also obtain a carbide-tipped blade; this blade will be the most useful.

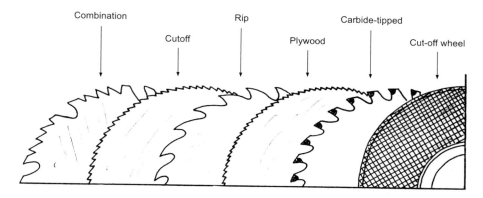

Combination        Rip        Carbide-tipped

Cutoff        Plywood        Cut-off wheel

**Figure 5.6**   Circular saw blades.

**Figure 5.7**   Mat knife.

## Drill Bits

When using a drill bit, always mark the material with a small dent or dimple. This will ensure that the drill bit does not walk (move) off of the intended area to be drilled. If you are going to drill steel, drill slowly while applying pressure. This will actually cause the drill to work better, as the bit will not heat up and dull the tip.

*Note*: Always wear your safety goggles when drilling.

When drilling aluminum, drill at a higher speed. Be sure that your drill bit is perpendicular to the surface. This position is called normal to the surface (90 degrees or a right angle).

## Mat Knife

The mat knife or utility knife (Figure 5.7) is a tool you will use virtually every day. You will cut gels, filters, show card, and foam core with it.

## Tape Measure

I recommend that you get yourself a good, strong 25 to 30 ft. tape with a locking tab (Figure 5.8). Learn to read a tape properly. They are usually divided into sixteenths of an inch. You can get metric ones, as well.

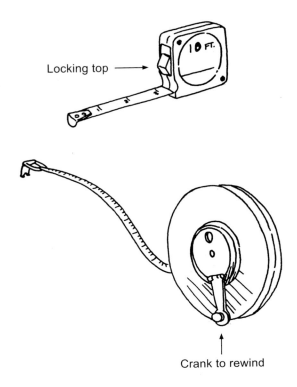

Locking top

Crank to rewind

**Figure 5.8** Reel tape measure.

## Reel Tape Measure

This type of tape measure comes in 50 and 100 ft. lengths and longer. They are very handy for set work.

---

**T.O.T.**

An average credit card is 3-3/8 in. long and 2-1/4 in. wide. You now have a second measuring device in your pocket (and don't forget that a dollar bill is 6 in. long).

---

**T.O.T.**

The spread of most folks' arms is pretty close to their height (measure your span and see). This means that you always have a "tape" handy.

**T.O.T.**
If you need to mark an exact measurement on a piece of wood to be cut, never use the beginning or tip of your tape measure. Measure from the number 1, then subtract an inch.

**T.O.T.**
Practice walking off an area after you know the exact distance. Do this four or five times, then note how many steps it took. You will be able to walk off an area and get a ballpark measurement after you calculate what each step represents. I usually err on the long side. It is better to have a little extra than to be short. This does not mean you should not have the right tools for the job, but this is a quick fix when you need it.

## Claw Hammer

The two basic types of claw hammer are the curved claw and the ripping claw (straight claw) (Figure 5.9). The curved claw provides better leverage for pulling nails. I use a straight-claw hammer with a convex (bell-shaped) face on the hammer head. It allows me to drive a nail flush with little or no marring. There is also a mesh or waffle-faced hammer, which is used mostly for driving large-headed nails during framing work. The mesh helps to keep the hammer from glancing off the nail head. Hammers come in many different head weights; pick one you can handle. I use a 16-oz. Estwing.

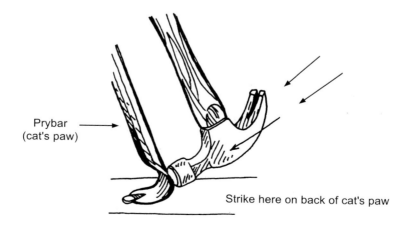

Prybar (cat's paw)

Strike here on back of cat's paw

**Figure 5.9** Claw hammer.

> **T.O.T.**
> I recommend an Estwing hammer. Get a straight claw type, which is easier for pulling nails. I use a smooth face so I don't leave marks.

## Personal Tools

Here is what I think you should start with when building your tool belt. These are general recommendations and the minimum needed.

> **T.O.T.**
> Only buy quality tools. Cheap ones will fail you when you need them most. (I promise you this.)

### Personal Tool Belt

- Your own personal headset for use with the walkie-talkies used on the set
- Padded suspenders, if you use them
- Pouch with several compartments
- Large 90-degree ring hammer holder (makes it easy to remove and install your hammer when you're up on a ladder)
- Tape measure, 30-ft. long by 3/4 to 1 in. wide
- Gloves ("hand shoes")
- Hammer, 16 oz.
- 4-in-1 screwdriver
- Allen wrench set
- Pliers (rubber-insulated handles)
- Dikes (rubber handles)/sidecutters/wirecutters
- Needlenose pliers (rubber handles)
- Miniature flashlight (2 in.)
- Black photo tape
- Clothespins (C-47s)
- Mat knife
- Torpedo level
- Bull's-eye level
- Nail and screw pouches (this does not mean you have to carry 5 pounds of each; carry about a dozen)
- #8 and #16 penny double-headed nails
- #8 drywall screws (1 in., 1-5/8 in., 2 in., 3 in.)
- Scissors (small pair)
- Mini-vise grips
- Leatherman knife

## *Everyday Basic Tools for a Grip's Personal Toolbox*

I suggest that you carry the following tools in a hand-carried toolbox or tool (ditty) bag. This does not mean that you have to carry *all* of them on you at any given time—just make sure that you have these available near the set.

- (1) Hammer, claw type
- (5) Common screwdrivers, different sizes
- (1) Phillips head screwdrivers, different sizes
- (1) Reed and Prince screwdriver
- (1) Staple gun
- (1) Allen wrench set, 1/16 in. to 5/8 in. standard
- (1) Socket set, 3/8-in. drive, 1/4 in. up to 1 in.
- (1) Open-end box set, 1/4 in. to 1 in.; extra 3/8-in., 7/16-in., 1/2-in., and 9/16-in. open-end box—a box ratchet is very handy (*Note*: The 9/16-in. wrench is the most used; have two.)
- (1) Rubber-handled pliers/lineman pliers
- (1) Channel locks, rubber handle
- (1) Vise grip
- (1) 30-ft. tape measure
- (1) Torpedo level, 6 in.
- (1) Hacksaw
- (1) 4-in-1 file
- (2) Crescent wrenches (open to 1 in.)
- (1) Needlenose pliers, rubber handle
- (1) Mat knife
- (1) Flashlight
- Cam wedges
- Clothespins
- Push pins, box of 100
- Safety pins, 20
- Baling wire spool, 50 ft.
- Staples, spares
- #16 double-head nails
- #8 double-head nails
- Drywall screws, 1 in. and 1-5/8 in. to 2-1/2 in.
- Chalk, white or yellow
- Automatic tape gun (ATG)
- 3/8-in. drill bit (standard size 1/4-in. drill bit)

### T.O.T.

I recommend that you carry carabineer clips in your tool box. They are handy when you want to send several things up high, say to the perms. Tie a bowline and just clip on the carabineer. You now have a quick release.

### Power Tools

These are the tools I carry in a milk crate that I bought:

- 7-1/4 in. circular saw, 110-volt A/C electric type (and a worm drive model for power cutting)
- Power screwdriver, battery operated
- Jig saw, electric, any good one
- Drill with 1/2-in. chuck (reversible, electric, variable-trigger speed)

### Useful Items to Also Carry

- Compass with 360-degree plate—use to check sun direction on location

**T.O.T.**

If you can afford it, buy yourself an electric rotozip. It is an excellent tool to cut a little mouse hole in a set wall. Save the panel that you cut out and tape it to the back of the set wall near the hole in case it has to go back in.

### Recommended Personal Gear

### Clothing for Sets

- Personal bag (always have your bag close by)
- Rain gear (you may be on a set that has a rain scene, or it may just rain on what was a sunny day)
- Change of clothes (you sometimes get filthy or wet)
- Ball cap or hat
- Two pairs of sunglasses (they break or get lost)
- Aspirin
- Toothbrush
- Battery-operated clock

**T.O.T.**

If you have a SCUBA card, photocopy it, because you have to fax a copy to production now and then so they can rent equipment.

> **T.O.T.**
> Copy your passport, driver's license, and Social Security card. Keep them in a safe place. You will usually have to provide a copy of these items for payroll purposes—either your passport or your license and Social Security number.

> **T.O.T.**
> Make sure you have an up-to-date passport. I had mine for 10 years and never used it. Then, wham! I filled it up in a short time and had to get a second one. Jobs just pop up sometimes. Production loves to see that you have your stuff together. It makes for a lasting impression. I play a little game; it's called antic-ipation. Everyone is impressed with a person who is together. I know I harp on this a lot, but if just one thing from this book makes you look good, then I feel you have gotten your money's worth. I will eagerly share what little experience I have with anyone who wants to help themselves. But, like most things in life, there are no free rides.

### Clothing and Items for Location

Location gear is the same as set clothes but with more changes:

- Bathing suit (hotels have pools and spas)
- Plug-in clock with battery back-up (always use two clocks—one electric and one battery or wind-up; I use the large number type so I do not have to wake fully up and strain to see my clock)

*Note*: Never fully rely on a desk wake-up call. That's like certain death. You would not jump without a reserve chute would you?

- All your hygiene needs
- Aspirin
- Two pairs of work shoes (rotate them daily—your feet sweat and get the shoes moist, and you don't want to get raw feet)

I always tell my grips to "plan for the worst and hope for the best." If you follow this advice, you won't be let down—I promise you!

I also carry an empty, soft-sided, zip-up duffel bag inside my travel bag. This way I have something to carry any presents home in. Trust me, you will say to yourself on many occasions, "Hey, I'll probably never be in Moscow again," or, "What are the chances of me ever coming back to Lawrence, Kansas?" When I was in Moscow, I bought several Russian army hats and several sets of nesting dolls. You will make good money, and you will spend good money.

### *Personal Electronic Equipment (A Must)*

It is essential to carry your own electronic equipment, particularly a statewide pager (if possible) with voice mail. If you only have a numerical pager, you usually get the number, call it back, and ask, "Did someone there page me?" If you are calling a large production office, the receptionist may not have been informed that a page was sent to you. You may miss a call that could have paid for a full year of voice-mail service. So, be smart and get a voice-mail pager.

#### Cell Phone

A new era has arrived. If you don't answer the phone or quickly return a page, the calling party is under pressure to fill the slot with whomever else is available. This is true whether you are a newbie trying to break in or a regular trying to get more work. Once again, trust me on this. I have been on both sides of the fence. I have been told that production knows that, if I do not get back to them within 5 or 10 minutes after they have paged me, I am not in a place to call them back. That is a good reputation to have. I am a fanatic about returning a call quickly for work.

Once again, I promise you that, if your work is good, your attitude is great, and you return calls very quickly, then you are projecting a sense of "ready, willing, and able." A future employer is very impressed by that. In a short time you will become known for your quick replies. Here is an illustration for you. Suppose you look in a phone book for someone to replace a broken glass window, and the first company you call either does not answer the phone or you have to leave a message and they don't call you right back. I bet you then move right on down the list. It's human nature. I do not mean to sound preachy. I am just trying to get you your first job and propel you to the next and the next and the next.

---

**T.O.T.**

Develop what I call "set ears." Tune your hearing to the voices of the director, the cameraperson or director of photography (DP), the gaffer, and your boss (the key grip), as well as the best boy. If you hear that any one of them would like something, you as a grip should call out that it is on the way or that you will retrieve it. This shows that you have set consciousness and are willing to work.

THE GRIP BOOK **147**

**T.O.T.**

Answer all requests made over the radio by repeating what is needed. For example, suppose the key grip calls out, "Give me a baby plate, a C-stand arm, and a postage stamp single." You should then reply, "One baby plate, a C-stand arm and head, and a $10 \times 12$ open-ended single. Roger. Flying in." This example illustrates that both parties involved know what is needed. The key grip knows that the call was transmitted, and your acknowledgment confirms that it was received. Communication is a major player in the movie industry. I do not want to be redundant, but I do want to drive home key points that will aid you and make you look a little better than the next person who wants the job or during the next call back if they shrink the crew. The grip department is a team. I am not advocating upstaging your peers, but I *am* saying that you must give it your all.

**T.O.T.**

When the need arises, for safety reasons, a grip or anyone else can yell "Cut!"

# Filters and Gels

## Fluorescent Light Filters

Standard cool-white or daylight fluorescent tubes offer a reasonable approximation of photographic daylight except for their excessive green content. Two separate techniques are available to deal with this situation: (1) balance all sources to the fluorescent, or (2) balance the fluorescent to the sources. Rosco Product 3304 is applied to windows or daylight sources and 3306 is applied to 3200 K sources to balance them to the fluorescent lights. Rosco Products 3308, 3313, 3314, 3310, and 3311 are applied to fluorescent lights to convert them to either 3200 K or nominal daylight. A roll of the material is generally a little over 100 sq. ft. (54 in. by 25 ft.), and the products are optically clear.

| Roscoe Product No. | Name | Description |
|---|---|---|
| 3304 | Tough Plusgreen | Converts daylight to match fluorescents |
| 3315 | Tough 1/2 Plusgreen | Adds partial green to daylight and 3200 K sources for balancing with fluorescents and discharge lamps; equivalent to CC15 Green |
| 3316 | Tough 1/4 Plusgreen | Adds partial green to daylight and 3200 K sources for balancing with fluorescents and discharge lamps; equivalent to CC75 Green |
| 3306 | Tough Plusgreen | Converts 3200 K sources to match cool white fluorescent |
| 3308 | Tough Plusgreen | Converts cool-white fluorescent to nominal daylight by absorbing excess green |
| 3313 | Tough 1/2 | Partial green-absorbing filter equivalent to 0.15 cc Magenta; useful on some discharge sources |
| 3314 | Tough 1/4 | Partial green-absorbing filter equivalent to 0.075 cc Magenta; useful on some discharge sources |

| | | |
|---|---|---|
| 3310 | Fluorofilter | Converts cool-white fluorescent to 3200 K |
| 3311 | Fluorofilter | Same as 3310 in 4-ft. sleeves for covering lamps |

---

**T.O.T.**

Put tape on gel, then staple or pushpin gel up. This prevents tearing.

---

**T.O.T.**

For a gel on a frame, use magic markers to write the gel name and type in the corner; this will not show when a light is projected through it.

---

## Arc Light Filters

Rosco's Cinegel System offers a wide range of filters for carbon arcs, HMI, CID, and CSI lamps. They vary in the character and the amount of color correction provided to deal with the age of the lamps in use and other operating conditions. All materials are 100 sq. ft. and are fabricated in a deep-dyed base for optical and high-heat stability.

---

**T.O.T.**

A roll of gel is usually about 25 ft. long and about 4 ft. wide. This gives you enough gel to cover six 4 × 4 frames.

---

## Tungsten Conversion Filters

Rosco Tungsten Conversion Filters convert incandescent 3200 K sources to nominal daylight. These filters offer a deep-dyed base for optical clarity and high-heat stability. They are about 100 sq. ft. (54 in. wide).

| No. | Name | Description |
|---|---|---|
| 3202 | Tough Blue 50 (full blue) | Boosts 3200 K to nominal 5500 K daylight |
| 3204 | Tough Booster (half blue) | Boosts 3200 K to 4100 K |
| 3206 | Tough 1/2 Blue (quarter blue) | Boosts 3200 K to 3800 K |
| 3208 | Tough 1/4 Blue (third blue) | Boosts 3200 K to 3500 K |
| 3216 | Tough 1/8 Blue (eight blue) | Boosts 3200 K to 3300 K |

**T.O.T.**

Tape gel to the face of the frame on a zenon (high-density lamp); try not to touch the glass with your hand, as this will leave oil from your fingers on the glass that heats up and causes the unit to burn out more quickly.

## Neutral Density Filters

RoscoSun Neutral Density Filters reduce the level of incident daylight. Two of the materials also convert daylight to a nominal 3200 K. Except for RoscoScrim (54 in. wide), all roll materials are 100 sq. ft. (58 in. wide) and are optically clear.

| No. | Name | Description |
|---|---|---|
| 3402 | RoscoSun N3 | Reduces light intensity one stop |
| 3403 | RoscoSun N6 | Reduces light intensity two stops |
| 3404 | RoscoSun N9 | Reduces light intensity three stops |
| 3405 | RoscoSun 85N3 | Reduces light intensity one stop and converts daylight to nominal 3200 K |
| 3406 | RoscoSun 84N6 | Reduces light intensity two stops and converts daylight to nominal 3200 K. |
| 3809 | RoscoScrim | Perforated material (54 in. wide) that reduces light |

**T.O.T.**

Use water and a squeegee to put up gels on the inside of a window when you can't get to the outside of the window from the exterior (e.g., a high-rise). Photo Mount® spray can also be used or a small tab of ATG tape. If you ask what the DP is seeing, you can sometimes use photo black tape (it will look like part of the window frame).

**T.O.T.**

To reduce a bright spot on a translight (e.g., a spotlight in the picture), cut neutral density (ND) gel to the approximate shape and tape it on with cellophane or ATG tape tabs. Clean it up before you roll it up and send it back. You can also use Bobinett material.

**T.O.T.**

To cut a gel, such as a neutral density gel, for the inside of a lamp shade that will be seen on camera, here is a trick that will help. Roll the shade on a flat piece of ND gel while marking the gel with a marker. The shape will fit pretty close with just a little trimming. Now just apply a little dab of ATG tape to the inside of the lamp shade to hold the gel in place.

## Daylight Conversion Filters

RoscoSun Daylight Conversion Filters are used when shooting in an interior at a 3200 K balance. They are required at windows or other openings to convert incident daylight to an approximation of 3200 K. Partial conversions are utilized where less than full correction (a cooler or bluer daylight appearance) is preferred. All roll materials are 100 sq. ft. (58 in. wide) and optically clear.

| No. | Name | Description |
|---|---|---|
| 3401 | RoscoSun 85 | Converts 5500 K daylight to a nominal 3200 K |
| 3407 | RoscoSun CTO | Converts 5500 K daylight to a nominal 2900 K |
| 3408 | RoscoSun 1/2 CTO | Converts 5500 K daylight to a nominal 3800 K |

**T.O.T.**

Use ND gel inside a lamp shade or wall sconce glass to reduce light if no dimmer can be used.

# Techniques for Mounting the Camera

A camera can be mounted on aircraft, cars, motorcycles, jet skis, boats, parasails, and elsewhere, but you've got your work cut out for you. I will list a few things that are a must when mounting a camera. Remember that a camera and lens usually cost $50,000 to $500,000. No oops allowed. If you want to be able to say, "I'll be back," do it right. Here are a few hints. There are many ways to rig a vehicle. First, if you can get equipment from Modern, American, Matthews, or Norm's Studio Equipment (in North Hollywood, CA); either rent it or buy it. It will pay for itself over and over again—not only by the rental revenue but also by the impression it leaves with directors of photography, directors, and producers. You will look like a professional, and we all know what looks can do.

I use a combination of Modern and Speed-Rail® equipment. Seno Moussally (also known as "Yoda"), the owner of Modern, takes my designs, builds the rig exactly to my specifications, and usually enhances the design after he sees where I am going with it. All the other manufacturers mentioned have excellent equipment; I simply have developed a personal relationship with Seno. Eddie Phillips at Matthews is fantastic. He sold me my grip equipment. Norm, Jr., at Norm's, is a grip turned business executive who really knows the ins and outs, and Lance at American has always built a better mouse trap.

With reliable vendors, cellular telephones, and overnight delivery services, there is no reason not to get the right piece of equipment immediately. At Modern, Seno has a huge showroom of widgets, gadgets, tubes, sleeves, plates, and rigs already built. He really has "been there and rigged that." When I had four hours to rig a side-mounted camera on a brand new Mercedes, I drove the car to Modern, and Seno welded and fit what I needed on the spot. I drove back to the set, had a nice cup of coffee, and got the shots production needed. What I am trying to say is that I only *act* like a genius. I use the Albert Einsteins of the film industry to further my projects. I can't do it all, but I know who can, and I just gave you their names. Learn from the masters.

Here is a trick I use when I mount clamps on motorcycle frames. I apply 2-inch-wide paper tape to the area where I will apply the starter clamp. Then I put gaffer tape over the paper tape. The paper tape is easier to peel off the painted frame than gaffer tape is. After you have wrapped the gaffer tape 2 to 3 times around the frame, cut out a piece of rubber mat and wrap it only once around the frame, then attach the metal clamp. This system should hold the clamp in place without scraping or marring the tube of the motorcycle frame. Whenever you mount a camera on

**153**

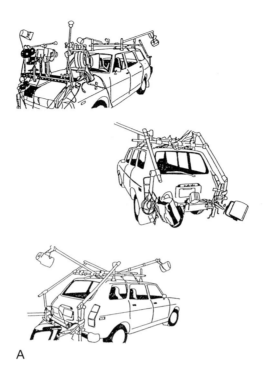

A

**Figure 7.1A** Speed-Rail rigs.

a motorcycle, try to get three or four starter points on each mount. This gives it stability, and when you are asked to adjust the rig angle of the camera, your work will be expedited. Trust me on this; no mount is rigged in stone. Film is moving art. Changes are often made. Be prepared for those changes.

At first it may seem like it takes a little longer to get started, but I promise you it will pay off for you. It's called planning ahead. They say advice is worth what it cost you; you paid for the advice in this book, so use it. This book is about my making you one of the best, safest, and fastest mount riggers out there.

A car, truck, boat, or other vehicle may have to have a camera mounted on it. This is where expertise and imagination come together. You may be called on to mount a camera on a bicycle, airplane, train, or even a jet ski. (Believe me, a jet ski can be fitted with a camera.) There are several types of mounts, but there are no specific mounts for specific applications. This is where you step in as a grip. You will have to use the basic mounts available and design your own. It seems tough at first, but if you are someone who likes to build things you will enjoy this. I have provided illustrations of mounts I have made with any materials at hand (Figure 7.1).

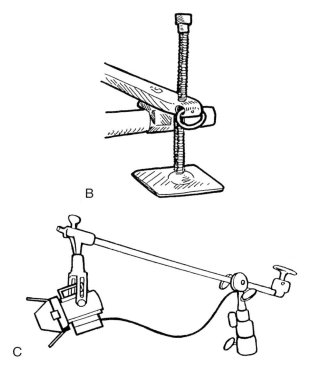

**Figure 7.1** B Adjustable leveling leg on hood mount C Gobo head and arm (c-stance head and arm) used as a menice arm to rig a small light.

Use the list of materials to get a basic idea of what you will need to design and rig your own mounts. You can use wood, metal, plastic, or anything else that works safely. Observe one of the Golden Rules: There are ten ways to do the same job, and usually they all work.

**T.O.T.**

Poor man's vehicle process: Put a lever under the frame of the car and pump it up and down while filming. It gives the effect of movement.

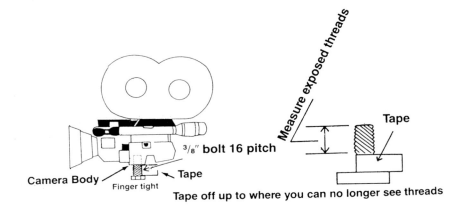

**Figure 7.2** Tape method.

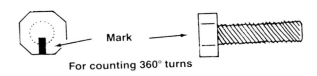

**Figure 7.3** Marker method.

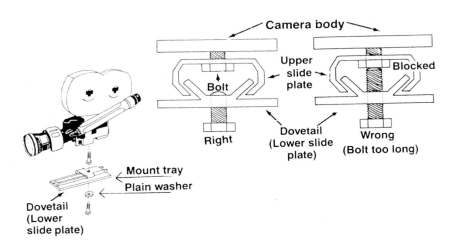

**Figure 7.4** Dovetail method.

## Speed-Rail® Tubing and Fittings

I prefer Speed-Rail® tubing and fittings. They can be assembled quickly, they are strong, and your rig will look like it was designed by a professional. You can add or subtract tubing by loosening two set screws. The standard-size tubing I have used most is 1–1/4 in. (1.680-in. OD; or, 3.2 mm with a 4.27-mm OD), although larger tubing can be used.

A trick of the trade for mounting a camera on a car, or any vehicle, is to find out whether the vehicle has been strip painted. Strip painting is temporary paint that peels off after you are finished with the vehicle. Strip painting sometimes is needed to match or change the color of a car for a certain scene. The car is then changed back to the original color for a matching scene, days or even weeks later. Our job as a grip is to ensure that the camera is mounted securely and safely without ruining the paint or damaging the car. Installing a camera on a mount you have safely and securely rigged on a vehicle usually is accomplished with one bolt—a 3/8 in. × 16 pitch bolt. This bolt cannot be too tight, or you will bend or pull the thread out of the $100,000 camera. If the bolt is too loose, the camera may move, ruining the shot and possibly your career (Figures 7.2, 7.3, 7.4). Screw the bolt into the base of the camera until it bottoms, mark the remaining threads with a marking pen or tape, back out the bolt, and measure the amount of threaded portion of the bolt that went into the camera body.

Another trick of the trade is knowing that usually about a 1/4 inch to 1/2 inch of thread can be inserted into the camera base. If you cannot mark the threaded portion of the bolt that is sticking out, mark the head of the bolt and count how many completed 360-degree counterclockwise revolutions or fractions thereof it takes to back out the bolt. Record this information to use later when you are mounting the camera for your shot. Never insert the bolt too deeply, but do not use too few of the threads either. My suggestion is to know how deep the bolt can and will go into the camera body, measure the thickness of the plate or mounting surface, and add this and the thickness of a flat washer to the length of the bolt. I use a washer (usually flat) because, when tightening the bolt to the base, the bolt grinds (galls) its way into the metal and produces a locking action. These mounts usually are expensive and usually are rented from a rental house. You do not want to ruin an expensive mount when an inexpensive washer can take the beating instead. It shows you are a professional. If too much bolt enters the base of the camera, the camera will jam or short circuit. You must work with someone who has experience before you start mounting cameras (Figure 7.4). A dovetail plate is a slide plate for the base of a camera. It allows quick mounting and dismounting of a camera. Insert a bolt through the mount plate base to the dovetail (slide plate) to ensure that the thread of the bolt does not exceed the height of the wings or lip of the dovetail plate. If the threads are too high, the camera will not slide on the plate. This should tell you that something is wrong. You should not have any problems if you use this plate. If there is no dovetail (slide plate) to use, you must mount the camera body directly with a bolt, as described earlier.

## Power Grip or Super Grip (Mounting Technique)

(Figure 7.5)

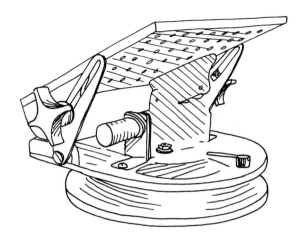

**Figure 7.5**  Adjustable plate on super grip.

## Camera Clamp

Fastened with a screw drive for greater holding power, a 16-mm clamp is specially designed for a lightweight film or television camera. A 35-mm camera clamp is a heavy-duty camera clamp. The clamps have a steel core and are cadmium plated and electropainted. (Figure 7.6)

**Figure 7.6**  Camera clamp.

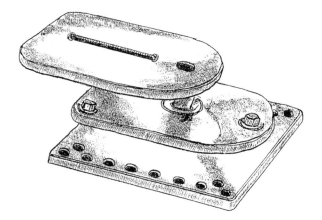

**Figure 7.7**   Ball level head.

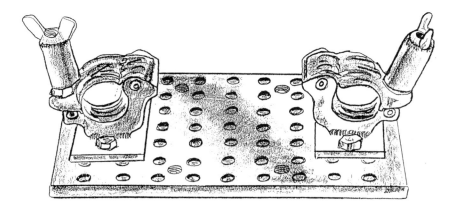

**Figure 7.8**   Cheese plate with grid clamp adapters (Modern Equipment Company).

## Minislider SR-71 Dolly (Mounting Technique)

The minislider dolly requires no assembly. Figures 7.34 and 7.35 illustrate two different types. It is a skate-wheel dolly that glides securely within black anodized aluminum channel beams. Wheel tension can be adjusted to control slider flow. A locking brake allows rigid camera positioning. Beam end clamps have 1-1/4-in. Speed-Rail® flanges mounted to facilitate rigging (the Speed-Rail®, elbows, and tees are not included). The package includes one set of 4-ft. (1.2-m) beams; optional 8-ft. (2.4 m) beams also are available. A longer channel beam can be used. The minislider dolly comes with a Mitchell plate on 4-in. (10-cm) riser stands. The Mitchell plate can be secured to the dolly base for lower mounting of a fluid head or secured to the underside of the dolly base for use with a remote or Weaver Steadman head.

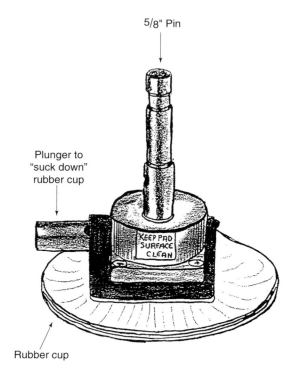

**Figure 7.9** Small super grip.

**Figure 7.10** Junior grid clamp 1 1/8″ receiver (Modern Equipment Company).

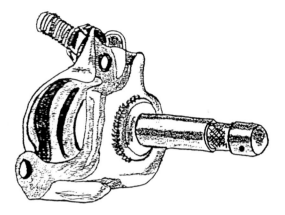

**Figure 7.11**   Baby grid clamp 5/8″ pin (Modern Equipment Company).

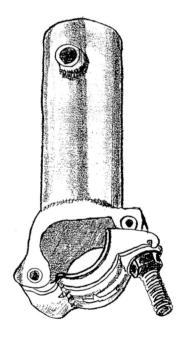

**Figure 7.12**   Speed-Rail® to grid clamp adapter (Modern Equipment Company).

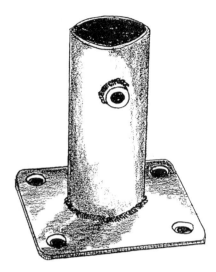

**Figure 7.13** Speed-Rail® flange plate (Modern Equipment Company).

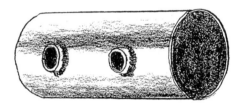

**Figure 7.14** Speed-Rail® sleeve/coupler (Modern Equipment Company).

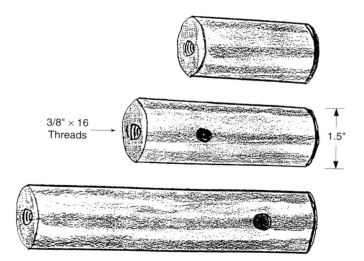

3/8" × 16
Threads

1.5"

**Figure 7.15** Starter plugs (smooth) for Speed-Rail® 1 1/2″ (Modern Equipment Company).

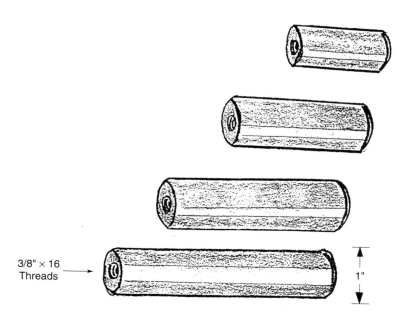

3/8" × 16
Threads

1"

**Figure 7.16** Starter plugs (smooth) for Speed-Rail® 1″ (Modern Equipment Company).

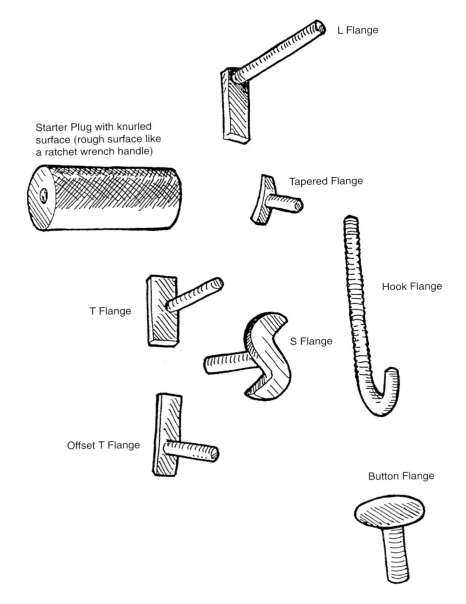

L Flange

Starter Plug with knurled
surface (rough surface like
a ratchet wrench handle)

Tapered Flange

Hook Flange

T Flange

S Flange

Offset T Flange

Button Flange

**Figure 7.17** Speed-Rail® starter plug flanges for auto frames (3/8″ × 16 pitch thread) (Modern Equipment Company).

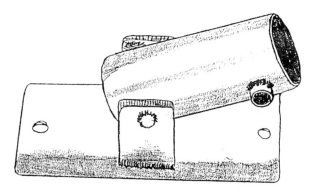

**Figure 7.18**   Speed-Rail® swivel flange (Modern Equipment Company).

**Figure 7.19**   Speed-Rail® double coupler swivel (Modern Equipment Company).

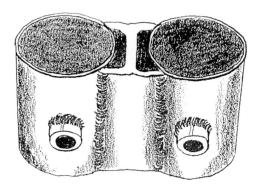

**Figure 7.20**   Speed-Rail® double coupler (Modern Equipment Company).

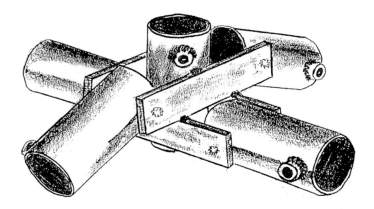

**Figure 7.21**   4 Way Swivel Coupler for Speed-Rail® (Modern Equipment Company).

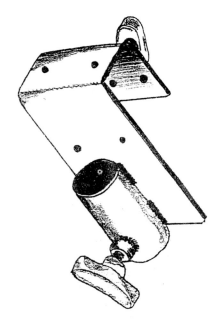

**Figure 7.22**   No nail hanger.

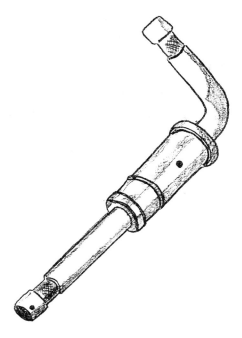

**Figure 7.23** Baby 5/8″ to junior 1 1/8″ pin adapter 90% 5/8″ angle pin (Modern Equipment Company).

**Figure 7.24** Baby pin 5/8″ to spade adapter (Modern Equipment Company).

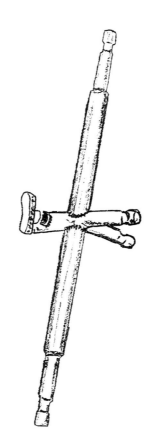

**Figure 7.25** 4 way baby pin 5/8″ offset pin and receiver (Modern Equipment Company).

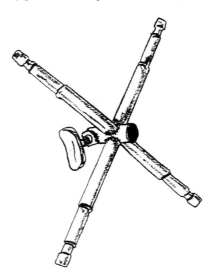

**Figure 7.26** 4 way star offset pin 5/8″ pin and receiver (Modern Equipment Company).

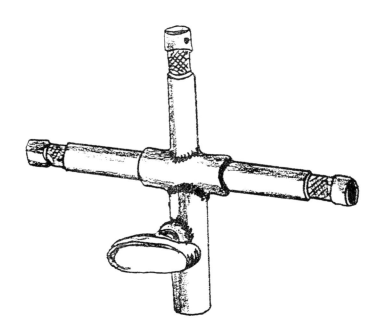

**Figure 7.27**  3 way baby pin 5/8″ pin and receiver (Modern Equipment Company).

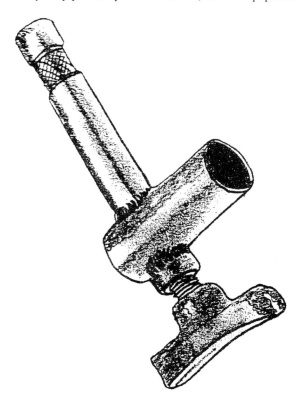

**Figure 7.28**  Junior receiver 1 1/8″ to baby pin 5/8″ (Modern Equipment Company).

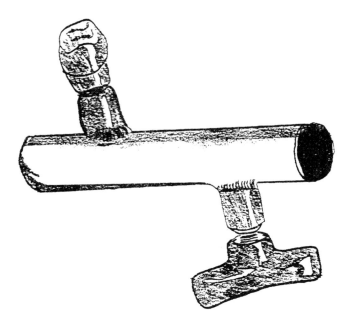

**Figure 7.29** Baby pin to baby pin adapter 5/8″ receiver (Modern Equipment Company).

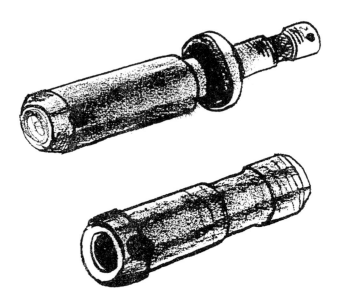

**Figure 7.30** Junior pin 1 1/8″ to baby pin 5/8″ receiver/adapter (Modern Equipment Company).

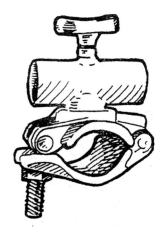

**Figure 7.31** Junior grip clamp.

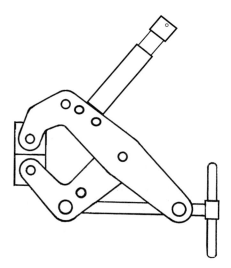

**Figure 7.32** Speed clamp (Timco Company).

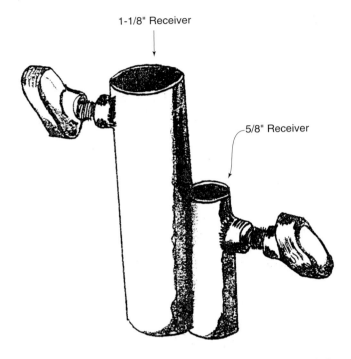

1-1/8" Receiver

5/8" Receiver

**Figure 7.33** Junior 1 1/8″ receiver to baby pin 5/8″ receiver (Modern Equipment Company).

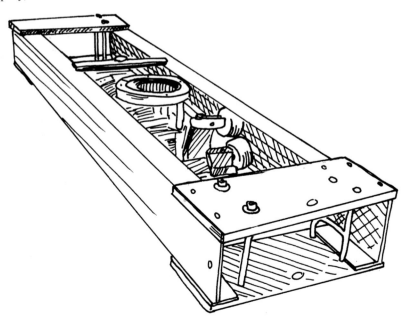

**Figure 7.34** Boxed slider with mitchell mount.

## SR-71 Dolly Features

- Ultra smooth linear bearing movement
- Quick and easy setup with no assembly required
- Carrying case
- Four models: 2-ft., 3-ft., 5-ft., 6-ft.
- Use with any camera movement from 0 to 6 in.
- Use with any Mitchell detail head

Mounting suggestions:

- Two apple boxes as a sliding high hat
- Any camera dolly to make adjustments
- Any camera dolly to make camera moves without a track
- Tripod to make camera moves
- Speed-Rail® pipe for a sliding car mount
- Process trailer to make moves without a dolly track
- Car to make moves on the interior of a car
- Undersling on a crane arm to make the crane arm more versatile
- Condor to make camera moves wherever the Condor takes you
- Camera car to add a new dimension to camera car moves

It is easy to be creative with the SR-71. (Figure 7.35) The manufacturer is available for questions and comments. To apply these mounting suggestions, as well as many others, the manufacturer strongly suggests employing a qualified grip. The manufacturer can be reached at (323) 769-0650 or by fax at (323) 461-2338. I have used this piece of equipment on many car shoots, and the camera operators have been very pleased with the shots they have gotten. Don't limit your shots to car shoots, though.

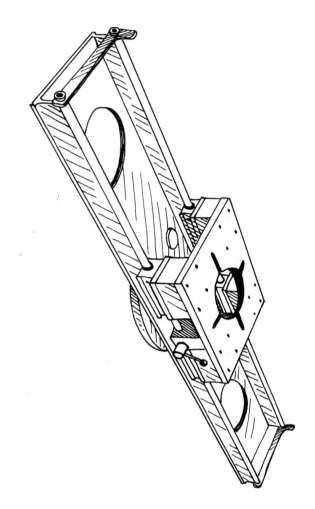

**Figure 7.35** SR-71 dolly slider with mitchell plate.

## ShowRig Truss System

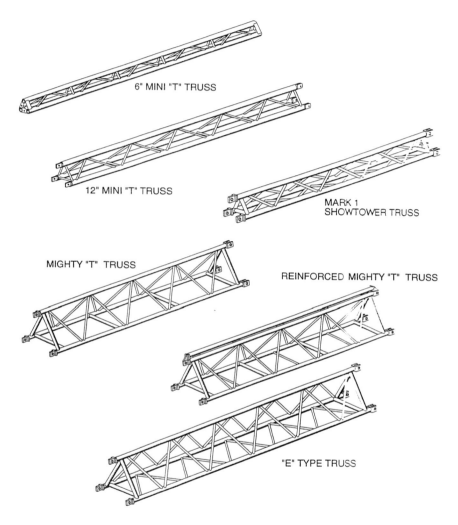

**Figure 7.36** Triangle trusses.

PATENT PENDING

Designed and Manufactured by
**SGPS,Inc**.

• Use it for framing translights, painted backings and green screens.

• Mini T is a low profile truss that has been designed as a
lighter weight, stiffer alternative to steel water pipe and irrigation pipe.

•6" Mini-"T' weighs 62 lbs. per 20 ft. section
A 20 ft. piece of 1 1/2" schedule 40 black water
pipe weighs 54.5 lbs. Three times the rigidity
for almost the same weight.

• Our framing corners are designed so the single
pipe is on the inside for easy tensioning of soft
goods in the frame.

• A 20 ft. section is easily carried by one person.

• Hang curtains and masking on less points.

Chords are made using
1 1/4" Speed Rail

**Unit Weight**
• 20 ft 60 lbs.

Securely bolts together using
Grade 8 Hardened Bolts

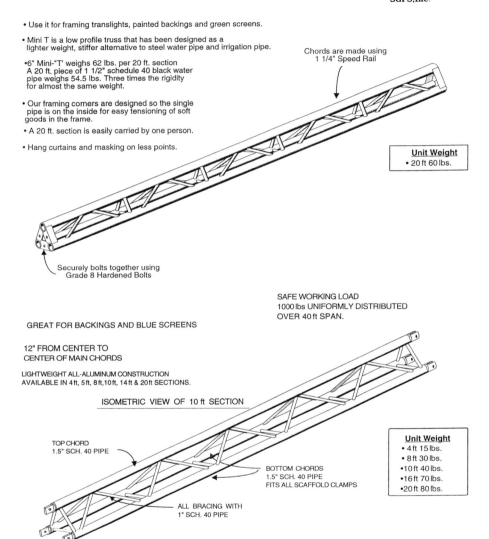

SAFE WORKING LOAD
1000 lbs UNIFORMLY DISTRIBUTED
OVER 40 ft SPAN.

GREAT FOR BACKINGS AND BLUE SCREENS

12" FROM CENTER TO
CENTER OF MAIN CHORDS

LIGHTWEIGHT ALL-ALUMINUM CONSTRUCTION
AVAILABLE IN 4 ft, 5 ft, 8 ft,10 ft, 14 ft & 20 ft SECTIONS.

ISOMETRIC VIEW OF 10 ft SECTION

TOP CHORD
1.5" SCH. 40 PIPE

BOTTOM CHORDS
1.5" SCH. 40 PIPE
FITS ALL SCAFFOLD CLAMPS

ALL BRACING WITH
1" SCH. 40 PIPE

**Unit Weight**
• 4 ft 15 lbs.
• 8 ft 30 lbs.
•10 ft 40 lbs.
•16 ft 70 lbs.
•20 ft 80 lbs.

**Figure 7.36** *(Continued)* ShowRig triangle trusses.

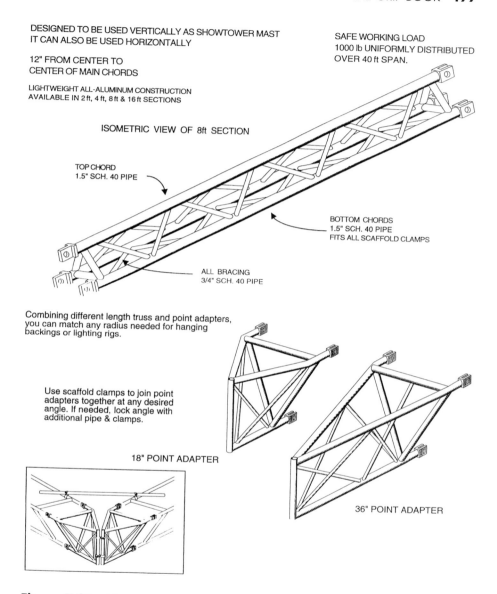

DESIGNED TO BE USED VERTICALLY AS SHOWTOWER MAST
IT CAN ALSO BE USED HORIZONTALLY

SAFE WORKING LOAD
1000 lb UNIFORMLY DISTRIBUTED
OVER 40 ft SPAN.

12" FROM CENTER TO
CENTER OF MAIN CHORDS

LIGHTWEIGHT ALL-ALUMINUM CONSTRUCTION
AVAILABLE IN 2 ft, 4 ft, 8 ft & 16 ft SECTIONS

ISOMETRIC VIEW OF 8ft SECTION

TOP CHORD
1.5" SCH. 40 PIPE

BOTTOM CHORDS
1.5" SCH. 40 PIPE
FITS ALL SCAFFOLD CLAMPS

ALL BRACING
3/4" SCH. 40 PIPE

Combining different length truss and point adapters,
you can match any radius needed for hanging
backings or lighting rigs.

Use scaffold clamps to join point
adapters together at any desired
angle. If needed, lock angle with
additional pipe & clamps.

18" POINT ADAPTER

36" POINT ADAPTER

**Figure 7.36** *(Continued)* ShowRig triangle trusses and end adapters (18″ and 36″).

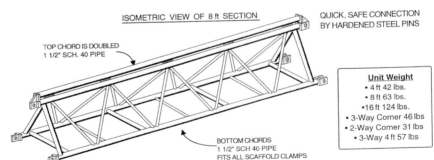

SAFE WORKING LOAD
2,000 lb UNIFORMLY
DISTRIBUTED OVER 40 ft SPAN

23 1/4" OD OF CORDS

LIGHTWEIGHT ALL-ALUMINUM CONSTRUCTION
AVAILABLE IN 2 ft, 4 ft, 8 ft, & 16 ft SECTIONS
EVERY CONCEIVABLE ADAPTER IN STOCK.
INTER-CONNECTS WITH OUR "E"-TYPE TRUSS

QUICK SAFE CONNECTION
BY HARDENED STEEL PINS

ISOMETRIC VIEW OF 8 ft SECTION

TOP CHORD
1 1/2" SCH. 40 PIPE

BOTTOM CHORDS
1 1/2" SCH 40 PIPE (SPEEDRAIL)
FITS ALL SCAFFOLD CLAMPS

**Unit Weight**
• 4 ft 30 lbs.
• 8 ft 50 lbs.
• 16 ft 100 lbs

THIS TRUSS CAN BE RIGGED INVERTED
FOR LIGHT WEIGHT LOADS SUCH AS
SKY PANS OR CYCS. COMBINING DIFFERENT
LENGTHS OF TRUSS AND OUR TWO LENGTHS
OF FLEXIBLE ANGLE ADAPTERS, JUST ABOUT
ANY SHAPE CAN BE ACHIEVED.

SAFE WORKING LOAD
3,000 lb UNIFORMLY
DISTRIBUTED OVER 40 ft SPAN

DESIGNED FOR OUT-DOOR APPLICATIONS

LIGHTWEIGHT ALL-ALUMINUM CONSTRUCTION
AVAILABLE IN 3'6", & 16 ft SECTIONS
TWO & THREE WAY ADAPTORS IN STOCK.

ISOMETRIC VIEW OF 8 ft SECTION

QUICK, SAFE CONNECTION
BY HARDENED STEEL PINS

TOP CHORD IS DOUBLED
1 1/2" SCH. 40 PIPE

BOTTOM CHORDS
1 1/2" SCH 40 PIPE
FITS ALL SCAFFOLD CLAMPS

**Unit Weight**
• 4 ft 42 lbs.
• 8 ft 63 lbs.
• 16 ft 124 lbs.
• 3-Way Corner 46 lbs
• 2-Way Corner 31 lbs
• 3-Way 4 ft 57 lbs

THIS UNIQUE DESIGN ALLOWS THIS
TRUSS TO HANDLE SOME WIND LOADING,
MAKING THIS TRUSS THE IDEAL CHOICE
FOR LARGE EXTERIOR DIFFUSION FRAMES.
EITHER GROUND SUPPORTED OR CRANE FLOWN.

**Figure 7.36** *(Continued)* ShowRig triangle trusses.

SAFE WORKING LOAD 2,000 lbs
UNIFORMLY DISTRIBUTED OVER 40 ft SPAN

**Also Known as MARK 2 SHOWTOWER MAST TRUSS**

23 1/4" OD OF CHORDS

LIGHTWEIGHT ALL-ALUMINUM CONSTRUCTION
AVAILABLE IN 5 ft, 10 ft, & 20 ft SECTIONS
EVERY CONCEIVABLE ADAPTER IN STOCK.
INTER-CONNECTS WITH OUR MIGHTY "T" TRUSS

ISOMETRIC VIEW OF 10 ft SECTION

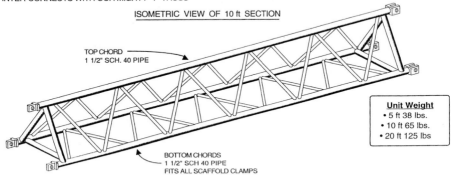

TOP CHORD
1 1/2" SCH. 40 PIPE

Unit Weight
• 5 ft 38 lbs.
• 10 ft 65 lbs.
• 20 ft 125 lbs

BOTTOM CHORDS
1 1/2" SCH 40 PIPE
FITS ALL SCAFFOLD CLAMPS

QUICK, SAFE CONNECTION
BY HARDENED STEEL PINS

**Figure 7.36** *(Continued)* ShowRig triangle truss.

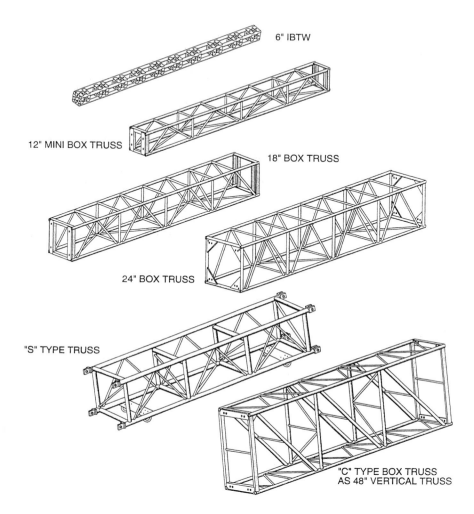

**Figure 7.36** *(Continued)* ShowRig box trusses.

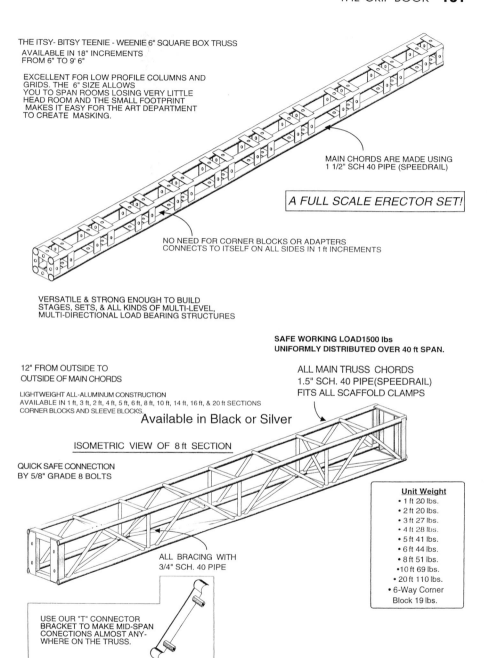

THE ITSY- BITSY TEENIE - WEENIE 6" SQUARE BOX TRUSS
AVAILABLE IN 18" INCREMENTS
FROM 6" TO 9' 6"

EXCELLENT FOR LOW PROFILE COLUMNS AND
GRIDS. THE 6" SIZE ALLOWS
YOU TO SPAN ROOMS LOSING VERY LITTLE
HEAD ROOM AND THE SMALL FOOTPRINT
MAKES IT EASY FOR THE ART DEPARTMENT
TO CREATE MASKING.

MAIN CHORDS ARE MADE USING
1 1/2" SCH 40 PIPE (SPEEDRAIL)

*A FULL SCALE ERECTOR SET!*

NO NEED FOR CORNER BLOCKS OR ADAPTERS
CONNECTS TO ITSELF ON ALL SIDES IN 1 ft INCREMENTS

VERSATILE & STRONG ENOUGH TO BUILD
STAGES, SETS, & ALL KINDS OF MULTI-LEVEL,
MULTI-DIRECTIONAL LOAD BEARING STRUCTURES

**SAFE WORKING LOAD 1500 lbs
UNIFORMLY DISTRIBUTED OVER 40 ft SPAN.**

12" FROM OUTSIDE TO
OUTSIDE OF MAIN CHORDS

ALL MAIN TRUSS CHORDS
1.5" SCH. 40 PIPE (SPEEDRAIL)
FITS ALL SCAFFOLD CLAMPS

LIGHTWEIGHT ALL-ALUMINUM CONSTRUCTION
AVAILABLE IN 1 ft, 3 ft, 2 ft, 4 ft, 5 ft, 6 ft, 8 ft, 10 ft, 14 ft, 16 ft, & 20 ft SECTIONS
CORNER BLOCKS AND SLEEVE BLOCKS.
Available in Black or Silver

ISOMETRIC VIEW OF 8 ft SECTION

QUICK SAFE CONNECTION
BY 5/8" GRADE 8 BOLTS

**Unit Weight**
- 1 ft 20 lbs.
- 2 ft 20 lbs.
- 3 ft 27 lbs.
- 4 ft 28 lbs.
- 5 ft 41 lbs.
- 6 ft 44 lbs.
- 8 ft 51 lbs.
- 10 ft 69 lbs.
- 20 ft 110 lbs.
- 6-Way Corner
  Block 19 lbs.

ALL BRACING WITH
3/4" SCH. 40 PIPE

USE OUR "T" CONNECTOR
BRACKET TO MAKE MID-SPAN
CONECTIONS ALMOST ANY-
WHERE ON THE TRUSS.

**Figure 7.36** *(Continued)* ShowRig box trusses.

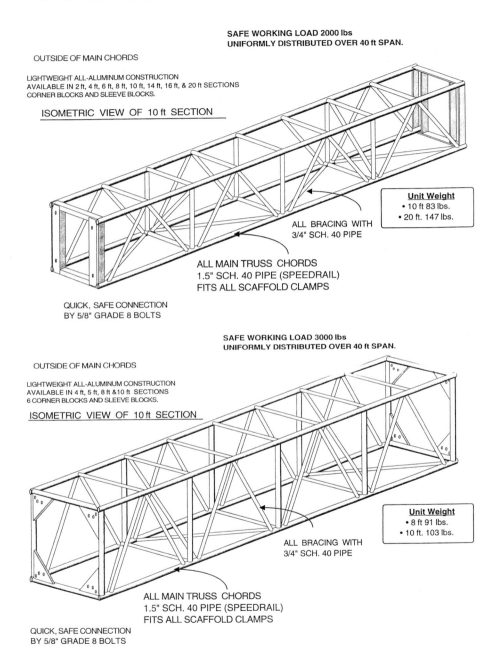

**SAFE WORKING LOAD 2000 lbs**
**UNIFORMLY DISTRIBUTED OVER 40 ft SPAN.**

OUTSIDE OF MAIN CHORDS

LIGHTWEIGHT ALL-ALUMINUM CONSTRUCTION
AVAILABLE IN 2 ft, 4 ft, 6 ft, 8 ft, 10 ft, 14 ft, 16 ft, & 20 ft SECTIONS
CORNER BLOCKS AND SLEEVE BLOCKS.

ISOMETRIC VIEW OF 10 ft SECTION

**Unit Weight**
• 10 ft 83 lbs.
• 20 ft. 147 lbs.

ALL BRACING WITH
3/4" SCH. 40 PIPE

ALL MAIN TRUSS CHORDS
1.5" SCH. 40 PIPE (SPEEDRAIL)
FITS ALL SCAFFOLD CLAMPS

QUICK, SAFE CONNECTION
BY 5/8" GRADE 8 BOLTS

**SAFE WORKING LOAD 3000 lbs**
**UNIFORMLY DISTRIBUTED OVER 40 ft SPAN.**

OUTSIDE OF MAIN CHORDS

LIGHTWEIGHT ALL-ALUMINUM CONSTRUCTION
AVAILABLE IN 4 ft, 5 ft, 8 ft & 10 ft SECTIONS
6 CORNER BLOCKS AND SLEEVE BLOCKS.

ISOMETRIC VIEW OF 10 ft SECTION

**Unit Weight**
• 8 ft 91 lbs.
• 10 ft. 103 lbs.

ALL BRACING WITH
3/4" SCH. 40 PIPE

ALL MAIN TRUSS CHORDS
1.5" SCH. 40 PIPE (SPEEDRAIL)
FITS ALL SCAFFOLD CLAMPS

QUICK, SAFE CONNECTION
BY 5/8" GRADE 8 BOLTS

**Figure 7.36** *(Continued)* ShowRig box trusses.

SAFE WORKING LOAD **4,000 lb** UNIFORMLY
DISTRIBUTED OVER **40 ft SPAN**

26" HIGH BY 22.1/2" WIDE

LIGHTWEIGHT ALL-ALUMINUM CONSTRUCTION,
YET BUILT FOR VERY HEAVY LOADS
1 TON & 1/2 TON MOTORS CAN BE MOUNTED INTERNALLY.
AVAILABLE IN 4 ft, & 8 ft SECTIONS
STANDARD ANGLE ADAPTERS AND CORNER BLOCKS IN STOCK.

ISOMETRIC VIEW OF 8 ft SECTION

QUICK, SAFE CONNECTION
BY HARDENED STEEL PINS

TOP CHORD
1 1/2" SCH. 40 PIPE

**Unit Weight**
• 4 ft 50 lbs.
• 8 ft 100 lbs.

FOR ADDED STRENGTH THE
BOTTOM CHORD IS 1 1/2" SCH 80 PIPE
FITS ALL SCAFFOLD CLAMPS

COMES COMPLETE WITH WHEELS

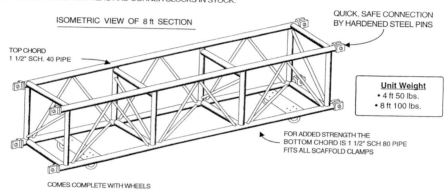

WHEN USED IN A VERTICAL ORIENTATION
THIS TRUSS IS CAPABLE OF SPANNING **80 ft**,
WITH A SAFE WORKING LOAD OF **2000 lbs**
UNIFORMLY DISTRIBUTED.

48 in HIGH BY 18 in WIDE
LIGHTWEIGHT, HIGH STRENGTH
ALUMINUM CONSTRUCTION

AVAILABLE IN 20 ft, 10 ft, 4 ft, & 2 ft SECTIONS

ISOMETRIC VIEW OF 10 ft SECTION

**Unit Weight**
• 4 ft 80 lbs.
• 10 ft 127 lbs.

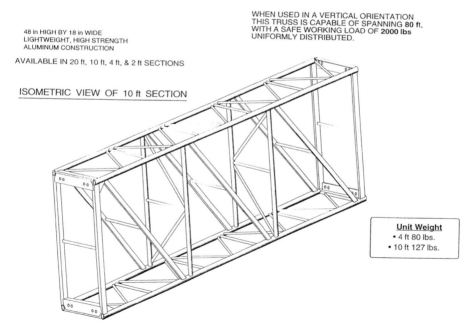

**Figure 7.36** *(Continued)* ShowRig box trusses.

WHEN USED IN A HORIZONTAL ORIENTATION
THIS TRUSS IS CAPABLE OF SPANNING **40 ft**,
WITH A SAFE WORKING LOAD OF
**2000 lbs** UNIFORMLY DISTRIBUTED.

18 in BY 48 in LIGHTWEIGHT HIGH STRENGTH
ALUMINUM CONSTRUCTION

AVAILABLE IN 20 ft, 10 ft, 4 ft, & 2 ft SECTIONS

ISOMETRIC VIEW OF 10 ft SECTION

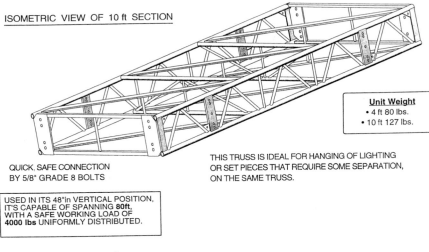

**Unit Weight**
• 4 ft 80 lbs.
• 10 ft 127 lbs.

QUICK, SAFE CONNECTION
BY 5/8" GRADE 8 BOLTS

THIS TRUSS IS IDEAL FOR HANGING OF LIGHTING
OR SET PIECES THAT REQUIRE SOME SEPARATION,
ON THE SAME TRUSS.

USED IN ITS 48"in VERTICAL POSITION,
IT'S CAPABLE OF SPANNING **80ft**,
WITH A SAFE WORKING LOAD OF
**4000 lbs** UNIFORMLY DISTRIBUTED.

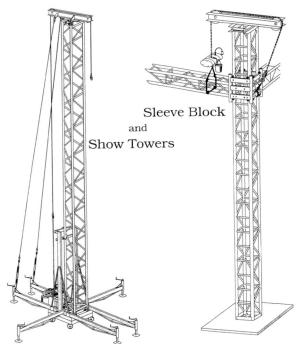

Sleeve Block
and
Show Towers

**Figure 7.36** *(Continued)* ShowRig truss tower system.

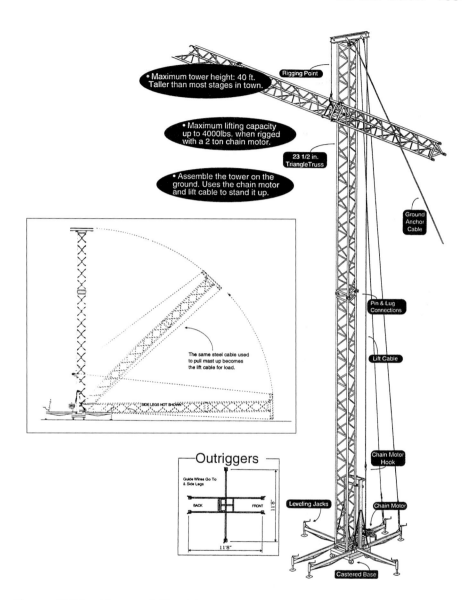

• Maximum tower height: 40 ft. Taller than most stages in town.

Rigging Point

• Maximum lifting capacity up to 4000lbs. when rigged with a 2 ton chain motor.

23 1/2 in. TriangleTruss

• Assemble the tower on the ground. Uses the chain motor and lift cable to stand it up.

Ground Anchor Cable

The same steel cable used to pull mast up becomes the lift cable for load.

SIDE LEGS NOT SHOWN

Pin & Lug Connections

Lift Cable

Outriggers

Guide Wires Go To & Side Legs

BACK

FRONT

11'8"

11'8"

Chain Motor Hook

Leveling Jacks

Chain Motor

Castered Base

**Figure 7.36** *(Continued)* ShowRig tower system.

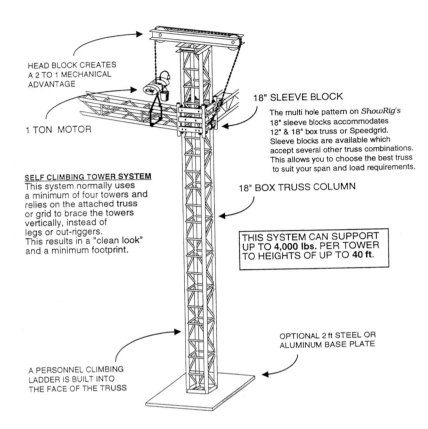

HEAD BLOCK CREATES
A 2 TO 1 MECHANICAL
ADVANTAGE

1 TON MOTOR

**SELF CLIMBING TOWER SYSTEM**
This system normally uses
a minimum of four towers and
relies on the attached truss
or grid to brace the towers
vertically, instead of
legs or out-riggers.
This results in a "clean look"
and a minimum footprint.

18" SLEEVE BLOCK

The multi hole pattern on *ShowRig's*
18" sleeve blocks accommodates
12" & 18" box truss or Speedgrid.
Sleeve blocks are available which
accept several other truss combinations.
This allows you to choose the best truss
to suit your span and load requirements.

18" BOX TRUSS COLUMN

THIS SYSTEM CAN SUPPORT
UP TO **4,000 lbs.** PER TOWER
TO HEIGHTS OF UP TO **40 ft.**

OPTIONAL 2 ft STEEL OR
ALUMINUM BASE PLATE

A PERSONNEL CLIMBING
LADDER IS BUILT INTO
THE FACE OF THE TRUSS

**Figure 7.36** *(Continued)* ShowRig tower system.

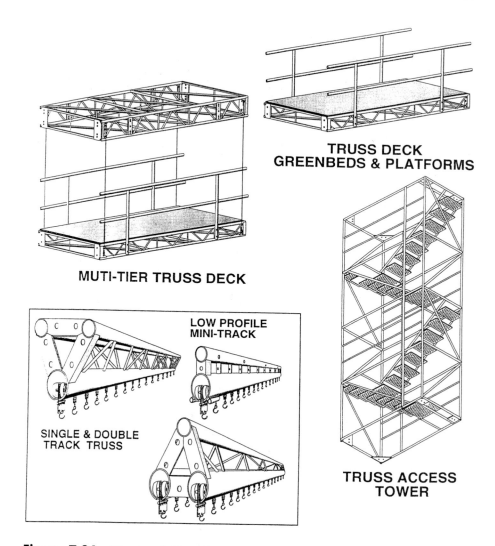

**TRUSS DECK GREENBEDS & PLATFORMS**

**MUTI-TIER TRUSS DECK**

**LOW PROFILE MINI-TRACK**

**SINGLE & DOUBLE TRACK TRUSS**

**TRUSS ACCESS TOWER**

**Figure 7.36** *(Continued)* ShowRig truss deck, platforms, green bead tower, and track chords systems.

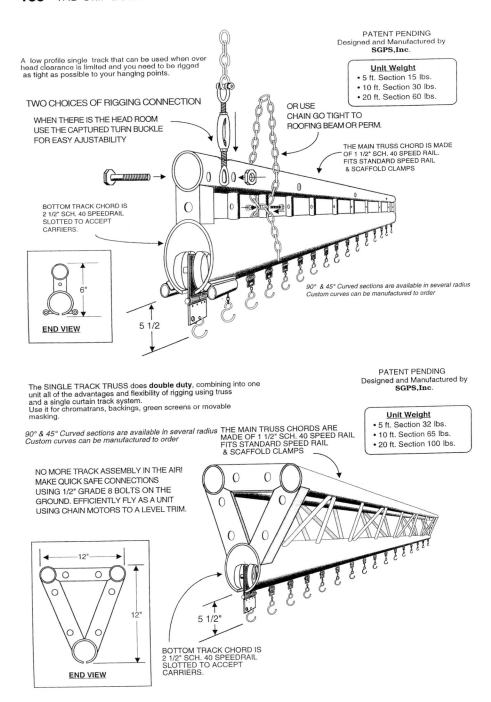

PATENT PENDING
Designed and Manufactured by
**SGPS,Inc.**

A low profile single track that can be used when over head clearance is limited and you need to be rigged as tight as possible to your hanging points.

**Unit Weight**
- 5 ft. Section 15 lbs.
- 10 ft. Section 30 lbs.
- 20 ft. Section 60 lbs.

TWO CHOICES OF RIGGING CONNECTION

WHEN THERE IS THE HEAD ROOM USE THE CAPTURED TURN BUCKLE FOR EASY AJUSTABILITY

OR USE
CHAIN GO TIGHT TO
ROOFING BEAM OR PERM.

THE MAIN TRUSS CHORD IS MADE OF 1 1/2" SCH. 40 SPEED RAIL. FITS STANDARD SPEED RAIL & SCAFFOLD CLAMPS

BOTTOM TRACK CHORD IS 2 1/2" SCH. 40 SPEEDRAIL SLOTTED TO ACCEPT CARRIERS.

6"

**END VIEW**

5 1/2

*90° & 45° Curved sections are available in several radius Custom curves can be manufactured to order*

PATENT PENDING
Designed and Manufactured by
**SGPS,Inc.**

The SINGLE TRACK TRUSS does **double duty**, combining into one unit all of the advantages and flexibility of rigging using truss and a single curtain track system.
Use it for chromatrans, backings, green screens or movable masking.

**Unit Weight**
- 5 ft. Section 32 lbs.
- 10 ft. Section 65 lbs.
- 20 ft. Section 100 lbs.

*90° & 45° Curved sections are available in several radius Custom curves can be manufactured to order*

THE MAIN TRUSS CHORDS ARE MADE OF 1 1/2" SCH. 40 SPEED RAIL FITS STANDARD SPEED RAIL & SCAFFOLD CLAMPS

NO MORE TRACK ASSEMBLY IN THE AIR! MAKE QUICK SAFE CONNECTIONS USING 1/2" GRADE 8 BOLTS ON THE GROUND. EFFICIENTLY FLY AS A UNIT USING CHAIN MOTORS TO A LEVEL TRIM.

12"

12"

5 1/2"

BOTTOM TRACK CHORD IS 2 1/2" SCH. 40 SPEEDRAIL SLOTTED TO ACCEPT CARRIERS.

**END VIEW**

**Figure 7.36** *(Continued)*

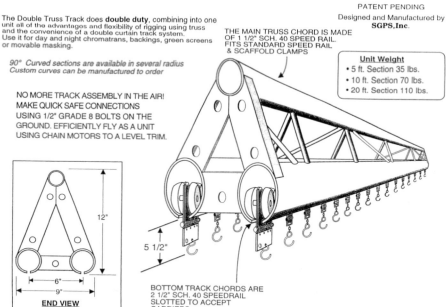

PATENT PENDING
Designed and Manufactured by
**SGPS,Inc.**

The Double Truss Track does **double duty**, combining into one unit all of the advantages and flexibility of rigging using truss and the convenience of a double curtain track system. Use it for day and night chromatrans, backings, green screens or movable masking.

*90° Curved sections are available in several radius Custom curves can be manufactured to order*

NO MORE TRACK ASSEMBLY IN THE AIR! MAKE QUICK SAFE CONNECTIONS USING 1/2" GRADE 8 BOLTS ON THE GROUND. EFFICIENTLY FLY AS A UNIT USING CHAIN MOTORS TO A LEVEL TRIM.

THE MAIN TRUSS CHORD IS MADE OF 1 1/2" SCH. 40 SPEED RAIL. FITS STANDARD SPEED RAIL & SCAFFOLD CLAMPS

**Unit Weight**
• 5 ft. Section 35 lbs.
• 10 ft. Section 70 lbs.
• 20 ft. Section 110 lbs.

END VIEW

12"
6"
9"

5 1/2"

BOTTOM TRACK CHORDS ARE 2 1/2" SCH. 40 SPEEDRAIL SLOTTED TO ACCEPT CARRIERS.

A safe and cost effective full featured greenbed system for places that "studio" beds don't work. This system can be rigged or ground supported in any warehouse or aircraft hanger.

THIS SYSTEM COMBINES THE STRUCTURAL STRENGTH OF AN ALUMINUM TRUSSING SYSTEM WITH A CONVENTIONAL GREENBED STYLE DECK SO YOU CAN SPAN THE DISTANCES BETWEEN THE BUILDINGS'S STRUCTURAL BEAMS.

LIGHT WEIGHT, HIGH STRENGTH ALUMINUM CONSTRUCTION ALLOWS FOR EASY ACCESS AND GREATER DECK CAPACITY WITHOUT EXCEEDING THE LOAD LIMITS OF THE BUILDING

**Unit Weight**
• 4' x 4' Deck 90 lbs.
• 4' x 10' Deck 223 lbs.

DECKS ARE AVAILABLE IN 2 FT, 3 FT & 4 FT WIDE VERSIONS. VARIOUS LENGTHS ALONG WITH CORNER SECTIONS & "T" CONNECTIONS, ACCOMMODATES YOUR EXACT LAYOUT REQUIREMENTS

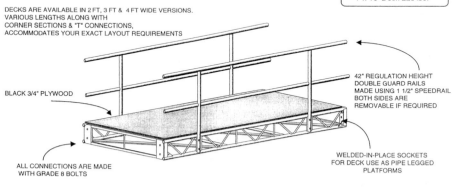

42" REGULATION HEIGHT DOUBLE GUARD RAILS MADE USING 1 1/2" SPEEDRAIL BOTH SIDES ARE REMOVABLE IF REQUIRED

BLACK 3/4" PLYWOOD

WELDED-IN-PLACE SOCKETS FOR DECK USE AS PIPE LEGGED PLATFORMS

ALL CONNECTIONS ARE MADE WITH GRADE 8 BOLTS

DECKS CAN BE CONNECTED SIDE BY SIDE TO CREATE WIDE WORKING PLATFORMS

**Figure 7.36** *(Continued)* ShowRig track chords and deck systems.

1 Ton CM Load Star
• Unit Weight w/ 60 ft Chain 147 lbs
• Shipping Weight 2 Motors w/ Case 421 lbs

1/2 Ton CM Load Star
• Unit Weight w/ 40 ft Chain 79 lbs
• Unit Weight w/ 60 ft Chain 91 lbs
• Shipping Weight 4 Motors w/ Crate 495 lbs

300 Lb. CM Pro Star
• Unit Weight w/ 40 ft Chain 39 lbs

This Power Distribution and control unit can control from 1 to 6 motors. Each motor circuit can be controlled separately. Because the PD is compact and light weight it can be mounted on the truss, easily hauled up into the perms or left on the floor taking up very little space.

The power connection is on the back panel. Power cable comes with each PD. For the power tie-in we can provide bare ends, sister lugs, or tweko connectors. Additionally on the back panel is a power output allowing for the use of "jumpers" to feed other PDs, eliminating the need for multiple power tie-ins.

**Power Requirement:**
For use with 1/2 ton motors   30 amps 208v/3 phase
For use with 1 ton motors   60 amps 208v/3 phase

Local Control
Motor Activation

Remote Control
Cable Connector

Motor Cable
Connector

Front View

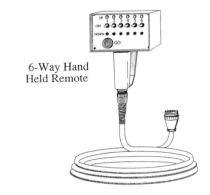

6-Way Hand
Held Remote

**Figure 7.36** *(Continued)* ShowRig chain hoist and power distribution and hand held remote systems.

# Cables, Slings, and Hardware

When picking cable for a project, I usually use aircraft-rated cable. It is strong and flexible and works nicely for most jobs. Seven by nineteen (see later) usually seems to work best. Use the fixture that allows you to accomplish the job safely. If you do not have a great deal of experience with cable, contact VER Sales in Burbank, California. They are as close to experts as anyone can be. I did a car spot for a Japanese manufacturer with a hot young actor. My crew had to fly a 60- by 80-foot frame with silk on it. We used aircraft cable locks, span sets, and a 70-ton crane with a spreader beam on it to distribute the weight. I tell this story because, years ago, when I first started keying, my budget was for rope, not cable. As my jobs grew I had to ask a lot of folks for a lot of advice. For this particular job, I went to VER Sales and explained that I really did not have a lot of experience, told them what the shot entailed, and asked them to help me decide what equipment I needed. Do not try to be a know-it-all. Plenty of folks are willing and available to help.

Following is a list of different types of hardware. This is only a glimpse of the equipment, cables, and attaching hardware that I have used over a period of years. The facts and figures sometimes change, and the charts are only for reference. Contact the various manufacturers and vendors before you head into the unknown. I really can't emphasize that enough. This book contains a few examples to get you started; devise what you think you may need, map it out, and then call a local merchant or the manufacturer.

## Miniature Cable

Miniature cable line is perfect for special effects and mechanical design that require sharp bends and confined space situations (Figure 8.1):

- $1 \times 7$—One center wire with six wires laid around the center; more flexible than $1 \times 3$; used for push–pull applications and for conductive needs with low flexibility.
- $7 \times 7$—Most standard cable construction; six $1 \times 7$ outside strands cabled around a $1 \times 7$ center; very flexible, good cycle life, and breaking strength.
- $1 \times 19$—Twelve wires laid around a $1 \times 7$ center; more flexible than $1 \times 7$ in push–pull and conductive applications; almost as high breaking strength as $1 \times 7$ with same diameter.

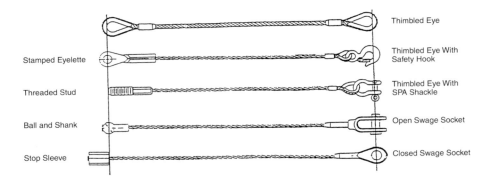

Stamped Eyelette

Threaded Stud

Ball and Shank

Stop Sleeve

Thimbled Eye

Thimbled Eye With
Safety Hook

Thimbled Eye With
SPA Shackle

Open Swage Socket

Closed Swage Socket

**Figure 8.1a** Miniature cable ends.

Proper

**Figure 8.1b** Hand-held nico press for sleeves.

- $7 \times 19$—Most flexible standard construction for cable; six $1 \times 19$ strands around a $1 \times 19$ center; lower breaking strength, more expensive than $7 \times 7$; long cycle life.

## Wire Rope

Wire rope consists of three basic components. These components vary in complexity and configuration to produce ropes for specific purposes or characteristics. The three basic components of a standard wire rope design are (1) wires that form the strand, (2) multiwire strands laid in a helix around a core, and (3) the core.

### Wires

Wire for rope is made in several materials and types, including steel, iron, stainless steel, Monel metal, and bronze. By far the most widely used material is high carbon steel, which is available in a variety of grades, each of which has properties related to the basic curve for steel rope wire. Wire rope manufacturers select the wire type that is most appropriate for the requirements of the finished product.

#### Steel

The strength of steel wire is appropriate to the particular grade of the wire rope in which the wires are used. Grades of wire rope are referred to as traction steel (TS), improved plow steel (MPS), plow steel (PS), improved steel (IPS), and extra-improved plow steel (EIP). These names originated at the earliest stages of development of wire rope and have been retained as references to the strength of a particular size and grade of rope. The plow steel strength curve forms the basis for calculating the strength of all steel rope wires. The tensile strength (measured in pounds per square inch, or psi) of any grade of steel wire is not constant. It varies with diameter and is highest in the smallest wires. The most common finish for steel wire is *bright* or *noncoated*. Steel wire also may be galvanized, which means it is coated with zinc. *Drawn galvanized* wire has the same strength as bright wire, but wire galvanized at a required finished size usually is 10% lower in strength. In certain applications, *tinned* wire is used, but tin does not provide the sacrificial (*i.e.*, cathodic) protection for steel that zinc does. Different coatings are available for other applications.

#### Iron

Iron wire is actually drawn from low-carbon steel and has a fairly limited use except in older elevator installations. When iron is used for other than elevator applications, it is most often galvanized.

### Stainless Steel

Stainless steel ropes are made of American Iron and Steel Institute (AISI) types 302/304, 316, and 305 (listed in order of frequency of use). Contrary to general belief, hard-drawn stainless steel type 302/304 is magnetic. Type 316 is less magnetic, and type 305 has a permeability low enough to qualify as nonmagnetic.

### Monel Metal

Monel metal is steel that contains 68% nickel. Monel metal wire usually is type 400 and conforms to federal specification QQ-N-281.

### Bronze

Bronze wire usually is type A phosphor bronze (Composite Design and Analysis Code [CDA] 510), although other bronzes can be specified.

### *Strands*

Strands are made up of two or more wires laid in one of many specific geometric arrangements or in combinations of steel wires and other materials such as natural or synthetic fibers. A strand can be composed of any number of wires, and a rope can have any number of strands.

### *Core*

The core is the foundation of a wire rope. It is made of materials that support the strands under normal bending and loading conditions. Core materials include fibers (hard vegetable and synthetic) or steel. A steel core consists of a strand or an independent wire rope.

## Spreader Beams

Load spreaders are used when loads to be lifted on a single hoist must be picked up and supported at two or more suspension points. Load spreaders can be furnished in a large number of practical designs to suit any lifting or handling condition (Figure 8.2).

## Sling Types

Various types of slings are shown in Figure 8.3. The grip hoist Dynafor MWX Miniweigher is a new method of check-weighing and load measurement. Dynafor MWX Miniweighers rely on microprocessor-based electronics and offer new

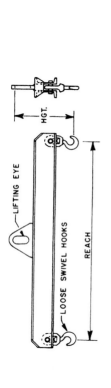

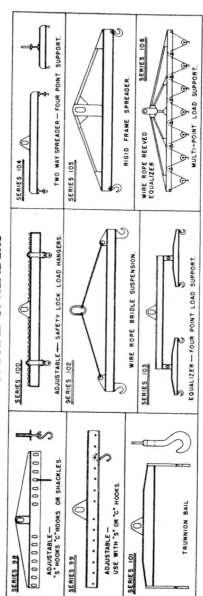

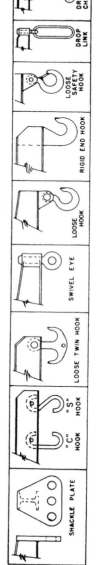

**Figure 8.2** Spreader beams.

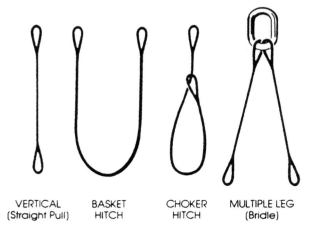

VERTICAL      BASKET     CHOKER     MULTIPLE LEG
(Straight Pull)    HITCH      HITCH      (Bridle)

**Figure 8.3a**   Slings.

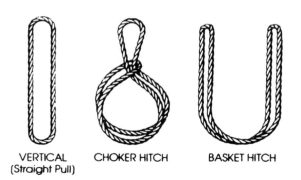

VERTICAL     CHOKER HITCH     BASKET HITCH
(Straight Pull)

**Figure 8.3b**   Slings.

standard functions and systems. Features of the Dynafor MWX Miniweigher include (Figure 8.4):

- It is operated via three push-button controls: (1) on–off, (2) 100% tare with return to total load applied, and (3) peak hold to show the maximum load applied.
- It provides up to 700 hours of operation before a battery charge is required (has a low-battery indicator); automatic shutdown after 20 minutes and variable response rate save battery power.

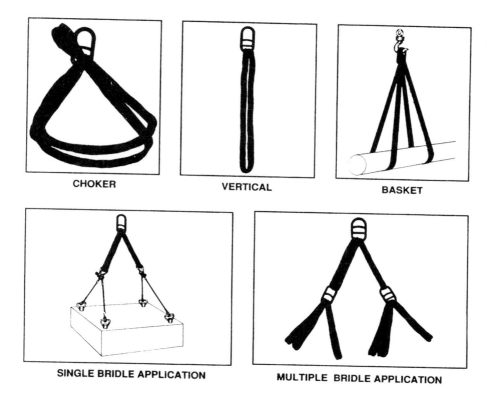

**Figure 8.3c** Bridle slings.

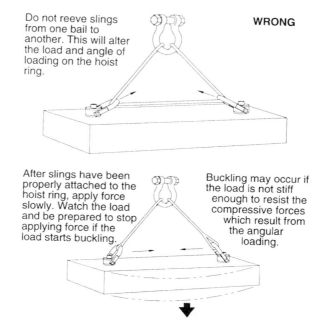

Do not reeve slings from one bail to another. This will alter the load and angle of loading on the hoist ring.

**WRONG**

After slings have been properly attached to the hoist ring, apply force slowly. Watch the load and be prepared to stop applying force if the load starts buckling.

Buckling may occur if the load is not stiff enough to resist the compressive forces which result from the angular loading.

**Figure 8.3d** Correct and incorrect attached hoist ring.

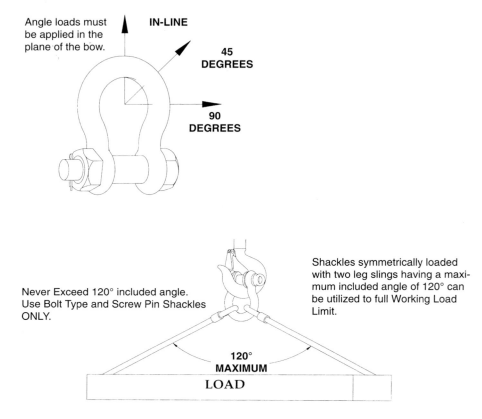

**Figure 8.3e** Shackles.

• The choice of unit measurement—kilograms, tons, pounds, short tons, daN, or kN—is displayed on the LCD.
• An overload indicator helps prevent overloading the equipment and systems.
• Unit is set at automatic zero when switched on.
• It has an output connection to handheld display and controls, to a personal computer, or interface for processing or printing the information.

## Glossary of Cables and Slings

• Alloy steel chain—The only chain recommended for overhead lifting.
• Angle of lift—Angle between the horizontal surface of the load and the lift chain, measured in degrees; should never be less than 30 degrees.
• Elongation—The effect on the chain of severe overload or exposure to shock load.

**Figure 8.4** Dynafor MWX Miniweigher.

- Grade 30—Proof coil chain; a general utility chain of low-carbon steel used for many everyday applications. *Grade 30 is not to be used for lifting or hoisting applications.*
- Grade 40—High test chain; a higher carbon steel chain that is considerably stronger than grade 30, meaning that a lighter chain can often do similar work. *Grade 40 is not to be used for lifting or hoisting applications.*
- Grade 70—Transport tie-down or binding chain; a high-strength, lightweight boron manganese steel chain designed for load-binding applications. *Grade 70 is not to be used for lifting or hoisting applications.*
- Grade 80—High-strength alloy chain with a high strength-to-weight ratio. Grade 80 is used predominantly for lifting and hoisting applications. *Grade 80 is the only chain recommended for lifting and hoisting.*

## Staging Systems
### *Ferrellels*

The features of the Ferrellel™ system are a scissors lift and a variable height feature that allows the deck to change height in seconds with no loose legs (Figure 8.5). The operator reaches under each end, squeezes the lock-pin lever, and raises

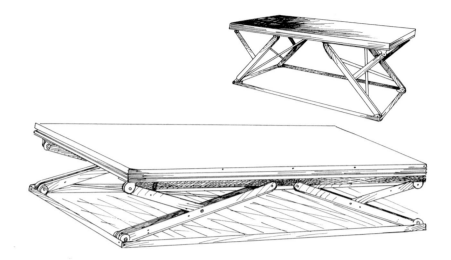

**Figure 8.5** Ferrellels.

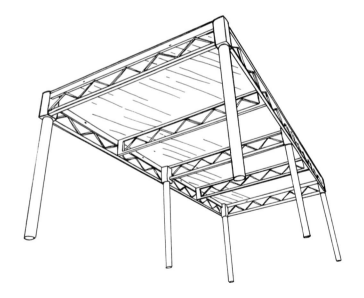

**Figure 8.6** Steeldeck.

or lowers the deck to 16, 24, 32, or 40 inches. Quick-lock extrusions connect decks together quickly with no bolts or screws. One end can be locked higher than the other to produce a ramp. Strong and solid, Ferrellels are engineered to support 160 pounds live load per square foot. The understructure is all aluminum with no welded joints. The enclosed base provides exceptional stability and distributes weight over a large footprint. I have used Ferrellels since I first learned of their existence. It is the Swiss Army knife of tables, platforms, and portable stages. A Ferrellel is super quick to assemble and relatively inexpensive if you consider the time, material, and personnel it takes to build a riser or stage from scratch. Use Ferrellels—you will look like a million-dollar technician. It's the top gun for fast location work.

### Steeldeck

The combination of features in Steeldeck®, as with all systems, represents a compromise between the properties we want a unit to possess—strength, ease of use, portability, versatility—and what is possible in light of such constraints as materials and cost. What follows is the main features required of a modular staging system and examples of the advantages that Steeldeck offers in each area (Figure 8.6). The priority of these features often depends on the requirements of the customer, so this is not intended to be a definitive order. Some features are relevant to most users most of the time.

# Lifts

## Condors and Cherry Pickers

We are shooting on a rooftop, 30 feet up. We need to have a moonlight system to fly high above and an eye-level shooting platform. What do we need to accomplish this? What are the factors to consider?

1. Where is the building?
2. What is the ground access?
3. Are there high-tension wires overhead?
4. What size moon (how big a light) do we need?
5. Will a person have to ride the basket? At what angle?
6. Does it have to be a four-wheel-drive unit?
7. Are we on a hill?
8. Can I use the outriggers?
9. Is the ground level?

These are a few, but not all, of the factors you have to think about and ask questions about. Here are a few more:

1. What size shooting crew do we need?
2. Will there be any light on the shooting basket and will it require an electrician?
3. Are we shooting level, below level, or as an above look-down?
4. Does the camera crew know how to work the lift?

These are not dumb questions; they must be answered before you do anything. Do not assume anything.

First let's talk about a Condor. This is a company name that has come to be synonymous with the name of the device. Condors are also called cherry pickers or high lifts, among other names. A cherry picker or Condor usually has two-wheel drive unless you ask for four-wheel drive. It is white or brightly colored and bears the name of the rental company, which would be fantastic if we were shooting a spot for that company. I usually request a cherry picker with an arm painted flat black, which reduces reflection problems. If you do not remember to order an arm that is painted black and a problem arises, you can always use a long piece of duvatyne cloth. This was a common way to black out an arm before manufacturers began painting the arms black. My advice is always to order a black arm. Sometimes day shoots end up as night shoots, and a lift with a black arm almost disappears at night.

Most cherry pickers or Condors have an elliptical tail travel. This means the lift is very slender when it is lined up straight with the base. When you rotate the base section, the tail extends past the sides of the wheel base. Sometimes this blocks access. If necessary, a Condor model that has zero tail swing is available. This means that nothing extends past the wheel base. Use this type of Condor in a tight area. I do not always call for this type because they are not readily available with longer arms.

Some cherry pickers have an articulating arm. These are terrific pieces of equipment and take up less room than conventional devices. As with all pieces of equipment, however, there is a price to pay—usually in lift capacity. The angle and the length of an arm determine the weight capacity and use of the arm. Look over the charts. Call and ask or even go and see for yourself.

Cherry pickers and Condors come with a wide base or narrow base. If I have the room, I usually ask for a wide base for stability. Don't get me wrong—they are all very stable, but it usually gives me and other crew members (who do not normally ride these things) a greater sense of confidence. All other things being equal, I generally opt for the wider base. Figure 9.1 provides an example of the many boom arms/cherry pickers/Condors/lifts that are out there. The model, shape, and size of crane required may be different in each area you are filming. Know what is available and how to use it. Use the right tool for the job. Don't guess or try to make do.

## Scissors Lifts

Scissors lifts frighten me. I have used narrow ones to go high. They are safe, but this old guy does not like them. Scissors lifts come in narrow and wide models with and without outriggers (Figure 9.2). I prefer outriggers, but sometimes you just cannot use that type. Scissors lifts can be fueled by gasoline or propane, and even electric models are available. You certainly would not want to use a gas engine lift on a small enclosed stage. Some lifts have a platform that extends on one end; these are helpful for maneuvering over obstacles. When ordering a scissors lift, be as specific as you can be. Consider as many factors as you can to determine the proper piece of equipment. Do not use, move, or operate any piece of equipment until you are fully trained and fully confident that you can operate it safely.

## Suppliers

When you use any lift, determine the physical weight of the unit fully loaded with persons, material, and equipment; then decide whether you need to put double sheets of 3/4-in. (1.9 cm) plywood under each wheel to distribute the weight over a

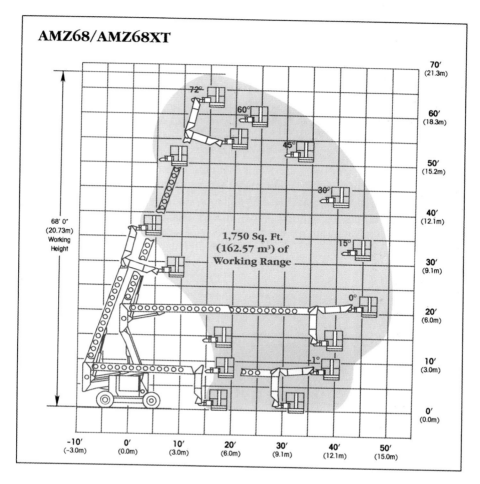

**Figure 9.1** Condor with articulating arm.

larger area. I always order at least eight sheets of plywood for a Condor or cherry picker shoot. Here's why. Say we start shooting at 7 a.m. on a city street. Around noon, the asphalt softens, and the wheels of the cherry picker will slowly settle into the softened asphalt and leave large ruts behind if you do not use double-sheet plywood. Trust me on this. This is not to say that the plywood will not leave a ridge, but it indicates that you have planned ahead as well as you can. As with any piece of equipment, call the supplier with any questions you might have. Suppliers are very knowledgeable about their equipment. They do not want anyone to get hurt, either. Do not try to figure it out on your own. Ask questions.

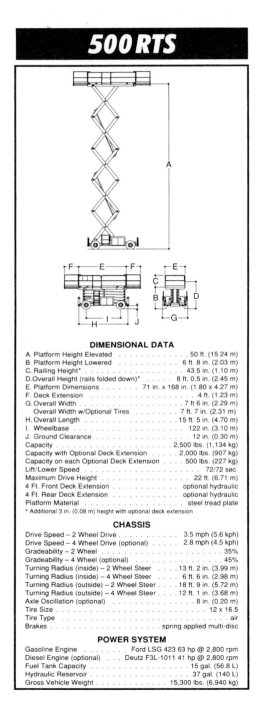

## 500 RTS

### DIMENSIONAL DATA

A. Platform Height Elevated . . . . . . . . . . . . . 50 ft. (15.24 m)
B. Platform Height Lowered . . . . . . . . . . . 6 ft. 8 in. (2.03 m)
C. Railing Height* . . . . . . . . . . . . . . . . . . . 43.5 in. (1.10 m)
D.Overall Height (rails folded down)* . . . . . 8 ft. 0.5 in. (2.45 m)
E. Platform Dimensions . . . . . . . 71 in. x 168 in. (1.80 x 4.27 m)
F. Deck Extension . . . . . . . . . . . . . . . . . . . . . . 4 ft. (1.23 m)
G.Overall Width . . . . . . . . . . . . . . . . . . . . 7 ft 6 in. (2.29 m)
    Overall Width w/Optional Tires . . . . . . . 7 ft. 7 in. (2.31 m)
H. Overall Length . . . . . . . . . . . . . . . . . . 15 ft. 5 in. (4.70 m)
I. Wheelbase . . . . . . . . . . . . . . . . . . . . . 122 in. (3.10 m)
J. Ground Clearance . . . . . . . . . . . . . . . . . 12 in. (0.30 m)
Capacity . . . . . . . . . . . . . . . . . . . . . 2,500 lbs. (1,134 kg)
Capacity with Optional Deck Extension . . . . . 2,000 lbs. (907 kg)
Capacity on each Optional Deck Extension . . . . 500 lbs. (227 kg)
Lift/Lower Speed . . . . . . . . . . . . . . . . . . . . . . 72/72 sec.
Maximum Drive Height . . . . . . . . . . . . . . . . 22 ft. (6.71 m)
4 Ft. Front Deck Extension . . . . . . . . . . . . optional hydraulic
4 Ft. Rear Deck Extension . . . . . . . . . . . . . optional hydraulic
Platform Material . . . . . . . . . . . . . . . . . . steel tread plate
\* Additional 3 in. (0.08 m) height with optional deck extension

### CHASSIS

Drive Speed – 2 Wheel Drive . . . . . . . . . . 3.5 mph (5.6 kph)
Drive Speed – 4 Wheel Drive (optional) . . . . . 2.8 mph (4.5 kph)
Gradeability – 2 Wheel . . . . . . . . . . . . . . . . . . . . . . 35%
Gradeability – 4 Wheel (optional) . . . . . . . . . . . . . . . . 45%
Turning Radius (inside) – 2 Wheel Steer . . . . 13 ft. 2 in. (3.99 m)
Turning Radius (inside) – 4 Wheel Steer . . . . 6 ft. 6 in. (2.98 m)
Turning Radius (outside) – 2 Wheel Steer . . . . 18 ft. 9 in. (5.72 m)
Turning Radius (outside) – 4 Wheel Steer . . . . 12 ft. 1 in. (3.68 m)
Axle Oscillation (optional) . . . . . . . . . . . . . . 8 in. (0.20 m)
Tire Size . . . . . . . . . . . . . . . . . . . . . . . . . . . 12 x 16.5
Tire Type . . . . . . . . . . . . . . . . . . . . . . . . . . . . . . air
Brakes . . . . . . . . . . . . . . . . . . . . spring applied multi-disc

### POWER SYSTEM

Gasoline Engine . . . . . . . . Ford LSG 423 63 hp @ 2,800 rpm
Diesel Engine (optional) . . . Deutz F3L-1011 41 hp @ 2,800 rpm
Fuel Tank Capacity . . . . . . . . . . . . . . . . . 15 gal. (56.8 L)
Hydraulic Reservoir . . . . . . . . . . . . . . . . . 37 gal. (140 L)
Gross Vehicle Weight . . . . . . . . . . . . 15,300 lbs. (6,940 kg)

**Figure 9.2** Scissor lift with extending platform.

**Figure 9.3a**  Example of a body harness.

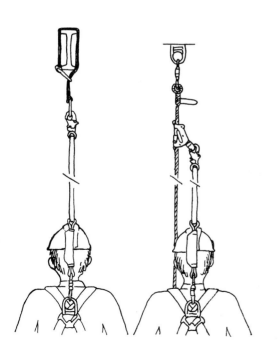

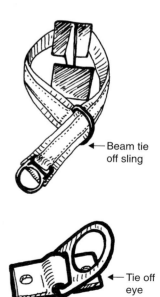

←Beam tie off sling

←Tie off eye

**Figure 9.3b**  Example of attach point.

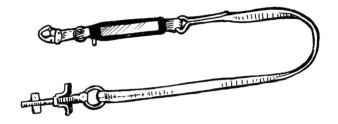

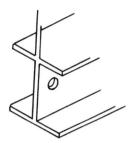

**Figure 9.3c** Tie off attachment for I-beam.

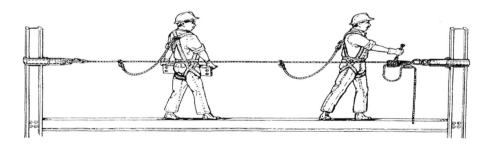

**Figure 9.3d** Body harness on cable.

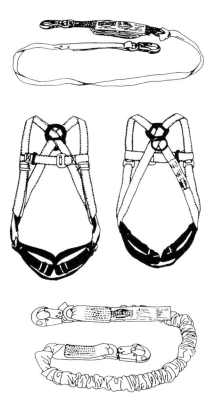

**Figure 9.3e**  Body harness and lanyard.

*Mike's note:* Too large costs extra money. Too small costs time and money. The dispatcher asks necessary questions about the details to avoid extra costs and to ensure that you have the proper size crane.

## Additional Equipment

The pieces of equipment shown in Figure 9.3 are helpful (and are now required by Local 80 Hollywood grips) and necessary for work with lifts, cherry pickers, or booms. Check with local unions and studios which piece of equipment harness is required.

# Cranes, Jibs, Arms, Dollies, and Heads

The following pages provide descriptions of and specifications for the cranes, jibs, and arms used in the industry.

1. Cranes, jibs, and arms can be set lower or higher depending on which base, dolly, tripod, or other crane they are being used with.
2. Some of these cranes, jibs, and arms may look short, but they may be the type that have kits or extensions to lengthen their reach or to change from remote operation to carrying a cameraperson or assistant.
3. The manufacturers' specs shown in their brochures indicate their recommended dollies, bases, or tripods. Please call the manufacturer or supplier if you have any questions about a crane, jib, or arm.

*Remember:* Read the manufacturer's specifications carefully!
*Caution:*

1. Do not operate any of these cranes, jibs, or arms without first being instructed on the proper operation of each unit.
2. Remember that the reach (length of arm) past the pivot point determines the actual height (plus base height and risers, if any).
3. See the manufacturer's instructions for full details on each piece of equipment.
4. The rigs (cranes, jibs, or arms) shown in this book are not all meant to support personnel, unless there is a note to the contrary.
5. Call the manufacturer of the arm or jib if the weight of the camera is an issue.

---

**T.O.T.**

During installation of a remote head on a jib arm or a crane arm in an underslung position, I have found it easier to loosen all four leveling bolts on the head, which allows the leveling head to move freely with its four-way tilting action. Set the remote head on the ground (or deck) with the threaded portion upward, if the head permits this position. With the arm balanced out, lower it to the threaded end of the remote, then gently slide the receiver hole over the threads of the remote, making sure not to damage the threads. Align the key way (slotted area), then install the winged/gland nut on the threads and rough

---

level it in place. Add weight to the bucket end of the jib or crane to rebalance the pivot point of the arm. Raise the arm to a working height (usually a six-step ladder under the arm will do nicely for judging the correct height). Now install the camera and safety. Rebalance the arm for the camera weight.

**T.O.T.**

Always move the crane arm after releasing the brake. This is a safety check to ensure that the brake is fully off.

## Cranes and Communication Systems

I highly recommend that, when you get a mobile crane, jib, or arm that will keep you some distance from the camera operator (*i.e.*, the camera operator is on a Titan crane or a Lenny arm with a remote), you ask production to rent you a communication system so you can hear the operator's requests. Any good sound department will set up a one-way system for you. The operator will have an open microphone and transmitter that will probably be an omnidirectional microphone. The operator will request movement in whichever direction is desired. He or she can speak in a normal voice, even so much as a whisper during a sound take. You and the other grips will have the receiver system (headsets) on so the grip operating the crane or arm knows what is requested. I use a system that a mixer (sound person) designed for my jobs.

I give full credit to Bob Dreebin, president of Roll Sound, for my rental system (800-468-7970). Call him, and he will set you up. I provide this information because if you cannot get the perfect piece of equipment to do the job right, you might as well use two tin cans and a string. Here is a basic system he has designed for this book:

- SM58 microphone or equivalent XLR-F to XLR-M cable Sony headphone amplifier with volume control or equivalent 1/4-inch phono mong to sub M-mini mall Comtec—72 transmitter or equivalent (comes in various frequencies a, b, c, d, e, f, etc.) (*Note:* The microphone must be kept in a clear area from the operator monitor (sweet spot) to prevent static.) 1 to 4 mono headsets and Comtex R-736 personal receivers.

*Huge note:* The size and weight are ever changing on cranes, jibs, arms, and dollies. The reference listed must be checked *before* you rely solely on them. Be smart! Check out the equipment with the manufacturer first. I don't want anyone hurt, killed, or to be sued! This is on you—am I clear?

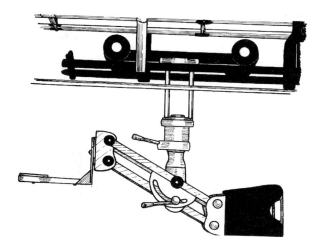

**Figure 10.1** Seno's Over/Under Jib Arm (Modern Equipment Company).

**Figure 10.2** Trovato Jr. (Trovato Manufacturing. Inc.).

The following cranes are listed from short to long arm length:

- **Seno's Over/Under Jib Arm** (Figure 10.1)
  *Lens height:* 2 feet/up from the base (depending on what this unit is mounted on)
  *Arm capacity:* 100 pounds
- **Trovato Jr.** (Figure 10.2)
  *Lens height:* 4 feet/up (depending on what this unit is mounted on)
  *Arm capacity:* 100 pounds
- **Trovato Tote Jib** (Figures 10.3–10.6)
  *Lens height:* 4 feet/up (depending on what this unit is mounted on)
  *Arm capacity:* 100 pounds

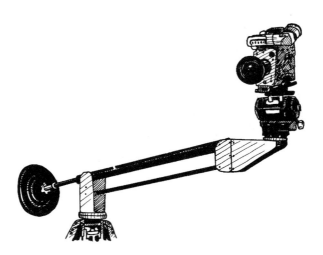

**Figure 10.3** Trovato Tote Jib (Trovato Manufacturing, Inc.).

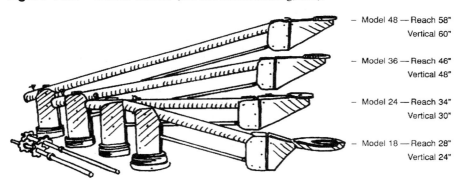

- Model 48 — Reach 58"
  Vertical 60"

- Model 36 — Reach 46"
  Vertical 48"

- Model 24 — Reach 34"
  Vertical 30"

- Model 18 — Reach 28"
  Vertical 24"

**Figure 10.4** Trovato Tote Jib (Trovato Manufacturing, Inc.).

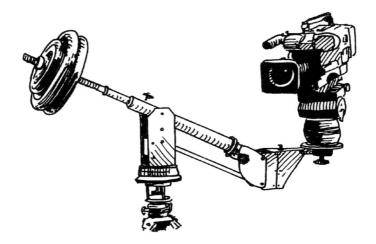

**Figure 10.5** Trovato Tote Jib (Trovato Manufacturing, Inc.).

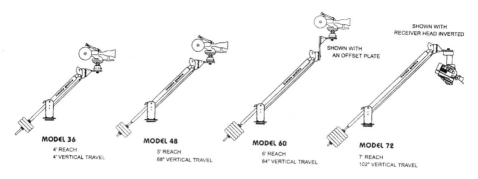

**Figure 10.6** Trovato Tote Jib (Trovato Manufacturing, Inc.).

**Figure 10.7** Euro-Jib.

- **Euro-Jib** (Figure 10.7)
  *Lens height:* 4 feet/up (depending on what this unit is mounted on)
  *Arm capacity:* 77 pounds
- **Liberty Range Jib** (Figure 10.8)
  *Lens height:* 5 feet/8 inches/up (depending on what this unit is mounted on)
  *Arm capacity:* 99 pounds
- **Egripment Mini-Jib/Arms Model 124** (Figure 10.9)
  *Lens height:* 5 feet/8 inches/up from the base (depending on what this unit is mounted on)
  *Arm capacity:* 99 pounds
- **Porta Jib** (Figure 10.10)
  *Lens height:* 6 feet/up (depending on what this unit is mounted on)
  *Arm capacity:* 90 pounds
- **Mini-Jib Liberty** (Figure 10.11)
  *Lens height:* 5 feet/8 inches/up (depending on what this unit is mounted on)
  *Arm capacity:* 99 pounds

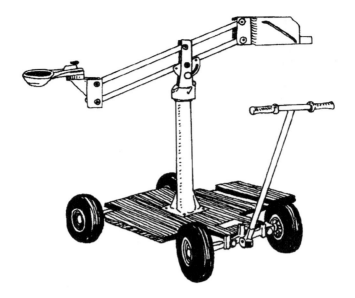

**Figure 10.8** Liberty Range Jib.

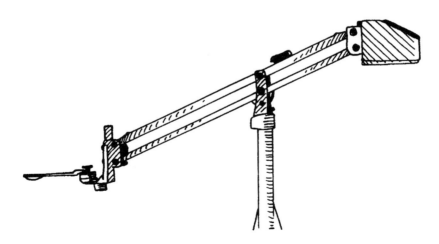

**Figure 10.9** Egripment Mini-Jib/Arm, Model 124.

**Figure 10.10a** Porta Jib on tripod.

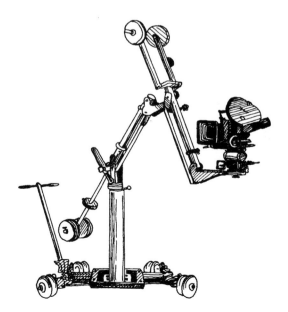

**Figure 10.10b** Porta Jib on dolly.

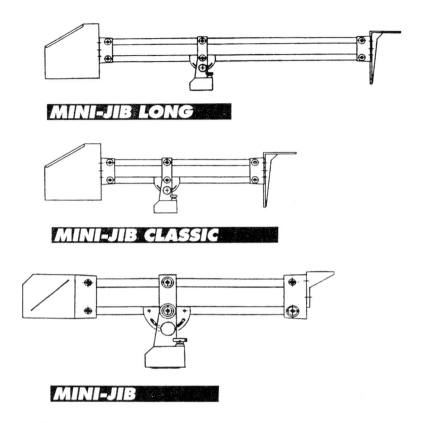

**Figure 10.11** Mini-Jibs.

- **Weaver-Steadman Five-Axis Fluid Crane** (Figure 10.12)
  *Lens height:* 6 feet/up (depending on what this unit is mounted on)
  *Arm capacity:* 90 pounds
- **JF Crossarm** (Figures 10.13 and 10.14)
  *Arm capacity:* 100 pounds
- **Maxi-Jib/Super Maxi-Jib** (Figure 10.15)
  *Lens height:* 16 feet/8 inches/up (depending on what this unit is mounted on)
  *Arm capacity:* 77 pounds
  *Note:* Remember that the heights given are a maximum, but the crane may be used in several shorter configurations. Check the manufacturer's specifications.
- **Seven Jib** (Figure 10.16)
  *Lens height:* 6 feet/4 inches/up (depending on what this unit is mounted on)
  *Arm capacity:* 45 pounds

THE GRIP BOOK **219**

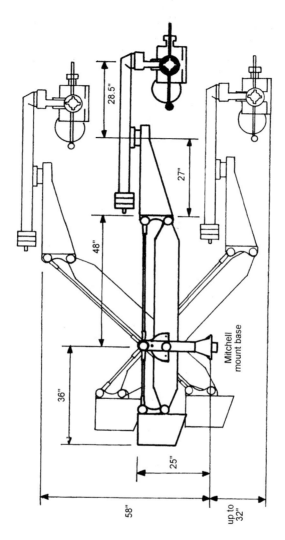

**Figure 10.12** Weaver-Steadman Five-axis Fluid Crane.

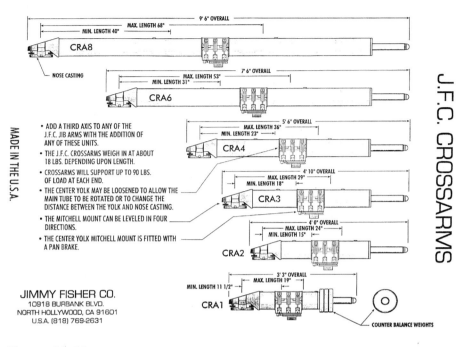

**Figure 10.13** J.F.C. Crossarm configurations.

**Figure 10.14** J.F. Crossarm on Fisher Dolly.

**Figure 10.15a** Maxi-Jib/Super Maxi-Jib (Egripment).

- **ZG Arm (Model 6-200)** (Figure 10.17)
  *Lens height:* 7 feet/up (depending on what this unit is mounted on)
  *Arm capacity:* 200 pounds
- **ZG Arm (Model 8-130, Ken Hill MFG)** (Figure 10.18)
  *Lens height:* 12 feet/up (depending on what this unit is mounted on)
  *Arm capacity:* 130 pounds.
- **ZG Arm (Model 11-100, Ken Hill MFG)** (Figure 10.19)
  *Lens height:* 14 feet/up (depending on what this unit is mounted on)
  *Note:* Training and demo reels are available; call K. Hill Manufacturing.
- **Javelin Crane Arm** (Figure 10.20)
  *Lens height:* 29 feet/4 inches up (depending on what this unit is mounted on)
  *Arm capacity:* 220 pounds
  *Note:* This crane can be assembled in seven different lengths and variations.
- **Piccolo Crane** (Figure 10.21)
  *Lens height:* 14 feet/up (depending on what this unit is mounted on)
  *Arm capacity:* 145 pounds
  *Note:* This crane will work on straight or curved track, supplied by the equipment manufacturer. It has its own integral track wheels.
- **Lightweight Jib** (Figure 10.22)
  *Lens height:* 8 feet/8 inches up (depending on what this unit is mounted on)
  *Arm capacity:* 65 pounds

**Figure 10.15b** Maxi-Jib configurations (Egripment).

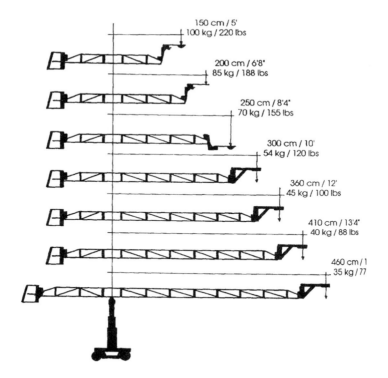

150 cm / 5'
100 kg / 220 lbs

200 cm / 6'8"
85 kg / 188 lbs

250 cm / 8'4"
70 kg / 155 lbs

300 cm / 10'
54 kg / 120 lbs

360 cm / 12'
45 kg / 100 lbs

410 cm / 13'4"
40 kg / 88 lbs

460 cm / 1
35 kg / 77

**Figure 10.15c**  Maxi-Jib configurations.

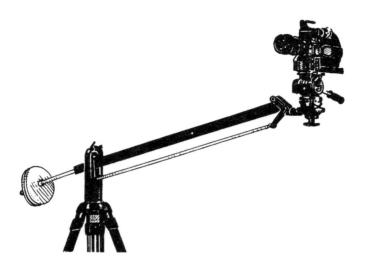

**Figure 10.16**  Seven Jib.

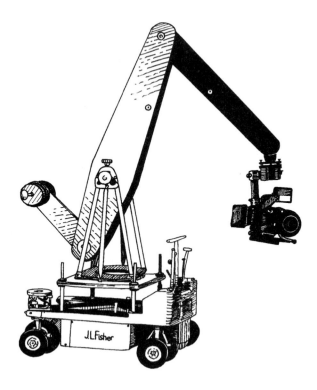

**Figure 10.17**   Z-Jib Arm (Model 6-200) on Fisher Dolly (Ken Hill Mfg.).

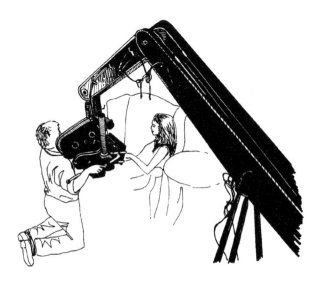

**Figure 10.18**   Z-Jib Arm, Model 8-130 (Ken Hill Mfg.).

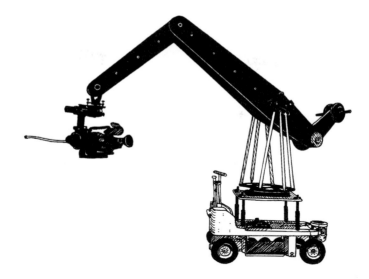

**Figure 10.19**  Z-Jib Arm, Model 11-100 (Ken Hill Mfg.).

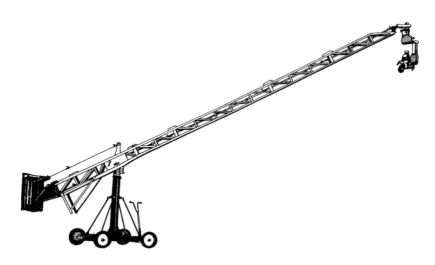

**Figure 10.20a**  Javelin Crane Arm (Egripment).

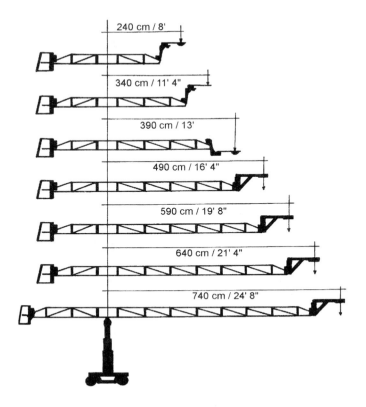

**Figure 10.20b** Javelin Crane Arm configurations (Egripment).

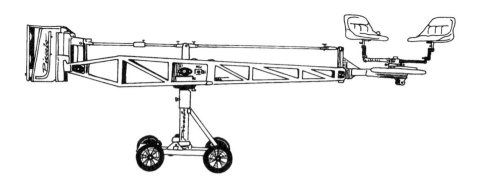

**Figure 10.21** Piccolo Crane (Egripment).

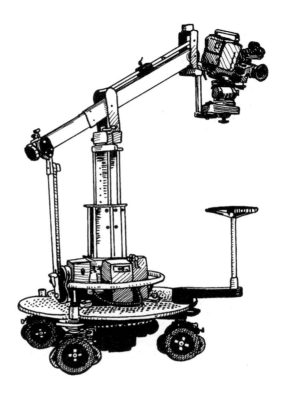

**Figure 10.22a**  Lightweight Jib on dolly.

**Figure 10.22b**  Lightweight Jib on track.

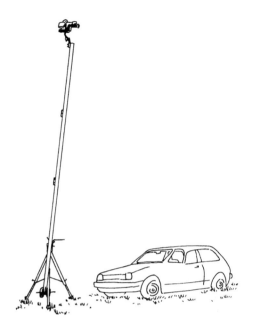

**Figure 10.23a** Jimmy Jib (Stanton).

- **Jimmy Jib (Junior to Giant)** (Figure 10.23)
  *Lens height:* 9 feet/30 feet/up from the base (depending on what this unit is mounted on)
  *Arm capacity:* 70 pounds
  *Note:* This jib can be adjusted to seven different configurations with some additional accessories.
- **Fisher Jib/Arm (Model 20)** (Figure 10.24)
  *Lens height:* 9 feet/5 inches up (depending on what this unit is mounted on)
  *Arm capacity:* 210 pounds
  *Note:* These heights or depths can be achieved only with the use of a 24-inch riser.
- **Fisher Jib/Arm (Model 21)** (Figure 10.25)
  *Lens height:* 11 feet/5 inches up (depending on what this unit is mounted on)
  *Arm capacity:* 210 pounds
  *Note:* These heights or depths can be achieved only with the use of a 24-inch riser.
- **Fisher Jib/Arm (Model 22)** (Figure 10.26)
  *Lens height:* 13 feet/up (depending on what this unit is mounted on)
  *Arm capacity:* 150 pounds
  *Note:* These heights or depths can be achieved only with the use of a 24-inch riser.

**Figure 10.23b**  Jimmy Jib (Stanton).

**Figure 10.23c**  Jimmy Jib (Stanton).

**Figure 10.23e** Jimmy Jib Head (Stanton).

**Figure 10.23d** Jimmy Jib Head (Stanton).

**Figure 10.23f** Jimmy Jib System (Stanton).

## MINIMUM AND MAXIMUM HEIGHT

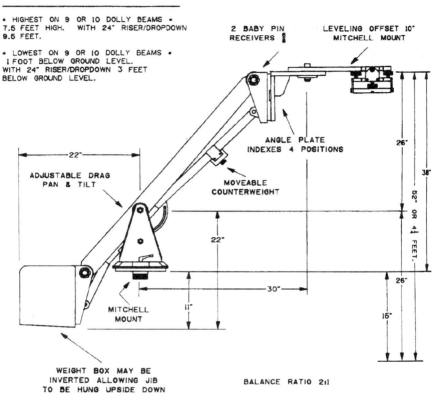

• HIGHEST ON 9 OR 10 DOLLY BEAMS •
7.5 FEET HIGH. WITH 24" RISER/DROPDOWN
9.5 FEET.

• LOWEST ON 9 OR 10 DOLLY BEAMS •
1 FOOT BELOW GROUND LEVEL.
WITH 24" RISER/DROPDOWN 3 FEET
BELOW GROUND LEVEL.

2 BABY PIN RECEIVERS

LEVELING OFFSET 10"
MITCHELL MOUNT

ANGLE PLATE
INDEXES 4 POSITIONS

26"

38"

ADJUSTABLE DRAG
PAN & TILT

22"

MOVEABLE
COUNTERWEIGHT

52" OR 4½ FEET.

22"

30"

26"

MITCHELL
MOUNT

11"

15"

WEIGHT BOX MAY BE
INVERTED ALLOWING JIB
TO BE HUNG UPSIDE DOWN

BALANCE RATIO 2:1

**Figure 10.24a** Fisher Jib, Model 20 (J.L. Fisher Mfg.).

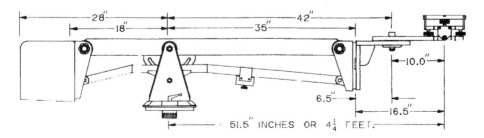

28"
18"
42"
35"
10.0"
6.5"
16.5"
51.5" INCHES OR 4¼ FEET.

**Figure 10.24b** Fisher Jib, Model 20 (J.L. Fisher Mfg.).

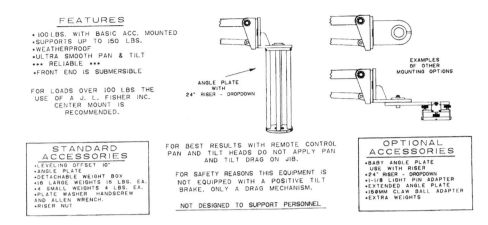

FEATURES

• 100 LBS. WITH BASIC ACC. MOUNTED
• SUPPORTS UP TO 150 LBS.
• WEATHERPROOF
• ULTRA SMOOTH PAN & TILT
••• RELIABLE •••
• FRONT END IS SUBMERSIBLE

FOR LOADS OVER 100 LBS THE
USE OF A J. L. FISHER INC.
CENTER MOUNT IS
RECOMMENDED.

ANGLE PLATE
WITH
24" RISER - DROPDOWN

EXAMPLES
OF OTHER
MOUNTING OPTIONS

STANDARD
ACCESSORIES
• LEVELING OFFSET 10"
• ANGLE PLATE
• DETACHABLE WEIGHT BOX
• 18 LARGE WEIGHTS 15 LBS. EA.
• 4 SMALL WEIGHTS 4 LBS. EA.
• PLATE WASHER HANDSCREW
  AND ALLEN WRENCH.
• RISER NUT

FOR BEST RESULTS WITH REMOTE CONTROL
PAN AND TILT HEADS DO NOT APPLY PAN
AND TILT DRAG ON JIB.

FOR SAFETY REASONS THIS EQUIPMENT IS
NOT EQUIPPED WITH A POSITIVE TILT
BRAKE. ONLY A DRAG MECHANISM.

NOT DESIGNED TO SUPPORT PERSONNEL

OPTIONAL
ACCESSORIES
• BABY ANGLE PLATE
  USE WITH RISER
• 24" RISER - DROPDOWN
• 1-1/8 LIGHT PIN ADAPTER
• EXTENDED ANGLE PLATE
• 150MM CLAW BALL ADAPTER
• EXTRA WEIGHTS

**Figure 10.24b** (continued) Fisher Jib/Arm accessories.

**Figure 10.24c** Fisher Arm, Model 20 on Fisher Dolly (Notice it is mounted on dolly arm due to its light weight.).

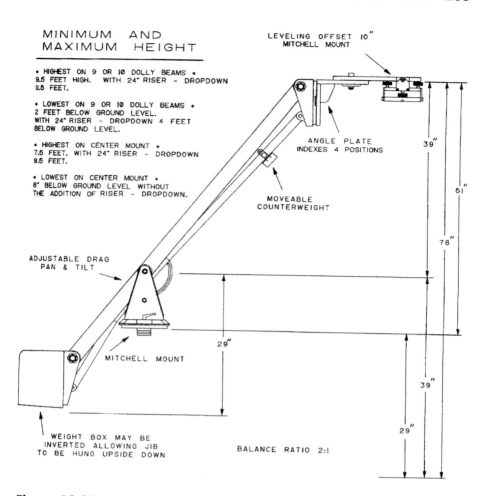

## MINIMUM AND MAXIMUM HEIGHT

• HIGHEST ON 9 OR 10 DOLLY BEAMS •
9.5 FEET HIGH. WITH 24" RISER - DROPDOWN
11.5 FEET.

• LOWEST ON 9 OR 10 DOLLY BEAMS •
2 FEET BELOW GROUND LEVEL.
WITH 24" RISER - DROPDOWN 4 FEET
BELOW GROUND LEVEL.

• HIGHEST ON CENTER MOUNT •
7.5 FEET. WITH 24" RISER - DROPDOWN
9.5 FEET.

• LOWEST ON CENTER MOUNT •
8" BELOW GROUND LEVEL WITHOUT
THE ADDITION OF RISER - DROPDOWN.

LEVELING OFFSET 10"
MITCHELL MOUNT

ANGLE PLATE
INDEXES 4 POSITIONS

MOVEABLE
COUNTERWEIGHT

ADJUSTABLE DRAG
PAN & TILT

MITCHELL MOUNT

WEIGHT BOX MAY BE
INVERTED ALLOWING JIB
TO BE HUNG UPSIDE DOWN

BALANCE RATIO 2:1

39"

51"

78"

39"

29"

29"

**Figure 10.25a** Fisher Jib/Arm, Model 21 (J.L. Fisher Mfg.).

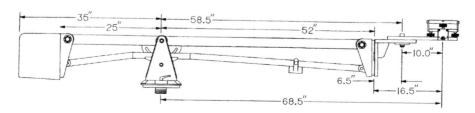

35"

25"

58.5"

52"

10.0"

6.5"

16.5"

68.5"

**Figure 10.25b** Fisher Jib/Arm, Model 21 (J.L. Fisher Mfg.).

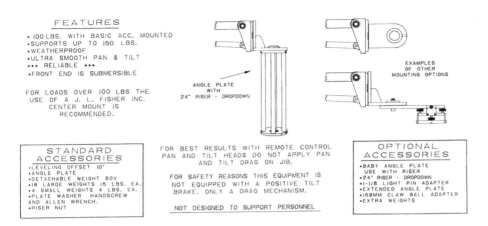

FEATURES

• 100 LBS. WITH BASIC ACC. MOUNTED
• SUPPORTS UP TO 150 LBS.
• WEATHERPROOF
• ULTRA SMOOTH PAN & TILT
• • • RELIABLE • • •
• FRONT END IS SUBMERSIBLE

FOR LOADS OVER 100 LBS THE
USE OF A J. L. FISHER INC.
CENTER MOUNT IS
RECOMMENDED.

ANGLE PLATE
WITH
24" RISER - DROPDOWN

EXAMPLES
OF OTHER
MOUNTING OPTIONS

STANDARD
ACCESSORIES
• LEVELING OFFSET 10"
• ANGLE PLATE
• DETACHABLE WEIGHT BOX
• 18 LARGE WEIGHTS 15 LBS. EA.
• 4 SMALL WEIGHTS 4 LBS. EA.
• PLATE WASHER HANDSCREW
  AND ALLEN WRENCH.
• RISER NUT

FOR BEST RESULTS WITH REMOTE CONTROL
PAN AND TILT HEADS DO NOT APPLY PAN
AND TILT DRAG ON JIB.

FOR SAFETY REASONS THIS EQUIPMENT IS
NOT EQUIPPED WITH A POSITIVE TILT
BRAKE. ONLY A DRAG MECHANISM.

NOT DESIGNED TO SUPPORT PERSONNEL

OPTIONAL
ACCESSORIES
• BABY ANGLE PLATE
  USE WITH RISER
• 24" RISER - DROPDOWN
• 1-1/8 LIGHT PIN ADAPTER
• EXTENDED ANGLE PLATE
• 150MM CLAW BALL ADAPTER
• EXTRA WEIGHTS

**Figure 10.25b**  (continued) Fisher Jib/Arm, Model 21 (J.L. Fisher Mfg.).

**Figure 10.25c**  Fisher Jib/Arm, Model 21, on spider dolly.

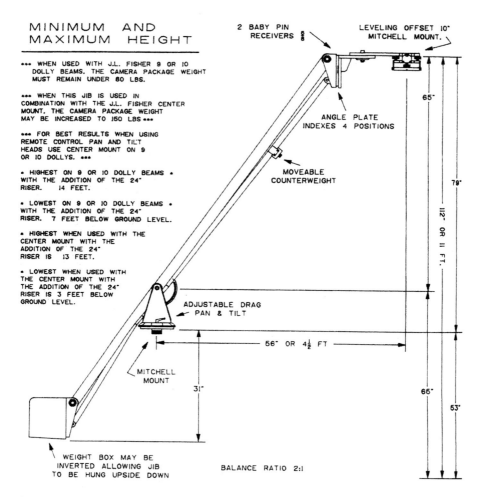

MINIMUM AND
MAXIMUM HEIGHT

••• WHEN USED WITH J.L. FISHER 9 OR 10
DOLLY BEAMS. THE CAMERA PACKAGE WEIGHT
MUST REMAIN UNDER 80 LBS.

••• WHEN THIS JIB IS USED IN
COMBINATION WITH THE J.L. FISHER CENTER
MOUNT. THE CAMERA PACKAGE WEIGHT
MAY BE INCREASED TO 150 LBS •••

••• FOR BEST RESULTS WHEN USING
REMOTE CONTROL PAN AND TILT
HEADS USE CENTER MOUNT ON 9
OR 10 DOLLYS. •••

• HIGHEST ON 9 OR 10 DOLLY BEAMS •
WITH THE ADDITION OF THE 24"
RISER.    14 FEET.

• LOWEST ON 9 OR 10 DOLLY BEAMS •
WITH THE ADDITION OF THE 24"
RISER.    7 FEET BELOW GROUND LEVEL.

• HIGHEST WHEN USED WITH THE
CENTER MOUNT WITH THE
ADDITION OF THE 24"
RISER IS   13 FEET.

• LOWEST WHEN USED WITH
THE CENTER MOUNT WITH
THE ADDITION OF THE 24"
RISER IS 3 FEET BELOW
GROUND LEVEL.

2 BABY PIN RECEIVERS

LEVELING OFFSET 10"
MITCHELL MOUNT.

ANGLE PLATE
INDEXES 4 POSITIONS

MOVEABLE
COUNTERWEIGHT

ADJUSTABLE DRAG
PAN & TILT

MITCHELL
MOUNT

31"

56" OR 4½ FT

65"

79"

112" OR 11 FT.

65"

53"

WEIGHT BOX MAY BE
INVERTED ALLOWING JIB
TO BE HUNG UPSIDE DOWN

BALANCE RATIO 2:1

**Figure 10.26a**    Fisher Jib/Arm, Model 22 (J.L. Fisher Mfg.).

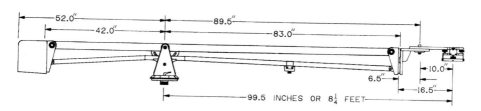

52.0"

42.0"

89.5"

83.0"

6.5"

10.0"

16.5"

99.5 INCHES OR 8¼ FEET

**Figure 10.26b**    Fisher Jib/Arm, Model 22 (J.L. Fisher Mfg.).

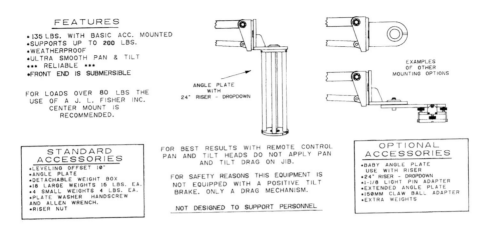

FEATURES

• 135 LBS. WITH BASIC ACC. MOUNTED
• SUPPORTS UP TO **200** LBS.
• WEATHERPROOF
• ULTRA SMOOTH PAN & TILT
••• RELIABLE •••
• FRONT END IS SUBMERSIBLE

FOR LOADS OVER 80 LBS THE
USE OF A J. L. FISHER INC.
CENTER MOUNT IS
RECOMMENDED.

EXAMPLES
OF OTHER
MOUNTING OPTIONS

ANGLE PLATE
WITH
24" RISER - DROPDOWN

STANDARD
ACCESSORIES
• LEVELING OFFSET 10"
• ANGLE PLATE
• DETACHABLE WEIGHT BOX
• 18 LARGE WEIGHTS 15 LBS. EA.
• 4 SMALL WEIGHTS 4 LBS. EA.
• PLATE WASHER HANDSCREW
 AND ALLEN WRENCH.
• RISER NUT

FOR BEST RESULTS WITH REMOTE CONTROL
PAN AND TILT HEADS DO NOT APPLY PAN
AND TILT DRAG ON JIB.

FOR SAFETY REASONS THIS EQUIPMENT IS
NOT EQUIPPED WITH A POSITIVE TILT
BRAKE. ONLY A DRAG MECHANISM.

NOT DESIGNED TO SUPPORT PERSONNEL

OPTIONAL
ACCESSORIES
• BABY ANGLE PLATE
 USE WITH RISER
• 24" RISER - DROPDOWN
• 1-1/8 LIGHT PIN ADAPTER
• EXTENDED ANGLE PLATE
• 150MM CLAW BALL ADAPTER
• EXTRA WEIGHTS

**Figure 10.26b**   (continued) Fisher Jib accessories.

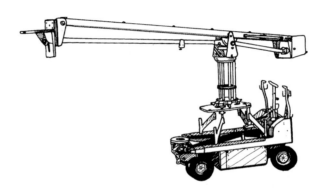

**Figure 10.26c**   Fisher Jib/Arm, Model 22, on Fisher Dolly #10 with center plate.

- **Chapman Crane Arm** (Figure 10.27)
  *Lens height:* 9 feet/6 inches up (depending on what this unit is mounted on)
  *Arm capacity:* 600 pounds
- **Aerocrane Jib/Arm** (Figure 10.28)
  *Lens height:* 9 feet/6 inches up (depending on what this unit is mounted on)
  *Arm capacity:* 75 pounds
- **Barber Baby Boom** (Figure 10.29)
  *Lens height:* 10 feet/up (depending on what this unit is mounted on)
  *Arm capacity:* 75 pounds
- **Barber Boom 20** (Figure 10.30)
  *Lens height:* 20 feet/up (depending on what this unit is mounted on)
  *Arm capacity:* 50 pounds

**Figure 10.27a** Chapman Crane Arm mounted on Chapman Titan (Chapman/Leonard).

**Figure 10.27b** Chapman Crane Arm on Chapman Olympian (Chapman/Leonard).

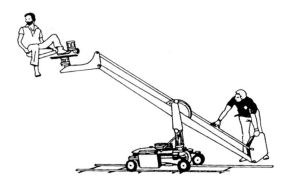

**Figure 10.27c** Chapman Crane Arm on Chapman Dolly Base on track (Chapman/Leonard).

**Figure 10.27d** Chapman Crane Arm with extention (Chapman/Leonard).

**Figure 10.27e** Chapman Crane Arm on Olympian (Chapman/Leonard).

**Figure 10.27f** Chapman Crane Arm with Skorkel Camera System (Chapman/Leonard).

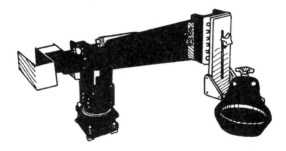

**Figure 10.28a** Aero Jib/Arm.

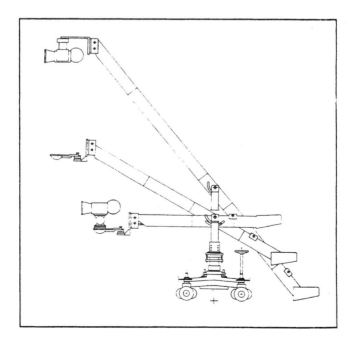

**Figure 10.28b** Aero Jib/Arm.

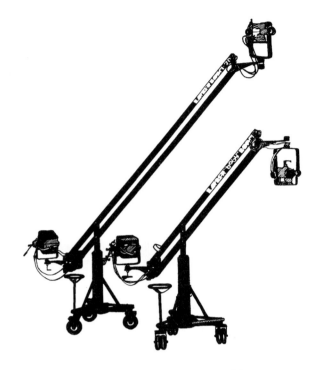

**Figure 10.29a** Barber Baby Boom and Barber Boom 20.

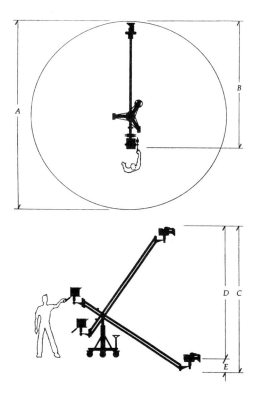

**Figure 10.29b** Barber Baby Boom.

**Figure 10.29c** Barber Baby Boom head positions (top and bottom slung).

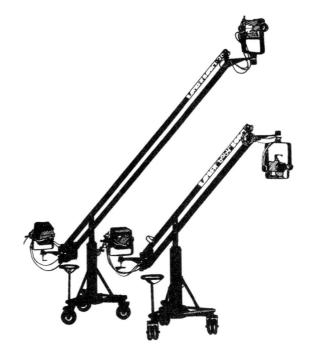

**Figure 10.30a** Barber Boom 20 and Baby Boom.

**Figure 10.30b** Barber Boom Head (top slung).

**Figure 10.30c** Barber Boom Head (under slung).

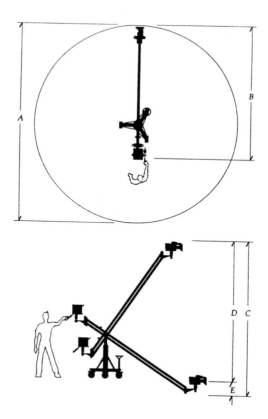

**Figure 10.30d** Barber Boom Travel.

- **MC-88 Crane** (Figure 10.31)
  *Lens height:* 24 feet/up (depending on what this unit is mounted on)
  *Arm capacity:* 105 pounds
- **Straight Shoot'R (PDM Mfg. Co.)** (Figure 10.32)
  *Lens height:* 9 feet/2 inches up (depending on what this unit is mounted on)
  *Arm capacity:* 110 pounds

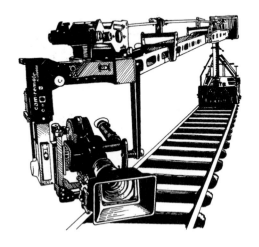

**Figure 10.31a**  MC-88 Crane on track.

**Figure 10.31b**  MC-88 Crane on dolly.

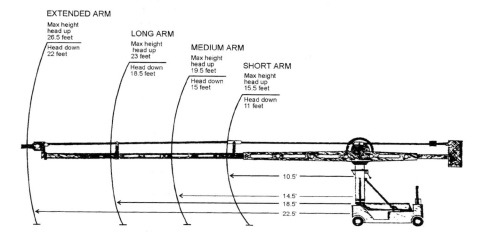

EXTENDED ARM
Max height
head up
26.5 feet
Head down
22 feet

LONG ARM
Max height
head up
23 feet
Head down
18.5 feet

MEDIUM ARM
Max height
head up
19.5 feet
Head down
15 feet

SHORT ARM
Max height
head up
15.5 feet
Head down
11 feet

10.5'
14.5'
18.5'
22.5'

**Figure 10.31c** MC-88 Crane specs (Matthews).

**Figure 10.32a** Straight Shoot'R (PDM Mfg. Co.).

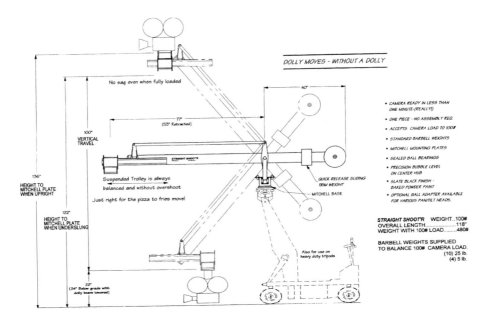

**Figure 10.32b**  Straight Shoot'R.

- **Pegasus Crane (Standard and Super)** (Figure 10.33)
  *Lens height:* 12 feet/8 inches up (depending on what this unit is mounted on)
  *Arm capacity:* 110 pounds
- **V.I.P. Four-in-One Crane** (Figure 10.34)
  *Lens height:* 13 feet/ up (depending on what this unit is mounted on)
  *Arm capacity:* 110 pounds
- **Super Jib** (Figure 10.35)
  *Lens height:* 13 feet/7 inches up (depending on what this unit is mounted on)
  *Arm capacity:* 331 pounds
- **Technocrane** (Figure 10.36)
  *Lens height:* 20 feet/ 2 inches up (depending on what this unit is mounted on)
  *Arm capacity:* 80 pounds
  *Highlights:* Technocrane can telescope during a shot, from a reach of 6 to 20 feet, at up to 8 feet per second. The crane can be mounted on top of Technocrane's truck, allowing a higher reach.
- **Super Technocrane** (Figure 10.37)
  *Lens height:* 30 feet/up (depending on what this unit is mounted on)
  *Arm capacity:* 80 pounds

**Figure 10.33a** Pegasus Crane with crew (Panther).

**Figure 10.33b** Pegasus Crane Remote (Panther).

**Figure 10.33c** Pegasus Crane Base (Panther).

# The Panther Pegasus Crane...

**... is the answer for grips, DP's and camera operators who want that little bit more from a crane.**

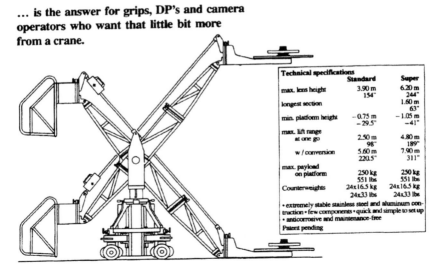

| Technical specifications | | |
|---|---|---|
| | **Standard** | **Super** |
| max. lens height | 3.90 m | 6.20 m |
| | 154" | 244" |
| longest section | | 1.60 m |
| | | 63" |
| min. platform height | −0.75 m | −1.05 m |
| | −29.5" | −41" |
| max. lift range | | |
| at one go | 2.50 m | 4.80 m |
| | 98" | 189" |
| w / conversion | 5.60 m | 7.90 m |
| | 220.5" | 311" |
| max. payload | | |
| on platform | 250 kg | 250 kg |
| | 551 lbs | 551 lbs |
| Counterweights | 24x16.5 kg | 24x16.5 kg |
| | 24x33 lbs | 24x33 lbs |

• extremely stable stainless steel and aluminum construction • few components • quick and simple to set up • anticorrosive and maintenance-free

Patent pending

Panther Pegasus Crane standard version

**Figure 10.33d** Panther Pegasus Crane standard version (Panther).

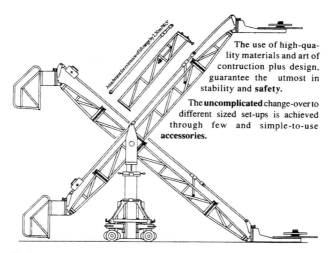

The use of high-qua-
lity materials and art of
contruction plus design,
guarantee the utmost in
stability and **safety.**

The **uncomplicated** change-over to
different sized set-ups is achieved
through few and simple-to-use
**accessories.**

Panther Pegasus Crane in extended version

**Figure 10.33d** (continued) Panther Pegasus Crane in extended version.

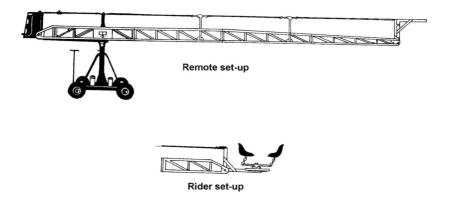

Remote set-up

Rider set-up

**Figure 10.34a** V.I.P. Four-in-one Crane.

**Figure 10.34b** V.I.P. Crane.

**Figure 10.35** Super Jib (Panther).

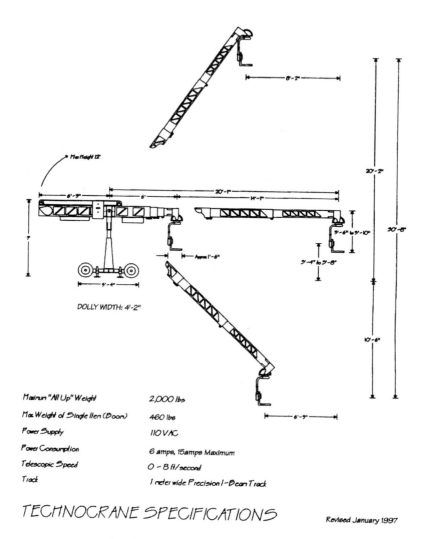

Max Height 12'

20'-2"

8'-2"

6'-5"   6'   20'-1"   14'-1"

7'

5'-4"

DOLLY WIDTH: 4'-2"

Appro 1'-6"

30'-6"

5'-6" to 5'-10"

5'-4" to 5'-8"

10'-6"

6'-5"

| | |
|---|---|
| Maximum "All Up" Weight | 2,000 lbs |
| Max Weight of Single Item (Boom) | 460 lbs |
| Power Supply | 110 VAC |
| Power Consumption | 6 amps, 15amps Maximum |
| Telescopic Speed | 0 - 8 ft/second |
| Track | 1 meter wide Precision I-Beam Track |

*TECHNOCRANE SPECIFICATIONS*

Revised January 1997

**Figure 10.36a**   Technocrane specifications.

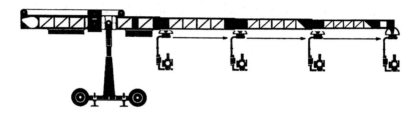

**Figure 10.36b**   Horizontal reach of the Technocrane.

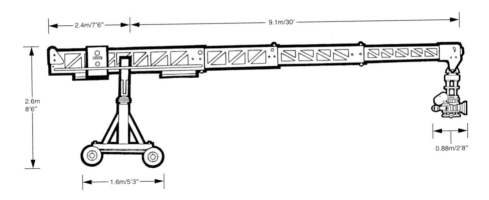

**Figure 10.37** Super Technocrane.

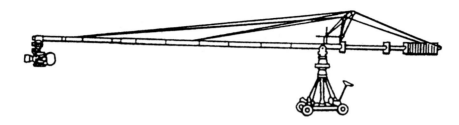

**Figure 10.38** Louma.

- **Louma** (Figure 10.38)
  *Lens height:* 27 feet/up (depending on what this unit is mounted on)
  *Arm capacity:* 74 pounds
  *Note:* Louma can also be used on the Titan and Super Nova cranes. The crane's attaching base (to dolly or crane) is a Mitchell mount base.
- **Enlouva II Crane** (Figure 10.39)
  *Lens height:* 24 feet/up (depending on what this unit is mounted on)
  *Arm capacity:* 140 pounds
- **Enlouva IIIA Crane** (Figure 10.40)
  *Lens height:* 25 feet/up (depending on what this unit is mounted on)
  *Arm capacity:* 140 pounds
  *Note:* Above measurements are based on a dolly column height of 48 inches.
- **Cam-Mate Crane/Jib/Arm** (Figure 10.41)
  *Lens height:* 28 feet/6 inches up (depending on what this unit is mounted on)
  *Arm capacity:* 550 pounds
- **The Crane (Mathews Studio Equipment)** (Figure 10.42)
  *Lens height:* 25 feet/up(depending on what this unit is mounted on)
  *Arm capacity:* 80 pounds
  *Note:* This crane is designed to support personnel!

**Figure 10.39** Enlouva II Crane (Camera Support System, Inc.).

**Figure 10.40a** Enlouva III Crane (Camera Support System, Inc.).

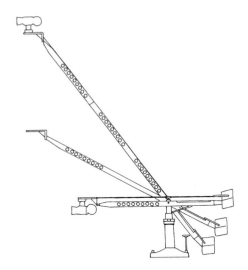

**Figure 10.40b**  Enlouva Crane (Camera Support System, Inc.).

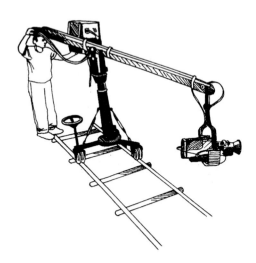

**Figure 10.41a**  Cam-Mate Crane/Jib/Arm.

**Figure 10.41b**   Cam-Mate Crane/Jib/Arm.

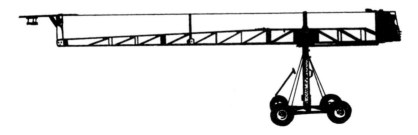

**Figure 10.42a**   The Crane (Matthews Studio Equipment).

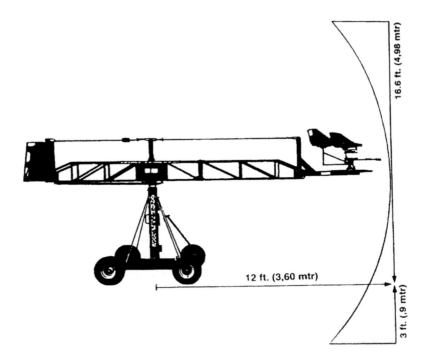

**Figure 10.42b** The Crane.

- **Giraffe Crane (Filmair)** (Figure 10.43)
  *Lens height:* 30 feet/up (depending on what this unit is mounted on)
  *Arm capacity:* 175 pounds
  *Note:* This crane is designed to support personnel!
- **Swiss Crane** (Figure 10.44)
  *Lens height:* 32 feet/up (depending on what this unit is mounted on)
  *Arm capacity:* 155 pounds
- **The Akēla Crane (Jr. and Sr.)** (Figure 10.45)
  *Lens height:* 32 feet/up (depending on what this unit is mounted on)
  *Arm capacity:* 225 pounds

## Motorized Cranes

The Chapman company is my top choice for motorized cranes. In my humble opinion, you will never find a safer or better engineered crane in the industry. Be safe, be smart, and call for a Chapman motorized crane. It is an Academy Award winner. *Note:* It is advised that the user of Chapman/Leonard equipment check with the manufacturer for the latest updates on *all* equipment. Leave nothing to chance. Be smart. Check first.

**Figure 10.43a** Giraffe Crane (Filmair).

**Figure 10.43b** Giraffe Crane Base (Filmair).

**Figure 10.44a** Swiss Crane (Filmair).

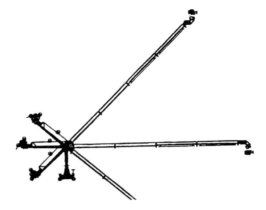

**Figure 10.44b** Swiss Crane.

**Figure 10.44c** Swiss Crane.

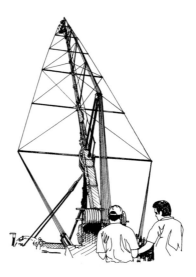

**Figure 10.45a**   The Akēla Crane (Jr. and Sr.).

## SPECIFICATIONS

| ARM REACH | LENS HEIGHT UNDERSLUNG | OVERALL ARM LENGTH | MAX. NOSE LOAD (INCLUDES REMOTE HEAD & CAMERA PKG.) |
|:---:|:---:|:---:|:---:|
| 32' | 32' | 41' | 225 lbs. |
| 39' | 39' | 48' | 200 lbs. |
| 46' | 46' | 55' | 175 lbs. |
| 53' | 53' | 62' | 150 lbs. |

Weight (w/chassis & weights) . . .3000 lbs.  
Dolly Dimension . . . . . . . . . . . . . .6' x 6'  
Pedestal Height . . . . . . . . . . . . . . . .9'  

Pedestal to rear . . . . . . . . . . . . . . . . .9'  
Steerable Dolly (Conventional) . . . . . . . . .1  
Operator (provided) . . . . . . . . . . . . . . .1  

*The Akela Jr. is lightweight and can be broken down into highly portable elements enabling assembly in the remotest of locations.

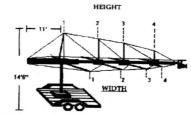

*Height from crane base w/o trailer to top of #1 pole is 13'6".  
*Optimum working space required is 17' back from the Pedestal.

**Figure 10.45b**   The Akēla Crane.

## SPECIFICATIONS (Akela Sr.)

| ARM REACH | LENS HEIGHT UNDERSLUNG | OVERALL ARM LENGTH | MAX. NOSE LOAD (includes remote head & camera pkg.) |
|---|---|---|---|
| 71'6" | 68' | 83' | 200 lbs. |
| 58'6" | 55' | 70' | 250 lbs. |
| 45'6" | 44' | 57' | 300 lbs. |

Weight (w/ Main Chassis & weights) ................ 7000 lbs.
Chassis w/Steering .......................................... 10'6" x 12'2"
Pedestal Pivot Point Height ............................... 10'
Overall Crane Height ......................................... 15'

Weight (w/Portable Chassis & weights) ............. 5000 lbs.
Chassis without Steering ............................... 8' x 10'
Pedestal to Rear .............................................. 12'
Operator (Provided) ......................................... 2
Setup Time ...................................................... 3 hrs.
Strike Time ...................................................... 2 hrs.

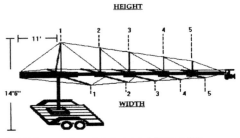

*Height from crane base w/o trailer to top of #1 pole is 13'6".
*Optimum working space required is 17' back from the Pedestal.

**Figure 10.45c**   The Akēla Crane.

## SPECIFICATIONS

| ARM REACH | LENS HEIGHT UNDERSLUNG | OVERALL ARM LENGTH | MAX. NOSE LOAD (INCLUDES REMOTE HEAD & CAMERA PKG.) |
|---|---|---|---|
| 85' | 79' | 94' | 100 lbs. |

### MAX. CAMERA WEIGHT............................45 lbs.

Weight (w/Main Chassis & weights) . . . . .8000 lbs.
Chassis w/Steering . . . . . . . . . . . . . .10'6" x 12'2"
Pedestal Pivot Point Height . . . . . . . . . . . . . .10'
Overall Crane Height . . . . . . . . . . . . . . . . . . .15'

Weight (w/Portable Chassis & weights) . .6000 lbs.
Chassis w/out Steering . . . . . . . . . . . . . . .8' x 10'
Pedestal to Rear . . . . . . . . . . . . . . . . . . . . . .12'
Operator (provided) . . . . . . . . . . . . . . . . . . . .2

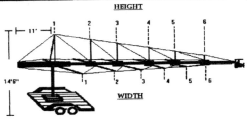

*Height from crane base w/o trailer to top of #1 pole is 13'6".
*Optimum working space required is 17' back from the Pedestal.

**Figure 10.45d**   The Akēla Crane.

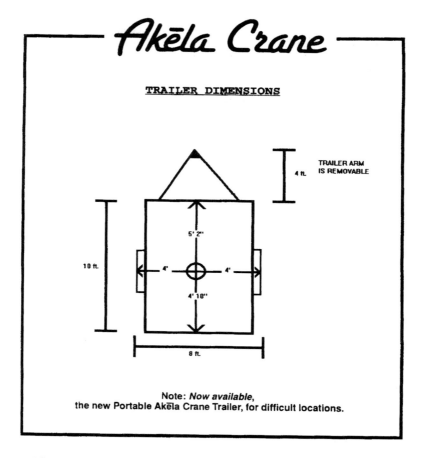

**Figure 10.45e**   The Akēla Crane.

### Super Nova

See Figure 10.46.

---

**T.O.T.**

*Good safety practice:* When you are letting a cameraperson off of a riding crane, step on the arm, have another grip take the place of the cameraperson, lock the brakes, put the arm on the chains, and reduce the lead or mercury for counterbalance.

---

### Titan II

See Figure 10.47.

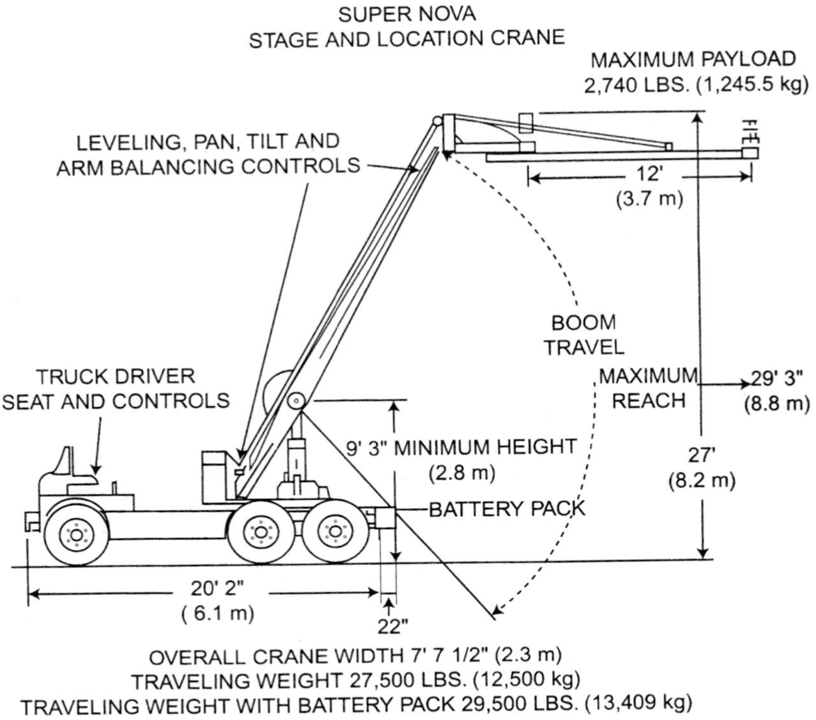

SUPER NOVA
STAGE AND LOCATION CRANE

MAXIMUM PAYLOAD
2,740 LBS. (1,245.5 kg)

LEVELING, PAN, TILT AND
ARM BALANCING CONTROLS

12'
(3.7 m)

BOOM
TRAVEL

TRUCK DRIVER
SEAT AND CONTROLS

MAXIMUM
REACH

29' 3"
(8.8 m)

9' 3" MINIMUM HEIGHT
(2.8 m)

27'
(8.2 m)

BATTERY PACK

20' 2"
( 6.1 m)

22"

OVERALL CRANE WIDTH 7' 7 1/2" (2.3 m)
TRAVELING WEIGHT 27,500 LBS. (12,500 kg)
TRAVELING WEIGHT WITH BATTERY PACK 29,500 LBS. (13,409 kg)

**MOBILE CRANE ACCESSORIES**

4' Hydraulic Riser - (Mobile Crane & Western Dolly)
Telescoping Arm Adapter - Mobile Crane
Super Nova Sideboard - (Set of 2)
Mobile Crane Long Sliding Tow Bar
Steel Leveling Head - Mobile Crane
Vehicle Tow Dolly - Mobile Crane
12" Camera Riser (Steel) - Mobile Crane
Mobile Crane Ramp / Riser
6' Camera Extension - Mobile Crane
12' Camera Extension - Mobile Crane
10' Camera Riser - Mobile Crane
Super Casper Mobile Crane Extension

2 Camera Plate - Mobile Crane, Steel
2 Cam. Plate Setup Package - Mobile Crane, Steel
3' Drop Down - Mobile Crane
6' Drop Down - Mobile Crane
10' Drop Down - Mobile Crane
Nitrogen Bottle & Regulator - Mobile Crane
180° Remote Camera Platform - Mobile Crane
Lead Bucket Extension - Mobile Crane
360° Remote Camera Platform - Mobile Crane
Nose Platform - SteadiCam Platform
Titan Track - 20' Single Piece
Super Nova Battery Pack

**Figure 10.46** Super Nova (Chapman).

| | | |
|---|---|---|
| Lens Height (with 12" Riser, Turret and Camera) | 27 ft. | 8.2 m |
| Base Mount Height | 23 ft. 6 in. | 7.2 m |
| Reach beyond Chassis to Lens | 17 ft. 3 in. | 5.5 m |
| Reach beyond Chassis with Extension | 29 ft. 3 in. | 8.8 m |
| Vertical Travel of Boom above Ground | 23 ft. | 7 m |
| Vertical Travel of Boom below Ground | 3 ft. 7 in. | 1.1 m |
| Chassis Width | 7 ft. 7 1/2 in. | 2.3 m |
| Chassis Length | 20 ft. 2 in. | 6.1 m |
| Chassis Length w/ Battery Pack | 22 ft. | 6.7 m |
| Minimum Chassis Height | 9 ft. 3 in. | 2.8 m |
| Fully Extended Boom Length | 30 ft. 11 in. | 9.4 m |
| Maximum Length of Boom and Chassis w/ Battery Pack | 39 ft. 2 in. | 11.9 m |
| Clearance Height for Man and Camera with Arm Level and Post down | 11 ft. | 3.4 m |
| Crane Traveling Weight | 27,500 lbs. | 12,500 kg |
| Crane Traveling Weight with Battery Pack | 29,500 lbs. | 13,409 kg |
| Arm Balancing Ratio | 2.5 : 1 | |
| Tread | 6 ft. 4 in. | 1.9 m |
| Wheel Base (Outside Wheels) | 13 ft. 10 1/2 in. | 4.2 m |
| Ground Clearance with Arm Level (Post up) | 8 ft. 5 in. | 2.6 m |
| Maximum Speed on Level Ground with Battery Power (ft./sec.) | 8 ft. 8 in./sec. | 2.6 m/sec. |
| Minimum Turn Radius to Extremity of Chassis | 23 ft. 3 in. | 7 m |
| *Maximum Payload (with Bucket Extension) | 2,740 lbs. | 1,245.5 kg |

## OTHER SUPER NOVA FEATURES

- Remote Controlled Power Steering for Rear Wheels
- Heavy Duty Braking Applied to All 6 Wheels
- Pans 360°
- Electric Powered for Silence
- Smooth, Automatic Leveling in Less Than 10 Seconds
- Hand or Foot / Geared or Belt Driven Camera Turrets
- Qualified Driver Dispatched with Every Order
- Battery Pack System for Remote Power to Cameras
- Battery Pack System for Remote Lighting Power for up to 12k HMI's

- Cruises at 50 mph
- Gasoline Engine for Highway Travel
- Defies Most Terrain
- Crab Steering Capabilities
- 6-Wheel Steering and 6-Wheel Drive
- Battery Powered Arm Brakes
- Push Button Balancing

*Payload Includes All Items (i.e. Man, Camera, Platform, Turret, Crane Arm, etc.) on Base Mount.

**Figure 10.46** (continued) Super Nova.

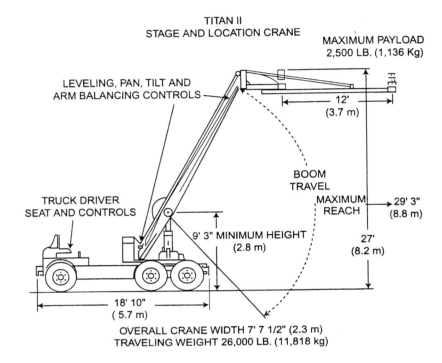

TITAN II
STAGE AND LOCATION CRANE

MAXIMUM PAYLOAD
2,500 LB. (1,136 Kg)

LEVELING, PAN, TILT AND
ARM BALANCING CONTROLS

12'
(3.7 m)

BOOM
TRAVEL

TRUCK DRIVER
SEAT AND CONTROLS

MAXIMUM
REACH

29' 3"
(8.8 m)

9' 3" MINIMUM HEIGHT
(2.8 m)

27'
(8.2 m)

18' 10"
( 5.7 m)

OVERALL CRANE WIDTH 7' 7 1/2" (2.3 m)
TRAVELING WEIGHT 26,000 LB. (11,818 kg)

**MOBILE CRANE ACCESSORIES**

4' Hydraulic Riser - (Mobile Crane & Western Dolly)
Telescoping Arm Adapter - Mobile Crane
Super Nova Sideboard - (Set of 2)
Mobile Crane Long Sliding Tow Bar
Steel Leveling Head - Mobile Crane
12" Camera Riser (Steel) - Mobile Crane
Mobile Crane Ramp / Riser
6' Camera Extension - Mobile Crane
12' Camera Extension - Mobile Crane
10' Camera Riser - Mobile Crane
Super Casper Mobile Crane Extension

2 Camera Plate - Mobile Crane, Steel
2 Cam. Plate Setup Package - Mobile Crane, Steel
3' Drop Down - Mobile Crane
6' Drop Down - Mobile Crane
10' Drop Down - Mobile Crane
Nitrogen Bottle & Regulator - Mobile Crane
180° Remote Camera Platform - Mobile Crane
Lead Bucket Extension - Mobile Crane
360° Remote Camera Platform - Mobile Crane
Nose Platform - SteadiCam Platform
Titan Track - 20' Single Piece

**Figure 10.47**   Titan II.

## SPECIFICATIONS

| | | |
|---|---:|---:|
| Lens Height (with 12" Riser, Turret and Camera) | 27 ft. | 8.2 m |
| Base Mount Height | 23 ft. 6 in. | 7.2 m |
| Reach beyond Chassis to Lens | 17 ft. 3 in. | 5.5 m |
| Reach beyond Chassis with Extension | 29 ft. 3 in. | 8.8 m |
| Vertical Travel of Boom above Ground | 23 ft. | 7 m |
| Vertical Travel of Boom below Ground | 3 ft. 7 in. | 1.1 m |
| Chassis Width | 7 ft. 7 1/2 in. | 2.3 m |
| Chassis Length | 20 ft. 2 in. | 6.1 m |
| Minimum Chassis Height | 9 ft. 3 in. | 2.8 m |
| Fully Extended Boom Length | 30 ft. 11 in. | 9.4 m |
| Maximum Length of Boom and Chassis | 37 ft. 4 in. | 11.4 m |
| Clearance Height for Man and Camera with Arm Level and Post Down | 11 ft. | 3.4 m |
| Crane Traveling Weight | 26,000 lbs. | 11,818 kg |
| Arm Balancing Ratio | 2.5 : 1 | |
| Gross Weight with 600 lb. Nose Load | 26,600 lbs. | 12,091 kg |
| Tread | 6 ft. 4 in. | 1.9 m |
| Wheel Base (Outside Wheels) | 13 ft. 10 1/2 in. | 4.2 m |
| Ground Clearance with Arm Level (Post up) | 8 ft. 5 in. | 2.6 m |
| Maximum Speed on Level Ground with Battery Power (ft./sec.) | 8.8 ft/sec. | 2.6 m/sec. |
| Outside Turn Radius of Chassis | 23 ft. 3 in. | 7 m |
| *Maximum Payload (with Bucket Extension) | 2,500 lbs. | 1,136.3 kg |

## OTHER TITAN II / NOVA FEATURES

- Remote Controlled Power Steering for Rear Wheels
- Heavy Duty Braking Applied to All 6 Wheels
- Battery Powered Hydraulic Arm Brakes
- Gasoline Engine and Electric Motor
- Hydraulic Leveling in Less Than 10 Seconds
- Hand or Foot Operated Camera Turrets
- Qualified Driver Sent with Every Order

- Cruises at 50 mph
- 6-Wheel Steering and 6-Wheel Drive
- Defies Most Terrain
- Partial Crabbing Ability
- Push Button Balancing
- Silent Operation
- Swings 360°

*Payload Includes All Items (i.e. Man, Camera, Platform, Turret, Crane Arm, etc.) on Base Mount.

*It is advised that the user of Chapman/Leonard equipment check with the manufacturer for the latest updates on *all* equipment.

**Figure 10.47**   (continued) Titan II features.

### T.O.T.

Before taking or building a crane on a stage floor, check to see if the stage is elevated. Sometimes you have to lay Titan track (large planks of wood that can hold the weight of the huge crane).

## Apollo

See Figure 10.48.

## Zeus

See Figure 10.49.

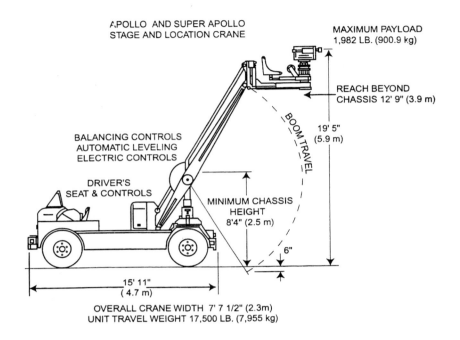

APOLLO AND SUPER APOLLO
STAGE AND LOCATION CRANE

MAXIMUM PAYLOAD
1,982 LB. (900.9 kg)

REACH BEYOND
CHASSIS 12' 9" (3.9 m)

BOOM TRAVEL

19' 5"
(5.9 m)

BALANCING CONTROLS
AUTOMATIC LEVELING
ELECTRIC CONTROLS

DRIVER'S
SEAT & CONTROLS

MINIMUM CHASSIS
HEIGHT
8'4" (2.5 m)

6"

15' 11"
( 4.7 m)

OVERALL CRANE WIDTH 7' 7 1/2" (2.3m)
UNIT TRAVEL WEIGHT 17,500 LB. (7,955 kg)

**MOBILE CRANE ACCESSORIES**

4' Hydraulic Riser - (Mobile Crane & Western Dolly)
Telescoping Arm Adapter - Mobile Crane
Super Nova Sideboard - (Set of 2)
Mobile Crane Long Sliding Tow Bar
Steel Leveling Head - Mobile Crane
Vehicle Tow Dolly - Apollo Crane
12" Camera Riser (Steel) - Mobile Crane
Mobile Crane Ramp / Riser
6' Camera Extension - Mobile Crane
12' Camera Extension - Mobile Crane
10' Camera Riser - Mobile Crane

Super Casper Mobile Crane Extension
2 Camera Plate - Mobile Crane, Steel
2 Cam. Plate Setup Package - Mobile Crane, Steel
3' Drop Down - Mobile Crane
6' Drop Down - Mobile Crane
10' Drop Down - Mobile Crane
Nitrogen Bottle & Regulator - Mobile Crane
180° Remote Camera Platform - Mobile Crane
Lead Bucket Extension - Mobile Crane
360° Remote Camera Platform - Mobile Crane
Nose Platform - SteadiCam Platform

**Figure 10.48** Apollo.

## SPECIFICATIONS

| | | |
|---|---|---|
| Lens Height (with 12 " Riser, Turret and Camera) | | |
| Base Mount Height | 19 ft. 5 in. | 5.9 m |
| Reach beyond Chassis to Lens | 15 ft. 11 in. | 4.9 m |
| Reach beyond Chassis with Extension | 12 ft. 9 in. | 3.9 m |
| Vertical Travel of Boom above Ground | 18 ft. 9 in. | 5.7 m |
| Vertical Travel of Boom below Ground | 15 ft. 5 in. | 4.7 m |
| Chassis Width | 10 1/2 in. | 27 cm |
| Chassis Length | 7 ft. 7 1/2 in. | 2.3 m |
| Minimum Chassis Height | 15 ft. 11 in. | 4.7 m |
| Fully Extended Boom Length | 8 ft. 4 in. | 2.5 m |
| Maximum Length of Boom and Chassis | 23 ft. | 7 m |
| Clearance Height for Man and Camera w/ Arm Level and Post down | 29 ft. 4 in. | 8.9 m |
| Crane Traveling Weight | 10 ft. 1 in. | 3 m |
| Arm Balancing Ratio | 17,500 lbs. | 7,955 kg |
| Tread | 1.9 : 1 | |
| Wheel Base | 6 ft. 4 in. | 1.9 m |
| Ground Clearance w/ Arm Level (Post Up) | 10 ft. 6 1/2 in. | 3.2 m |
| Maximum Speed on Level Ground with Battery Power (ft./sec.) | 7 ft. | 2.1 m |
| Minimum Turn Radius to Extremity of Chassis | 11.2 ft./ sec. | 3.4 m/ sec |
| *Maximum Payload | 21 ft. 2 in. | 6.5 m |
| | 1,982 lbs. | 900.9 kg |

## OTHER APOLLO FEATURES

- Remote Controlled Power Steering for Rear Wheels
- Heavy Duty Braking Applied to All 4 Wheels
- Battery Powered Hydraulic Arm Brakes
- Gasoline Engine and Electric Motor
- Hydraulic Leveling in Less Than 5 Seconds
- Hand or Foot Operated Camera Turrets
- Qualified Driver Sent with Every Order
- Super Apollo Comes with a Built-In Generator to Recharge

  Batteries while in Remote Locations

- Cruises at 50 mph
- 4-Wheel Steering and 4-Wheel Drive
- Defies Most Terrain
- Partial Crabbing Ability
- Swings 360 Degrees
- Battery Powered Arm Brakes
- Push Button Balancing

*Payload Includes All Items (i.e. Man, Camera, Platform, Turret, Crane Arm, etc.) on Base Mount.

*It is advised that the user of Chapman/Leonard equipment check with the manufacturer for the latest updates on *all* equipment.

**Figure 10.48**    (continued) Apollo features.

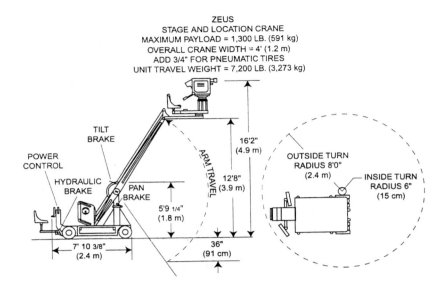

ZEUS
STAGE AND LOCATION CRANE
MAXIMUM PAYLOAD = 1,300 LB. (591 kg)
OVERALL CRANE WIDTH = 4' (1.2 m)
ADD 3/4" FOR PNEUMATIC TIRES
UNIT TRAVEL WEIGHT = 7,200 LB. (3,273 kg)

TILT BRAKE

POWER CONTROL

HYDRAULIC BRAKE

PAN BRAKE

ARM TRAVEL

16'2"
(4.9 m)

12'8"
(3.9 m)

5'9 1/4"
(1.8 m)

7' 10 3/8"
(2.4 m)

36"
(91 cm)

OUTSIDE TURN RADIUS 8'0"
(2.4 m)

INSIDE TURN RADIUS 6"
(15 cm)

**STAGE CRANE ACCESSORIES**

Aluminum Leveling Head - Stage Crane
6" Camera Riser - Crane
12" Camera Riser - Crane
3' Camera Riser - Crane
3' Camera Extension - Stage Crane
8' Camera Extension (Remote Use - Stage Crane Only)
10' Camera Extension (Remote Use - Stage Crane Only)
3' Camera Drop Down - Crane
Bucket Seat
Kidney Seat
4" Seat Arm - Stage Crane
6" Seat Arm - Stage Crane
12" Seat Arm - Stage Crane
19" Seat Arm - Stage Crane
3" Seat Riser - Stage Crane
6" Seat Riser - Stage Crane
12" Seat Riser - Stage Crane
Film (Hand-Operated) Turret - Geared

Film (Hand-Operated) Turret - Belted
Electric, Video / Film Turret
TV (Foot-Operated) Turret
Free Head Turret
Offset Turret
Hydraulic Jack & Handle
Stage Crane Tires (2nd Set) - Pneumatic
Stage Crane Tires (2nd Set) - Solid
Stage Crane Track (10' Section)
¼ Lead Weight
½ Lead Weight
Lead Weight
Stage Crane Slide Weight (8 lbs.)
Stage Crane Slide Weight (16 lbs.)
Lead Bucket Extension
Zeus Sideboard
Circular Platform w/ Rails - 48"
Circular Platform w/ Rails - 72"
Crane Steadicam Platform Adapter Package

**Figure 10.49**  Zeus.

**SPECIFICATIONS**

| | | |
|---|---|---|
| Lens Height (Turret) | 14 ft. | 4.3 m |
| Lens Height (Platform) | 16 ft. | 4.9 m |
| Base Mount Height | 10 ft. 6 in. | 3.2 m |
| *Maximum Payload (Turret) | 600 lbs. | 273 kg |
| *Maximum Payload for Front of the Arm (Platform) | 600 lbs. | 273 kg |
| *Maximum Payload for Back of the Arm (Platform) | 600 lbs. | 273 kg |
| Maximum Horizontal Reach (to Lens without Extension) | 9 ft. 6 in. | 2.9 m |
| Chassis Length | 7 ft. 3 in. | 2.2 m |
| Maximum Chassis Width | 6 ft. 2 1/2 in. | 1.9 m |
| Minimum Chassis Width | 34 1/2 in. | 88 cm |
| Center to Center Wheel Width for Track (Solid Wheel Setup) | 31 3/8 in. | 80 cm |
| Center to Center Wheel Width (Single Knobby Pneumatic Setup) | 45 1/2 in. | 1.2 m |
| Center to Center Width (Double Knobby Pneumatic Setup) | 65 in. | 1.7 m |
| Maximum Chassis Width (Knobby Pneumatic Wheel Setup) | 6 ft. 2 1/2 in. | 1.9 m |
| Minimum Chassis Height | 5 ft. 3 1/4 in. | 1.6 m |
| Normal Operating Weight Less Payload* | 5,200 lbs. | 2,364 kg |

**OTHER ATB II FEATURES**

- **Remote Actuator to Control Arm Independently** from the Camera Platform or Crane Operator Seat
- Built-In Charging System Operates on 110v or 220v
- Electric Powered for Smooth, Silent Operation in Forward and Reverse Modes
- Up to 12' of Vertical Boom Travel from Ground Level to Maximum Height
- Tires Come in Your Choice of Knobby, Pneumatic or Solid Track Wheels
- Selection of Turrets, Risers and Extensions, Aluminum Track Available upon Request
- 36 volt System Will Give Exceptional Performance and Acceleration along Sport Sidelines
- Comes with 48" Platform, Sideboards, Monitor Platform and Padding
- 360 Degree Arm Swing
- Versatility for Use with Film (Hand Operated) or TV (Foot Operated) Turrets
- Rocker Suspension
- Hydraulic Chassis and Parking Brake

*Payload Includes All Items (i.e. Man, Camera, Platform, Turret, Crane Arm, etc.) on Base Mount.

*It is advised that the user of Chapman/Leonard equipment check with the manufacturer for the latest updates on *all* equipment.

**Figure 10.49** (continued) Zeus.

## Electra II/Nike

See Figure 10.50.

## ATB II Sport Package

See Figure 10.51.

## Olympian

See Figure 10.52.

## Olympian II Hydraulic Lift Vehicle

See Figure 10.53.

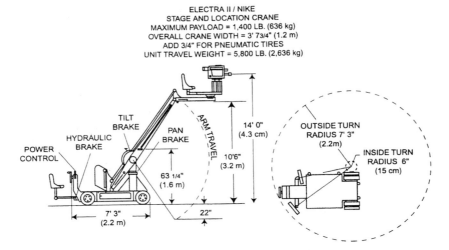

ELECTRA II / NIKE
STAGE AND LOCATION CRANE
MAXIMUM PAYLOAD = 1,400 LB. (636 kg)
OVERALL CRANE WIDTH = 3' 73/4" (1.2 m)
ADD 3/4" FOR PNEUMATIC TIRES
UNIT TRAVEL WEIGHT = 5,800 LB. (2,636 kg)

**STAGE CRANE ACCESSORIES**

Aluminum Leveling Head - Stage Crane
6" Camera Riser - Crane
12" Camera Riser - Crane
3' Camera Riser - Crane
3' Camera Extension - Stage Crane
8' Camera Extension (Remote Use - Stage Crane Only)
10' Camera Extension (Remote Use - Stage Crane Only)
3' Camera Drop Down - Crane
Bucket Seat
Kidney Seat
4" Seat Arm - Stage Crane
6" Seat Arm - Stage Crane
12" Seat Arm - Stage Crane
19" Seat Arm - Stage Crane
3" Seat Riser - Stage Crane
6" Seat Riser - Stage Crane
12" Seat Riser - Stage Crane
Film (Hand-Operated) Turret - Geared

Film (Hand-Operated) Turret - Belted
Electric, Video / Film Turret
TV (Foot-Operated) Turret
Free Head Turret
Offset Turret
Hydraulic Jack & Handle
Stage Crane Tires (2nd Set) - Pneumatic
Stage Crane Tires (2nd Set) - Solid
Stage Crane Track (10' Section)
¼ Lead Weight
½ Lead Weight
Lead Weight
Stage Crane Slide Weight (8 lbs.)
Stage Crane Slide Weight (16 lbs.)
Lead Bucket Extension
Zeus Sideboard
Circular Platform w/ Rails - 48"
Circular Platform w/ Rails - 72"
Crane Steadicam Platform Adapter Package

**Figure 10.50**   Electra II/Nike.

## SPECIFICATIONS

| | | |
|---|---|---|
| Lens Height (with 12 in. Riser) | 14 ft. | 4.3 m |
| Base Mount Height | 10 ft. 6 in. | 3.2 m |
| Reach beyond Chassis to Lens | 9 ft. 6 in. | 2.9 m |
| *Maximum Payload | 1,400 lbs. | 636 kg |
| Vertical Travel of Boom above Ground | 10 ft. | 3 m |
| Vertical Travel of Boom below Ground | 2 ft. | 60 cm |
| Chassis Width | 3 ft. 8 in. | 1.1 m |
| Outside dimensions w/ Pneumatic Tires | 3 ft. 9 1/2 in. | 1.2 m |
| Chassis Length | 7 ft. 3 in. | 2.2 m |
| Minimum Chassis Height | 5 ft. 3 1/2 in. | 1.6 m |
| Fully Extended Boom Length | 15 ft. 9 in. | 4.8 m |
| Maximum Length of Boom and Chassis | 16 ft. 9 in. | 5.1 m |
| Clearance Height for Man and Camera w/ Arm Level | 8 ft. | 2.4 m |
| Crane Weight w/Turret | 4,000 lbs. | 1,818 kg |
| Arm Balancing Ratio | 2 : 1 | |
| Tread | 39 7/8 in. | 1 m |
| Wheel Base | 5 ft. 1/2 in. | 1.5 m |
| Ground Clearance w/ Arm Level | 4 ft. 1 in. | 1.2 m |
| Maximum Speed on Level Ground | 9.8 ft. / sec. | 2.5 m / sec. |
| Outside Turn Radius | 6 ft. 3 in. | 1.9 m |
| Normal Operating Weight Less Payload | 5,200 lbs. | 2,364 kg |

## OTHER ELECTRA II / NIKE FEATURES

- Operates on 6 Tires (4 Front, 2 Rear)
- Solid or Pneumatic Tires Available
- On a Full Charge, Batteries Allow 24 Hours Use
- Charger Tapers off as Batteries Are Energized
- Battery Charge Pre-Set for either 110v or 220v
- Friction Brakes for Pan and Tilt Movement
- Selection of Turrets, Risers, Extensions and Aluminum Track
- Electric Powered for Smooth, Silent Operation in Forward / Reverse Modes

- Rocker Suspension
- Turnaround Front Wheels
- All Steel Construction
- Hydraulic Chassis / Parking Brake
- 360 Degree Arm Swing

*Payload Includes All Items (i.e. Man, Camera, Platform, Turret, Crane Arm, etc.) on Base Mount.

*It is advised that the user of Chapman/Leonard equipment check with the manufacturer for the latest updates on *all* equipment.

**Figure 10.50** (continued) Electra II/Nike features.

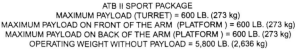

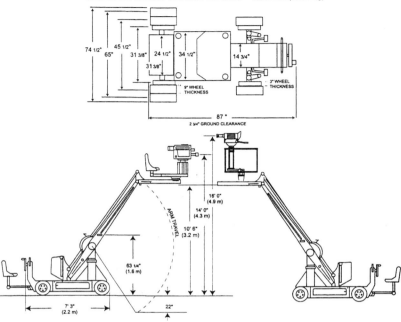

## ATB ACCESSORIES

CS / ATB 7" Riser
ATB Knobby Pneumatic Tires - (Set of 6)
ATB Solid Tires - (Set of 6)
ATB Sand Pneumatic Tires - (Set of 6)
ATB Golf Pneumatic Tires - (Set of 6)
ATB Stage Pneumatic Tires - (Set of 6)
ATB Front Mounted Low Deck
Sport ATB Dual Platform Setup
Aluminum Leveling Head - Stage Crane
6" Camera Riser - Crane
12" Camera Riser - Crane
Bucket Seat
Kidney Seat
4" Seat Arm - Stage Crane
6" Seat Arm - Stage Crane
12" Seat Arm - Stage Crane
19" Seat Arm - Stage Crane

3" Seat Riser - Stage Crane
6" Seat Riser - Stage Crane
12" Seat Riser - Stage Crane
Film (Hand-Operated) Turret - Geared
Film (Hand-Operated) Turret - Belted
TV (Foot-Operated) Turret
Free Head Turret
Offset Turret
Stage Crane Tires (2nd Set) - Pneumatic
Stage Crane Tires (2nd Set) - Solid
Stage Crane Track (10' Section)
¼ Lead Weight
½ Lead Weight
Lead Weight
Stage Crane Slide Weight (8 lbs.)
Stage Crane Slide Weight (16 lbs.)
Circular Platform w/ Rails - 48"
Crane Steadicam Platform Adapter Package

**Figure 10.51** ATB II Sport Package.

## SPECIFICATIONS

| | | |
|---|---|---|
| Lens Height (Turret) | 14 ft. | 4.3 m |
| Lens Height (Platform) | 16 ft. | 4.9 m |
| Base Mount Height | 10 ft. 6 in. | 3.2 m |
| *Maximum Payload (Turret) | 600 lbs. | 273 kg |
| *Maximum Payload for Front of the Arm (Platform) | 600 lbs. | 273 kg |
| *Maximum Payload for Back of the Arm (Platform) | 600 lbs. | 273 kg |
| Maximum Horizontal Reach (to Lens without Extension) | 9 ft. 6 in. | 2.9 m |
| Chassis Length | 7 ft. 3 in. | 2.2 m |
| Maximum Chassis Width | 6 ft. 2 1/2 in. | 1.9 m |
| Minimum Chassis Width | 34 1/2 in. | 88 cm |
| Center to Center Wheel Width for Track  (Solid Wheel Setup) | 31 3/8 in. | 80 cm |
| Center to Center Wheel Width (Single Knobby Pneumatic Setup) | 45 1/2 in. | 1.2 m |
| Center to Center Width (Double Knobby Pneumatic Setup) | 65  in. | 1.7 m |
| Maximum Chassis Width (Knobby Pneumatic Wheel Setup) | 6 ft. 2 1/2 in. | 1.9 m |
| Minimum Chassis Height | 5 ft. 3 1/4 in. | 1.6 m |
| Normal Operating Weight Less Payload* | 5,200 lbs. | 2,364 kg |

## OTHER ATB II FEATURES

- **Remote Actuator to Control Arm Independently** from the Camera Platform or Crane Operator Seat
- Built-In Charging System Operates on 110v or  220v
- Electric Powered for Smooth, Silent Operation in Forward and Reverse Modes
- Up to 12' of Vertical Boom Travel from Ground Level to Maximum Height
- Tires Come in Your Choice of Knobby, Pneumatic or Solid Track Wheels
- Selection of Turrets, Risers and Extensions, Aluminum Track Available upon Request
- 36 volt System Will Give Exceptional Performance and Acceleration along Sport Sidelines
- Comes with 48" Platform, Sideboards, Monitor Platform  and Padding
- 360 Degree Arm Swing
- Versatility for Use with Film (Hand Operated) or TV (Foot Operated) Turrets
- Rocker Suspension
- Hydraulic Chassis and Parking Brake

*Payload Includes All Items (i.e. Man, Camera, Platform, Turret, Crane Arm, etc.) on Base Mount.

*It is advised that the user of Chapman/Leonard equipment check with the manufacturer for the latest updates on *all* equipment.

**Figure 10.51**   ATB II features.

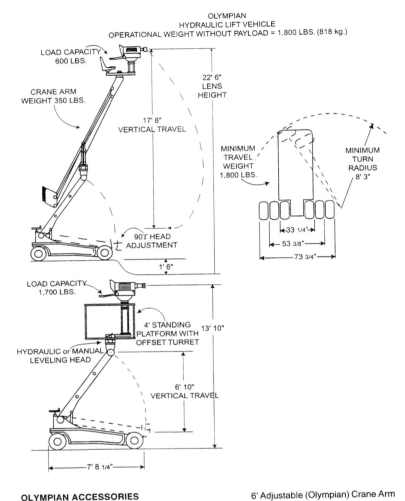

OLYMPIAN
HYDRAULIC LIFT VEHICLE
OPERATIONAL WEIGHT WITHOUT PAYLOAD = 1,800 LBS. (818 kg.)

LOAD CAPACITY
600 LBS.

CRANE ARM
WEIGHT 350 LBS.

22' 6"
LENS
HEIGHT

17' 8"
VERTICAL TRAVEL

MINIMUM
TRAVEL
WEIGHT
1,800 LBS.

MINIMUM
TURN
RADIUS
8' 3"

90° HEAD
ADJUSTMENT

33 1/4"
53 3/8"
73 3/4"

1' 6"

LOAD CAPACITY
1,700 LBS.

4' STANDING
PLATFORM WITH
OFFSET TURRET

13' 10"

HYDRAULIC or MANUAL
LEVELING HEAD

6' 10"
VERTICAL TRAVEL

7' 8 1/4"

**OLYMPIAN ACCESSORIES**
6" Mitchell Riser
Olympian Hydraulic Leveling Head
Olympian Track (10' Section)
Olympian 2' Camera Riser
Circular Platform w/ Rails - 48"
Circular Platform w/ Rails - 72"
Olympian Platform Monitor Bracket

6' Adjustable (Olympian) Crane Arm
6' (Olympian) Crane Arm
Olympian Balloon Tires - (Set of 8)
Olympian Solid Tires - (Set of 6)
Olympian Long Sideboard
Olympian Short Sideboard
Olympian II Camera Offset Plate
10' Fiberglass Ramp - Rated for 3,000 lbs.

**Figure 10.52** Olympian.

| | | |
|---|---|---|
| Lens Height (with Standard Film, TV, or Platform Setup) | 13 ft. 10 in. | 4.2 m |
| Lens Height (with Crane Arm Setup) | 22 ft. 6 in. | 6.9 m |
| Minimum Lens Height (with Crane Arm Setup, below Ground Level) | 1 ft. 6 in. | 46 cm |
| Reach beyond Chassis (with Film Setup) | 9 ft. | 23 cm |
| Reach beyond Chassis (with TV Setup) | 1 ft. 4 in. | 41 cm |
| Reach beyond Chassis (with Crane Arm (Film) Setup) | 10 ft. 9 in. | 3.3 m |
| Reach beyond Chassis (with Crane Arm (TV) Setup) | 8 ft. 7 in. | 2.6 m |
| *Maximum Payload | 1,700 lbs. | 798 kg |
| Vertical Travel (Standard Setup) | 6 ft. 10 in. | 2.1 m |
| Boom Travel (Crane Arm Setup) | 17 ft. 8 in. | 5.4 m |
| Chassis Single Wheel Width (Standard Setup Only) | 2 ft. 9 1/4 in. | 85 cm |
| Chassis Dual Wheel Width (Standard Setup Only) | 4 ft. 5 3/8 in. | 1.4 m |
| Chassis Triple Wheel Width | 6 ft. 1 3/4 in. | 1.9 m |
| Chassis Length | 7 ft. 8 1/4 in. | 2.3 m |
| Minimum Turn Radius | 8 ft. 3 in. | 2.5 m |
| Maximum Speed (with Full Charge) | 18 mph | 30 kph |
| Normal Operating Weight Less Payload* | 1,800 lbs. | 818 kg |

## OTHER OLYMPIAN FEATURES

- Two Motor Drive Enabling Speeds up to 18 mph
- Special Rear Steering Design with 20:1 Ratio
- Video Platform, Video or Film Turret Available
- Chassis Allows Removable Padded Barrier
- Large Balloon Tires (4psi to 30psi), for Movement in Sand
- Hydraulic Lift for Smooth, One-Man Operation
- Streamline Profile Does Not Interfere with Audience View
- Great for Football (or Other Sports) Sideline Coverage
- Complete Football Safety Package (Includes: Padding, Wheel Skirts, Cable Draggers)

- Rigid Single Beam Lift
- Flexibility in Camera Operator Setup
- Ability to Carry Crane Arm
- Hydraulic Leveling Accessory
- Detachable Sideboards
- Variable Camera Head Mount
- Ability To Be Used on or off Track
- Narrow Chassis w/ Variable Tire Widths

*Payload Includes All Items (i.e. Man, Camera, Platform, Turret, Crane Arm, etc.) on Base Mount.

*It is advised that the user of Chapman/Leonard equipment check with the manufacturer for the latest updates on *all* equipment.

**Figure 10.52** (continued) Olympian features.

OLYMPIAN II HYDRAULIC LIFT VEHICLE
MAXIMUM RATED PAYLOAD = 1,800 LBS. (818 kg)
OPERATING WEIGHT = 3,300 LBS. (1,500 kg)

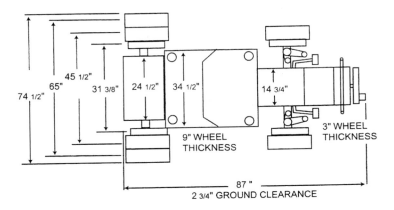

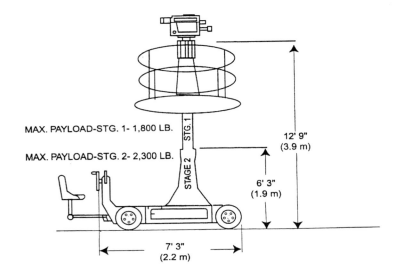

**OLYMPIAN II ACCESSORIES**
6" Mitchell Riser
Olympian 2' Camera Riser
Olympian Platform Monitor Bracket
Olympian II Camera Offset Plate
ATB Knobby Pneumatic Tires - (Set of 6)
Bucket Seat
Kidney Seat

**Figure 10.53** Olympian II.

## SPECIFICATIONS

| | | |
|---|---|---|
| Maximum Camera Mount Height | 12 ft. 9 in. | 3.9 m |
| Minimum Camera Mount Height | 6 ft. 3 in. | 1.9 m |
| *Maximum Payload - Stage 1 | 2,300 lbs. | 1,045.4 kg |
| *Maximum Payload - Stage 2 | 1,800 lbs. | 818.1 kg |
| Vertical Travel | 6 ft. 6 in. | 2 m |
| Minimum Ground Clearance | 2 3/4 in. | 7 cm |
| Chassis Deck Height | 16 in. | 41 cm |
| Maximum Chassis Length without Seat or Platform | 7 ft. 3 in. | 2.2 m |
| Maximum Chassis Width | 6 ft. 2 1/2 in. | 1.9 m |
| Minimum Chassis Width | 34 1/2 in. | 88 cm |
| Platform Diameter | 72 in. | 1.8 m |
| Platform Rail Height | 3 ft. 1 in. | 94 cm |
| Center to Center Wheel Width for Track (Solid Wheel Setup) | 31 3/8 in. | 80 cm |
| Center to Center Wheel Width (Single Knobby Pneumatic Setup) | 45 1/2 in. | 1.2 m |
| Center to Center Wheel Width (Double Knobby Pneumatic Setup) | 65 in. | 1.7 m |
| Wheel Base | 5 ft. 1 1/2 in. | 1.6 m |
| Speed | 13 ft./sec. | 4 m/sec. |
| Normal Operating Weight Less Payload* | 3,300 lbs. | 1,500 kg |

## OTHER OLYMPIAN II FEATURES

- Drive System Enables Speed of 13 ft./sec.
- Great for Football (or Other Sports) Sideline Coverage
- Streamline Profile Does Not Interfere with Audience View
- Relocated Hydraulic System Gives Driver Better Access
- Platform Mounts on Column for Easy Transportation
- Package Reduces to 2 ft. 10 1/2 in. for Transportation
- Complete Football Safety Package (Includes: Padding, Wheel Skirts, Cable Draggers)
- Electric Powered for Smooth Operation in Forward and Reverse Modes
- Over 6' of Vertical Camera Travel
- Built-In Battery Charger (110v/220v)
- Wraparound Platform Rail (38 in.)
- Silent Operation for Sound Stages
- Hydraulic Chassis and Parking Brake

*Payload Includes All Items (i.e. Man, Camera, Platform, Turret, Crane Arm, etc.) on Base Mount.

*It is advised that the user of Chapman/Leonard equipment check with the manufacturer for the latest updates on *all* equipment.

**Figure 10.53** (continued) Olympian II features.

# Cranes Mounted on Wheeled Bases

See Figure 11.1.

- **Felix** (Figures 11.2–11.4)
  *Lens height:* 9 feet/up from the base (depending on what this unit is mounted on)
  *Arm capacity:* 484 pounds
- **Piccolo** /(Figure 11.5)
  *Lens height:* 9 feet/5 inches/up (depending on what this unit is mounted on)
  *Arm capacity:* 550 pounds
- **Mini Skyking** (Figure 11.6)
  *Lens height:* 11 feet/6 inches/up (depending on what this unit is mounted on)
  *Arm capacity:* 550 pounds
- **Tulip** (Figure 11.7)
  *Lens height:* 12 feet/1 inch/up (depending on what this unit is mounted on)
  *Arms capacity:* 550 pounds
- **Super Maxi-Jib** (Figure 11.8)
  *Lens height:* 15 feet/4 inches/up (depending on what this unit is mounted on)
  *Arms capacity:* 77 pounds
- **Strada** (Figure 11.9)
  *Lens height:* 85 feet/up (depending on what this unit is mounted on)
  *Arms capacity:* 100 pounds

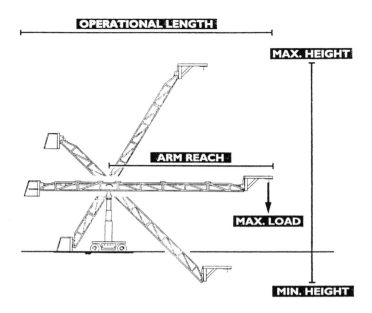

**Figure 11.1** Felix.

**Figure 11.2** Felix.

**Figure 11.3** Felix.

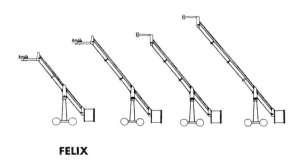

FELIX

**Figure 11.4** Felix.

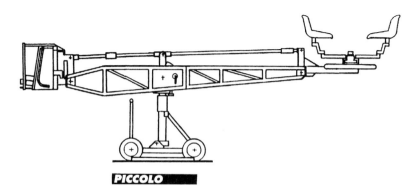

**Figure 11.5** Piccolo.

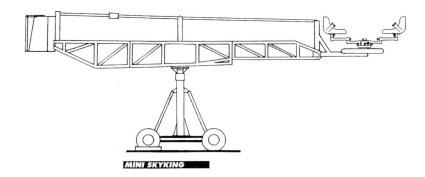

**Figure 11.6** Mini Skyking.

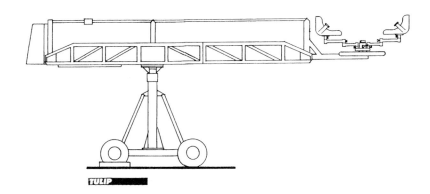

**Figure 11.7** Tulip.

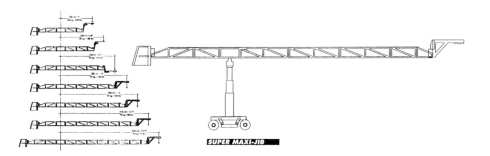

**Figure 11.8** Super Maxi-Jib.

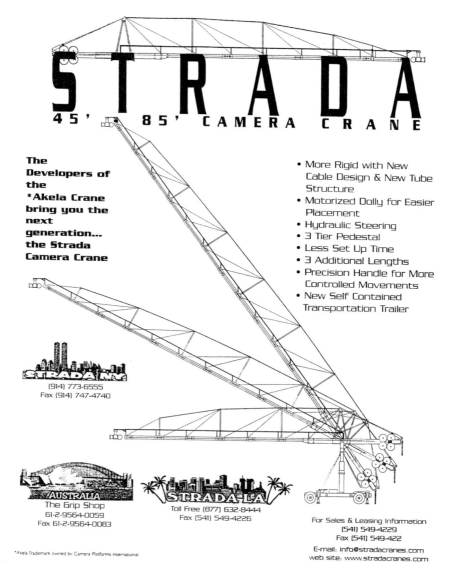

**The Developers of the *Akela Crane bring you the next generation... the Strada Camera Crane**

- More Rigid with New Cable Design & New Tube Structure
- Motorized Dolly for Easier Placement
- Hydraulic Steering
- 3 Tier Pedestal
- Less Set Up Time
- 3 Additional Lengths
- Precision Handle for More Controlled Movements
- New Self Contained Transportation Trailer

STRADA-NY
(914) 773-6555
Fax (914) 747-4740

AUSTRALIA
The Grip Shop
61-2-9564-0059
Fax 61-2-9564-0083

STRADA-LA
Toll Free (877) 632-8444
Fax (541) 549-4226

For Sales & Leasing Information
(541) 549-4229
Fax (541) 549-422
E-mail: info@stradacranes.com
web site: www.stradacranes.com

*Akela Trademark owned by Camera Platforms International

**Figure 11.9**  The Strada Crane.

# Lenny Arms

The Lenny Arms are built by the Chapman/Leonard company in North Hollywood. The company has designed many variations of the Lenny Arm to help film production get that special shot. Nothing has been left to chance. I have provided the phone number and website in the front of this book so you can see for yourself the huge amount of tools (arms, jibs, cranes, and dollies) as well as a vast inventory of additional equipment that they have available for service. Call, write, or e-mail them. They can help you with every aspect of successfully completing your shoot.

The Lenny Arms include (Figures 12.1–12.4):

1. Lenny Mini
2. Lenny Arm Plus
3. Lenny Arm II
4. Lenny Arm II Plus
5. Lenny Arm III

Not all Lenny Arms or configurations are shown.

### T.O.T.
Always move crane arm after releasing the brake. This is a safety check to ensure that the brake is fully off.

### T.O.T.
During installation of a remote head on a jib arm or a crane arm in an underslung position, I have found it easier to loosen all four leveling bolts on the head, which allows the leveling head to move freely with its four-way tilting action. Set the remote head on the ground (or deck) with the threaded portion upward, if the head permits this position. With the arm balanced out, lower it to the threaded end of the remote, then gently slide the receiver hole over the threads of the remote, making sure not to damage the threads. Align the key way (slotted area), then install the winged/gland nut on the threads and rough level it in place. Add weight to the bucket end of the jib or crane to rebalance the pivot point of the arm. Raise the arm to a working height (usually, a six-step ladder under the arm will do nicely for judging the correct height). Now install the camera and safety. Rebalance the arm for the camera weight.

# Examples of Lenny
## CABLE SYSTEM

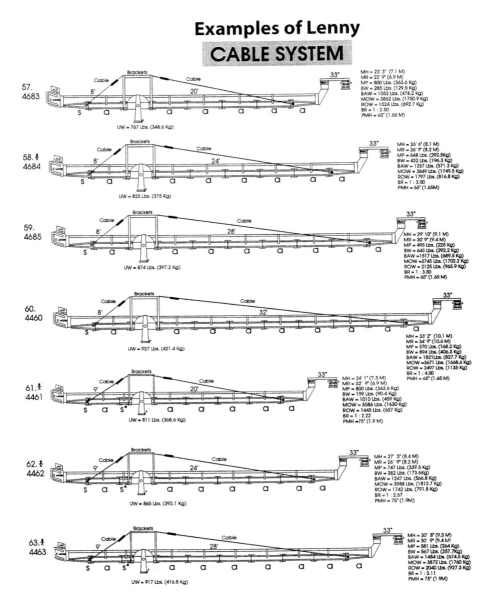

**57. 4683**

MH = 23' 3" (7.1 M)
MR = 22' 9" (6.9 M)
MP = 800 Lbs. (363.6 Kg)
BW = 285 Lbs. (129.5 Kg)
BAW = 1052 Lbs. (478.2 Kg)
MOW = 3852 Lbs. (1750.9 Kg)
ROW = 1524 Lbs. (692.7 Kg)
BR = 1 : 2.50
PMH = 65" (1.65 M)

UW = 767 Lbs. (348.6 Kg)

**58. 4684**

MH = 26' 6" (8.1 M)
MR = 26' 9" (8.2 M)
MP = 648 Lbs. (292.5Kg)
BW = 432 Lbs. (196.3 Kg)
BAW = 1257 Lbs. (571.3 Kg)
MOW = 3849 Lbs. (1749.5 Kg)
ROW = 1797 Lbs. (816.8 Kg)
BR = 1 : 3.00
PMH = 65" (1.65M)

UW = 825 Lbs. (375 Kg)

**59. 4685**

MH = 29' 10" (9.1 M)
MR = 30' 9" (9.4 M)
MP = 495 Lbs. (225 Kg)
BW = 643 Lbs. (292.2 Kg)
BAW =1517 Lbs. (689.5 Kg)
MOW =3745 Lbs. (1702.2 Kg)
ROW = 2125 Lbs. (965.9 Kg)
BR = 1 : 3.50
PMH = 65" (1.65 M)

UW = 874 Lbs. (397.2 Kg)

**60. 4460**

MH = 33' 2" (10.1 M)
MR = 34' 9" (10.6 M)
MP = 370 Lbs. (168.2 Kg)
BW = 894 Lbs. (406.3 Kg)
BAW =1821 Lbs. (827.7 Kg)
MOW =3671 Lbs. (1668.6 Kg)
ROW = 2497 Lbs. (1135 Kg)
BR = 1 : 4.00
PMH = 65" (1.65 M)

UW = 927 Lbs. (421.4 Kg)

**61. 4461**

MH = 24' 1" (7.3 M)
MR = 22' 9" (6.9 M)
MP = 800 Lbs. (363.6 Kg)
BW = 199 Lbs. (90.4 Kg)
BAW = 1010 Lbs. (459 Kg)
MOW = 3586 Lbs. (1630 Kg)
ROW = 1445 Lbs. (657 Kg)
BR = 1 : 2.22
PMH =75" (1.9 M)

UW = 811 Lbs. (368.6 Kg)

**62. 4462**

MH = 27' 5" (8.4 M)
MR = 26' 9" (8.2 M)
MP = 747 Lbs. (339.5 Kg)
BW = 382 Lbs. (173.6Kg)
BAW = 1247 Lbs. (566.8 Kg)
MOW = 3988 Lbs. (1812.7 Kg)
ROW = 1742 Lbs. (791.8 Kg)
BR = 1 : 2.67
PMH = 75" (1.9M)

UW = 865 Lbs. (393.1 Kg)

**63. 4463**

MH = 30' 8" (9.3 M)
MR = 30' 9" (9.4 M)
MP = 581 Lbs. (264 Kg)
BW = 567 Lbs. (257.7Kg)
BAW = 1484 Lbs. (674.5 Kg)
MOW = 3872 Lbs. (1760 Kg)
ROW = 2040 Lbs. (927.3 Kg)
BR = 1 : 3.11
PMH = 75" (1.9M)

UW = 917 Lbs. (416.8 Kg)

**Figure 12.1** Lenny Cable Systems.

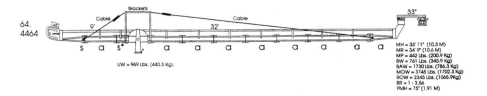

64.
4464

MH = 33' 11" (10.3 M)
MR = 34' 9" (10.6 M)
MP = 442 Lbs. (200.9 Kg)
BW = 761 Lbs. (345.9 Kg)
BAW = 1730 Lbs. (786.3 Kg)
MOW = 3745 Lbs. (1702.3 Kg)
ROW = 2345 Lbs. (1065.9Kg)
BR = 1 : 3.56
PMH = 75" (1.91 M)

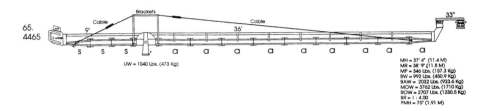

65.
4465

MH = 37' 4" (11.4 M)
MR = 38' 9" (11.8 M)
MP = 346 Lbs. (157.3 Kg)
BW = 992 Lbs. (450.9 Kg)
BAW = 2032 Lbs. (923.6 Kg)
MOW = 3762 Lbs. (1710 Kg)
ROW = 2707 Lbs. (1230.5 Kg)
BR = 1 : 4.00
PMH = 75" (1.91 M)

---

An additional increase in payload may be obtained by substituting the 3 wide bucket with a 4 wide bucket using this formula:
60 divided by Balance Ratio = payload increase.

An additional increase in payload may also be obtained by substituting the 3 wide bucket with a 5 wide bucket using this formula:
373 divided by BR = payload increase.

The auxiliary 5 wide bucket may be used with maximum 9 ft. back and maximum 36 ft. front in conjunction with cable system.

---

Bucket reaches ground.
(RECOMMENDED)

The Lenny Arm rear section combination should be configurated so that the bucket touches the ground before the Lenny Arm vertical travel limits are obtained.

Bucket does not reach ground.
(NOT RECOMMENDED)

WARNING: DO NOT EXCEED THE LISTED POST MOUNT HEIGHTS (PMH) VALUES TO AVOID INVALIDATING OUR SAFETY RECOMMENDATIONS.

---

*It is advised that the user of Chapman/Leonard equipment check with the manufacturer for the latest updates on *all* equipment.

**Figure 12.1** (continued) Lenny Cable System.

Lenny Arm II Plus® Mounting Choices

## The Lenny Arm II Plus can be mounted on these Chapman/Leonard products:

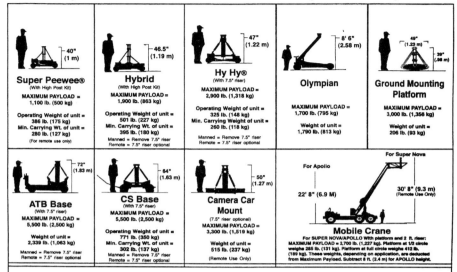

**Super Peewee®**
(With High Post Kit)
MAXIMUM PAYLOAD =
1,100 lb. (500 kg)

Operating Weight of unit =
386 lb. (175 kg)
Min. Carrying Wt. of unit =
280 lb. (127 kg)
(For remote use only)

**Hybrid**
(With High Post Kit)
MAXIMUM PAYLOAD =
1,900 lb. (863 kg)

Operating Weight of unit =
501 lb. (227 kg)
Min. Carrying Wt. of unit =
395 lb. (180 kg)
Manned = Remove 7.5" riser
Remote = 7.5" riser optional

**Hy Hy®**
(With 7.5" riser)
MAXIMUM PAYLOAD =
2,900 lb. (1,318 kg)

Operating Weight of unit =
325 lb. (148 kg)
Min. Carrying Weight of unit =
260 lb. (118 kg)
Manned = Remove 7.5" riser
Remote = 7.5" riser optional

**Olympian**

MAXIMUM PAYLOAD =
1,700 lb. (795 kg)

Weight of unit =
1,790 lb. (813 kg)

**Ground Mounting Platform**

MAXIMUM PAYLOAD =
3,000 lb. (1,356 kg)

Weight of unit =
206 lb. (93 kg)

**ATB Base**
(With 7.5" riser)
MAXIMUM PAYLOAD =
5,500 lb. (2,500 kg)

Weight of unit =
2,339 lb. (1,063 kg)

Manned = Remove 7.5" riser
Remote = 7.5" riser optional

**CS Base**
(With 7.5" riser)
MAXIMUM PAYLOAD =
5,500 lb. (2,500 kg)

Operating Weight of unit =
771 lb. (350 kg)
Min. Carrying Wt. of unit =
302 lb. (137 kg)
Manned = Remove 7.5" riser
Remote = 7.5" riser optional

**Camera Car Mount**
(7.5" riser optional)
MAXIMUM PAYLOAD =
3,300 lb. (1,519 kg)

Weight of unit =
515 lb. (237 kg)

(Remote Use Only)

**Mobile Crane**
For SUPER NOVA/APOLLO With platform and 2 ft. riser:
MAXIMUM PAYLOAD = 2,700 lb. (1,227 kg). Platform at 1/2 circle
weighs 285 lb. (131 kg). Platform at full circle weighs 412 lb.
(189 kg). These weights, depending on application, are deducted
from Maximum Payload. Subtract 8 ft. (2.4 m) for APOLLO height.

For Apollo    22' 8" (6.9 M)

For Super Nova    30' 8" (9.3 m)
(Remote Use Only)

The maximum height for the LENNY ARM II PLUS is calculated by using the bearings at both ends of the arm as points of reference. Assuming that the arm is at its maximum angle of elevation (56°) and that the rear bucket touches the ground, the max. height is calculated by multiplying the arm length by sin56°(.829). The forward bearing height is approximately the same as the camera lens height when the camera is underslung Additional height can be achieved by the use of risers, overslinging or by manned use.

The maximum payloads and operational weights for the LENNY ARM II PLUS have been calculated by assuming the configurations include the REMOTE NOSE (13.5 lb.) and a 24" CAMERA PLATE + LEVELING HEAD (26.5 lb.). Using other noses in addition to or without a 24" CAMERA PLATE + LEVELING HEAD will affect the figures for operational weights and maximum payloads. - Please consider these facts while deciding which configuration is to be chosen for a given task.

**To calculate specific operational weight for any given configuration, please use the following formula:**

Specific Operational Weight = BAW (Balanced arm weight, no payload.) + payload (camera weight, risers, etc.) + payload x balance ratio (Weight in bucket required to balance the given payload.)

**SPECIFIC OPERATIONAL HEIGHT ON ELEVATED PLATFORMS =**

PLATFORM MOUNT HEIGHT (Ground to mount) + FORWARD LENGTH OF ARM x .829 (Center post to fwd. bearing) + 1.1 ft. (.35 m) (Center post bearing to mount)

Actual Height (H) = MH - (PMH x BR - Actual Mount Height x BR)

*It is advised that the user of Chapman/Leonard equipment check with the manufacturer for the latest updates on *all* equipment.

**Figure 12.2** Mounting choices for Lenny Arm II.

## Lenny Arm® III   Mounting Options

## The Lenny Arm III can be mounted on these Chapman/Leonard products:

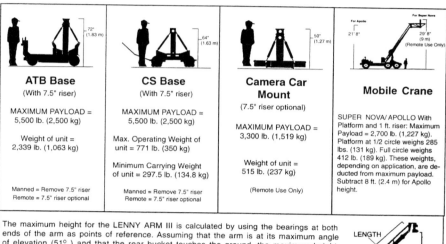

| ATB Base | CS Base | Camera Car Mount | Mobile Crane |
|---|---|---|---|
| (With 7.5" riser) | (With 7.5" riser) | (7.5" riser optional) | |
| MAXIMUM PAYLOAD = 5,500 lb. (2,500 kg) | MAXIMUM PAYLOAD = 5,500 lb. (2,500 kg) | MAXIMUM PAYLOAD = 3,300 lb. (1,519 kg) | SUPER NOVA/ APOLLO With Platform and 1 ft. riser: Maximum Payload = 2,700 lb. (1,227 kg). Platform at 1/2 circle weighs 285 lbs. (131 kg). Full circle weighs 412 lb. (189 kg). These weights, depending on application, are deducted from maximum payload. Subtract 8 ft. (2.4 m) for Apollo height. |
| Weight of unit = 2,339 lb. (1,063 kg) | Max. Operating Weight of unit = 771 lb. (350 kg) | Weight of unit = 515 lb. (237 kg) | |
| | Minimum Carrying Weight of unit = 297.5 lb. (134.8 kg) | | |
| Manned = Remove 7.5" riser | Manned = Remove 7.5" riser | (Remote Use Only) | |
| Remote = 7.5" riser optional | Remote = 7.5" riser optional | | |

The maximum height for the LENNY ARM III is calculated by using the bearings at both ends of the arm as points of reference. Assuming that the arm is at its maximum angle of elevation (51°) and that the rear bucket touches the ground, the maximum height is calculated by multiplying the arm length by sin 51° (.777). The forward bearing height is approximately the same as the camera lens height when the camera is underslung. Additional height can be achieved by the use of risers or by overslinging, and in manned use.

The maximum payloads and operational weights for the LENNY ARM III have been calculated by assuming the configurations include the REMOTE NOSE (17 lb.), a 24" CAMERA PLATE + LEVELING HEAD (26.5 lb.) and NOSE SEGMENT (82 lb.). Using other noses in addition to or without a 24" CAMERA PLATE + LEVELING HEAD will affect the figures for operational weights and maximum payloads. - Please consider these facts while deciding which configuration is to be chosen for a given task.

**To calculate specific operational weight for any given configuration, please use the following formula:**

| SPECIFIC OPERATIONAL HEIGHT ON ELEVATED PLATFORMS = |
|---|

| Specific Operational Weight | = | BAW (Balanced arm weight, no payload.) | + | payload (camera weight, risers, etc.) | + | payload x balance ratio (Weight in bucket required to balance the given payload.) |
|---|---|---|---|---|---|---|

| PLATFORM MOUNT HEIGHT (Ground to mount) | + | FORWARD LENGTH OF ARM x .777 (Center post to fwd. bearing) | + | 1.5 Ft. (.45 m) (Center post bearing to mount) |
|---|---|---|---|---|

Actual Height (H) = MH - (PMH x BR - Actual Mount Height x BR)

**WARNING:**  Never exceed the maximum payload values for any configuration. Chapman/Leonard Studio Equipment, Inc. will **NOT** guarantee the safety or performance of any alterations to the depicted arm configurations.

**Figure 12.3**   Mounting options for Lenny Arm III.

Lenny Arm® III  Configurations

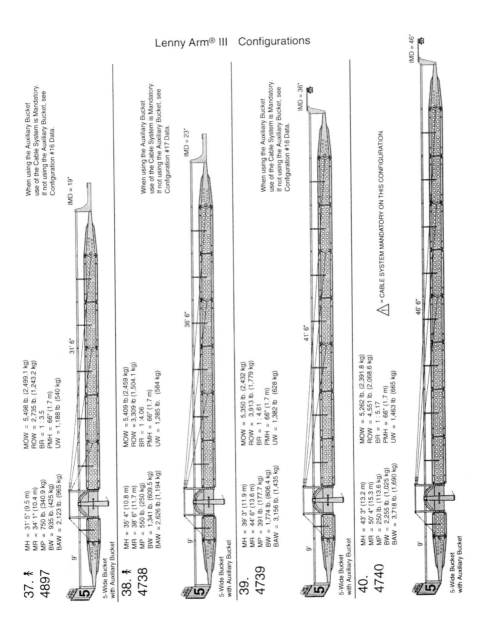

37. 🏃
4897

MH = 31' 5" (9.5 m)
MR = 34' 1" (10.4 m)
MP = 750 lb. (340.9 kg)
BW = 935 lb. (425 kg)
BAW = 2,123 lb. (965 kg)

MOW = 5,498 lb. (2,499.1 kg)
ROW = 2,735 lb. (1,243.2 kg)
BR = 1 : 3.5
PMH = 66' (1.7 m)
UW = 1,188 lb. (540 kg)

When using the Auxiliary Bucket
use of the Cable System is Mandatory.
If not using the Auxiliary Bucket, see
Configuration #16 Data.

5-Wide Bucket
with Auxiliary Bucket

38. 🏃
4738

MH = 35' 4" (10.8 m)
MR = 38' 6" (11.7 m)
MP = 550 lb. (250 kg)
BW = 1,341 lb. (609.5 kg)
BAW = 2,626 lb. (1,194 kg)

MOW = 5,409 lb. (2,459 kg)
ROW = 3,309 lb. (1,504.1 kg)
BR = 1 : 4.06
PMH = 66' (1.7 m)
UW = 1,285 lb. (584 kg)

When using the Auxiliary Bucket
use of the Cable System is Mandatory.
If not using the Auxiliary Bucket, see
Configuration #17 Data.

5-Wide Bucket
with Auxiliary Bucket

39.
4739

MH = 39' 3" (11.9 m)
MR = 44' 6" (13.6 m)
MP = 391 lb. (177.7 kg)
BW = 1,774 lb. (806.4 kg)
BAW = 3,156 lb. (1,435 kg)

MOW = 5,350 lb. (2,432 kg)
ROW = 3,913 lb. (1,779 kg)
BR = 1 : 4.61
PMH = 66' (1.7 m)
UW = 1,382 lb. (628 kg)

When using the Auxiliary Bucket
use of the Cable System is Mandatory.
If not using the Auxiliary Bucket, see
Configuration #18 Data.

5-Wide Bucket
with Auxiliary Bucket

40.
4740

MH = 43' 3" (13.2 m)
MR = 50' 4" (15.3 m)
MP = 250 lb. (113.6 kg)
BW = 2,255 lb. (1,025 kg)
BAW = 3,718 lb. (1,690 kg)

MOW = 5,262 lb. (2,391.8 kg)
ROW = 4,551 lb. (2,068.6 kg)
BR = 1 : 5.17
PMH = 66' (1.7 m)
UW = 1,463 lb. (665 kg)

⚠ = CABLE SYSTEM MANDATORY ON THIS CONFIGURATION.

5-Wide Bucket
with Auxiliary Bucket

**Figure 12.4a**  Some of the many Lenny Arm III configurations.

Lenny Arm® III  Configurations

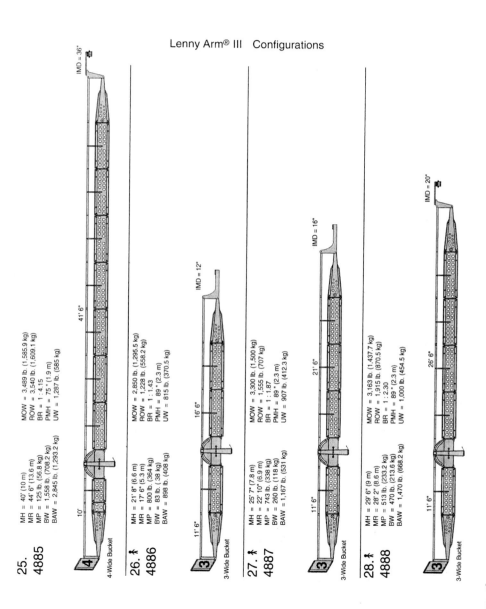

25.
4885

MH = 40' (10 m)
MR = 44' 6" (13.6 m)
MP = 125 lb. (56.8 kg)
BW = 1,558 lb. (708.2 kg)
BAW = 2,845 lb. (1,293.2 kg)

MOW = 3,489 lb. (1,585.9 kg)
ROW = 3,540 lb. (1,609.1 kg)
BR = 1 : 4.15
PMH = 75° (1.9 m)
UW = 1,287 lb. (585 kg)

4-Wide Bucket

26.
4886

MH = 21' 8" (6.6 m)
MR = 17' 6" (5.3 m)
MP = 800 lb. (364 kg)
BW = 83 lb. (38 kg)
BAW = 898 lb. (408 kg)

MOW = 2,850 lb. (1,295.5 kg)
ROW = 1,228 lb. (558.2 kg)
BR = 1 : 1.43
PMH = 89° (2.3 m)
UW = 815 lb. (370.5 kg)

3-Wide Bucket

27.
4887

MH = 25' 7" (7.8 m)
MR = 22' 10" (6.9 m)
MP = 743 lb. (338 kg)
BW = 260 lb. (118 kg)
BAW = 1,167 lb. (531 kg)

MOW = 3,300 lb. (1,500 kg)
ROW = 1,555 lb. (707 kg)
BR = 1 : 1.87
PMH = 89° (2.3 m)
UW = 907 lb. (412.3 kg)

3-Wide Bucket

28.
4888

MH = 29' 6" (9 m)
MR = 28' 2" (8.6 m)
MP = 513 lb. (233.2 kg)
BW = 470 lb. (213.6 kg)
BAW = 1,470 lb. (668.2 kg)

MOW = 3,163 lb. (1,437.7 kg)
ROW = 1,915 lb. (870.5 kg)
BR = 1 : 2.30
PMH = 89° (2.3 m)
UW = 1,000 lb. (454.5 kg)

3-Wide Bucket

**Figure 12.4b**  Some of the many Lenny Arm III configurations.

# Cablecam

## General Information

Cablecam can be suspended above any terrain, including mountains, forests, rivers, waterfalls, lakes, playing fields, roadways, stadiums, city streets, off-road terrain, and skiing courses (Figure 13.1). Cablecam is not temperature or moisture sensitive and runs smoothly in a wide range of conditions. Setup and breakdown of the system usually takes 1 or 2 days, depending on the location. Running spans of up to 2,000 feet (600 meters) are readily achievable with the standard 60-foot (18-meter) towers. Longer spans are possible with higher attachment points, such as larger towers, cranes, or the tops of buildings or stadiums. Dollies can boom up or down during a shot to match a landscape or to ascend or descend in relation to obstacles in the path of the dollies. This is accomplished by means of paying in or paying out high-line cable on or off a hydraulic winch. The dolly is 2 feet (0.6 meters) wide, which allows rigging through tight areas, such as between trees, through windows and doorways, and under lighting grids and scoreboards. The remote dolly can be safely flown close to pyrotechnical effects. *Note:* Cablecam now uses remote camera operation for greater safety. Check with Cablecam *before* you decide on which system to use. They are fantastic and will help you design the safest way to get your shot.

## Cablecam Motion Control System

The movement of the dolly and camera is programmed to repeat itself during each take. The computer can memorize dolly height, speed acceleration, deceleration, and direction. The computer can also memorize camera pan, tilt, roll, speed and aperture, zoom, and focus. The system can be set up to simultaneously trigger synchronized special effects sequences. These features eliminate the variables a filmmaker faces when combining camera tracking, stunt action, and pyrotechnical effects.

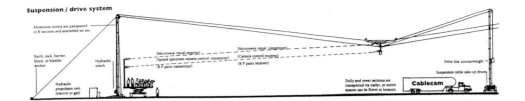

**Figure 13.1a** Cable cam over large area.

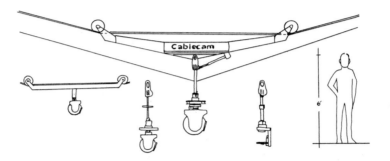

**Figure 13.1b** Cable cam head.

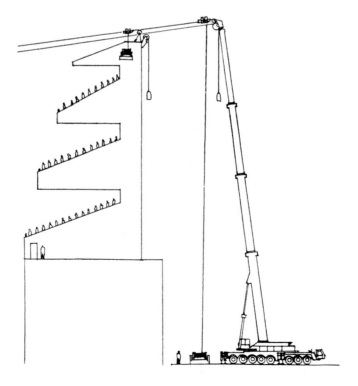

**Figure 13.1c** Cable cam at stadium.

# Dollies

The dollies described in this section are only a few of the types available (Figure 14.1). I believe that the examples chosen are the best the industry has to offer. Each dolly has its own characteristics, but all of the dollies do one basic thing—they are a mobile platform for the camera. This invention has saved the grip and camera department many hours of pain due to carrying a tripod with a camera on it. As you look through the charts and specifications for each dolly, decide for yourself which dolly is best suited for the job you are about to do.

> **T.O.T**
> When pushing the dolly, watch the actor with your peripheral vision. Look at your stop marks and watch the camera operator for any signals, such as a hand gesture to go up or down or in or out.

> **T.O.T.**
> Most dolly track is 24-1/2 inches wide from the center of the track rail to the center of the opposite track rail.

> **T.O.T.**
> Mark a small "V" with tape on your dolly control knobs. When one side of the "V" is directly in line with where the dolly arm begins to move up, the other edge is inline when it moves down. This technique is a great eyeball reference.

> **T.O.T.**
> *Rule of thumb:* Never arm more than four times without a pump up. Some dollies may arm up seven to eight times, but you do not want to run out of pressure in the middle of the shot.

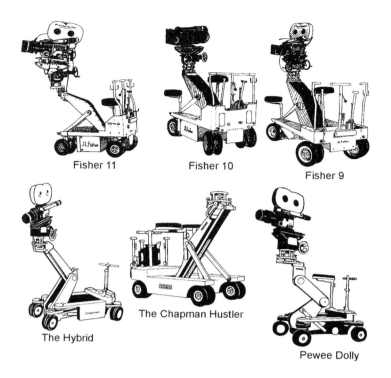

Fisher 11    Fisher 10    Fisher 9

The Chapman Hustler

The Hybrid

Pewee Dolly

**Figure 14.1** Various dollies from the J.L. Fisher Co. (top) and the Chapman Leonard Co. (bottom).

---

**T.O.T.**
Always replace the rubber tips on the track before transporting the dolly. This prevents damage.

---

## Doorway Dolly

As the name suggests, the doorway dolly (Figure 14.2) was designed to be an inexpensive camera dolly that is narrow enough to fit through most standard doorways. Over the years doorway dollies have been used not only for this purpose but also as efficient equipment transporters for camera cases, lighting fixtures, cable, and other pieces of equipment. Pneumatic tires are standard on the doorway dolly, but it can also be fitted with track wheels for use on straight dolly track. Steering is accomplished by using a pull handle (like a wagon). A new steering feature has been added recently that allows the operator to steer from onboard the dolly. This is accomplished by inserting the pull handle through the push bar at the front of the

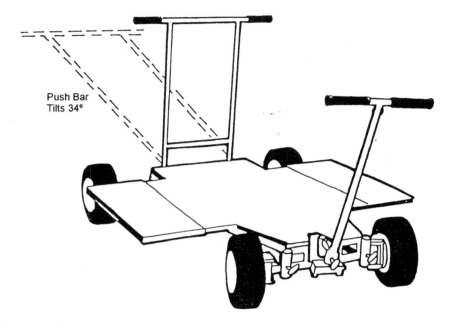

**Figure 14.2**  Doorway Dolly.

dolly. A recent addition available for the push bar is an angled fitting that allows the bar to tilt down 34 degrees for more clearance between the dolly and the dolly operator. The basic construction is a wooden platform attached to a steel tubing frame. The platform is fitted with a recessed camera tie-down area, and it is carpeted for a nonslip, low-maintenance surface. For extra-low-angle shots, the dolly can be inverted, thereby positioning the platform closer to the ground. This dolly also includes the ability to extend the rear wheels outward in order to provide greater operating stability.

## Western Dolly

A western dolly (Figure 14.3) is somewhat similar in design to the doorway dolly, but the western is much larger and is capable of transporting a heavier load. Its larger wheels offer a smoother, steadier ride than the smaller dollies. The western can be fitted with flotation track wheels and (unlike the doorway) can be operated on curved track. Applications for the western dolly include use as a camera dolly, equipment transporter, or low platform behind a camera car. For operator convenience, the push bar can be tilted down 34 degrees using a tilt adapter. The bar can also be side-mounted for close shots. When the western dolly is used inverted, the

**Figure 14.3** Western Dolly.

platform clearance is raised for use over rough terrain. Two recent additions to the western dolly include a turret assembly and pop-off wheels. The turret assembly allows for the mounting of two seats and a complete camera configuration supported by a Mitchell base. This is the standard mounting base for most cameras—it is flat with a key slot. The pop-off wheels allow for the quick removal of the dolly wheels for easy storage. The axle is incorporated into the wheel assembly to prevent the axle from becoming separated from the wheel upon removal.

## Tube Dolly

A tube dolly (Figure 14.4) is a specialized dolly originally designed to ride on sections of straight standard dolly track or tubing. The tube dolly was created to serve as a tracking platform for the older conventional-type crab dollies, which were not capable of being adapted for track use; the crab dolly would be physically loaded onto the tube dolly. The rear carriage of the tube dolly is adjustable back and forth to compensate for differing wheel lengths of crab dollies. Another application of the adjustable rear carriage is to serve as an outrigger platform for lighting or sound when the camera is riding on the main platform.

## Fisher #11 Crab Dolly

See Figure 14.5.

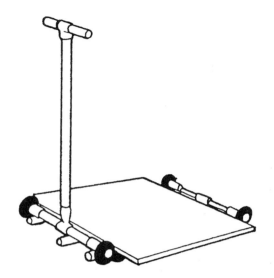

**Figure 14.4** Tube Dolly.

**Figure 14.5a** Fisher #11 Crab Dolly.

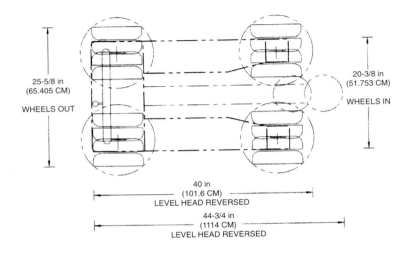

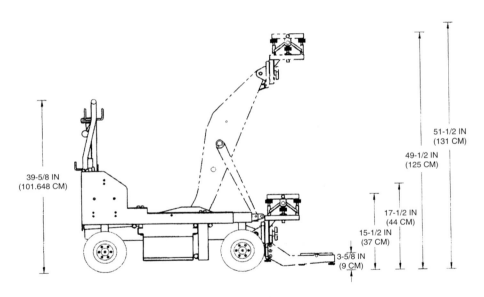

**Figure 14.5b** Fisher #11 Crab Dolly.

## Specifications for Fisher #11 Crab Dolly

| | | |
|---|---|---|
| Maximum elevation (without riser) | | |
| Head up | 51.125 in. | (129.858 cm) |
| Head down | 49.5 in. | (126 cm) |
| Minimum elevation (down position) | | |
| Head up | 17.5 in. | (44 cm) |
| Head down | 15.5 in. | (37 cm) |
| Minimum elevation (low-level head) | 3 in. | (7.62 cm) |
| Vertical beam travel | 33.375 in. | (84.773 cm) |
| Lift beam capacity | 200 bs. | (90.72 kg) |
| Lifts per system charge | 6 in. | 6 |
| Length (level head forward) | 44.75 in. | (114) |
| Length (level head reversed) | 40 in. | (101.6 cm) |
| Width for fully operational steering | 20.375 in. | (51.753 cm) |
| Width for fully operational steering | 25.75 in. | (65.405 cm) |
| Height (operating) | 39.625 in. | (100.648 cm) |
| Height (folded) | 23.125 in. | (58.738 cm) |
| Minimum turn radius (round) | 16.188 in. | (41.116 cm) |
| Minimum turn radius (conventional) | 33.5 in. | (85.09 cm) |
| Carrying weight | 307 lbs. | (139.25 kg) |

## Features

- Three-way steering system: crab, conventional, and round
- 80 to 240 volts AC or DC
- Multiposition level head
- Rotary knob or up–down lever
- Camera battery compartment
- Self-contained track system

## Standard Accessories

*Note*: These accessories should come with the Fisher #11 dolly:

- Two seats
- Two front boards (elephant ears or pork chops)
- Two high-side boards (31-1/2 in. [79 cm] long)
- Two low-side boards (11 in. [28 cm] long)
- One battery rack
- Two push posts
- Two carry handles (nickname: can openers)
- One knee bumper
- One power cord
- Front pins

## Optional Accessories

- Straight (square) track: 20 ft., 16 ft., 10 ft., 8 ft., 4 ft., 3 ft., or 2 ft.
- Curved track: 10-ft. diameter, 20-ft. diameter, 30-ft. diameter, or 70-ft. diameter
- Rotating offsets (four models to choose from)
- Low-level heads (two- or four-way level-type models)
- 45-degree seat offset
- 90-degree seat offset
- Seat riser
- Rotating seats
- Camera offsets: 10 in. or 24 in. (nickname: Ubangie)
- Universal adapter (converts a Mitchell base into a Ball base)
- Camera risers: 3 in., 6 in., or 12 in.
- 90-degree camera angle plate
- Round track adapter wheel set (boogie wheels)
- Diving boards (42 in. [107 cm] long)
- Lamp adapter
- Front board bridge
- Front track platform (low board with roller wheels)
- Ice skates
- Center mount kit (for large jib arms)
- Soft wheels (used as a softening effect)
- Monitor rack
- Cue board

**T.O.T.**
Spray oil or talcum powder on dolly wheels as you roll the dolly up and down the track. This transfers the lubricant to the needed area and makes less of a mess.

**T.O.T.**
If you are asked to work the dolly, do not roll over any cable because it may throw off the pin registry (the interior movement of the camera). It can also damage the dolly.

**T.O.T.**
Cut two full wedges to 3/4 in. at their highest point. This is a great way to get the dolly onto plywood.

## Fisher #10 Crab Dolly

See Figure 14.6.

### Specifications

| | | |
|---|---|---|
| Maximum elevation (without riser) | 62.625 in. | 159.068 cm |
| Minimum elevation (unaided) | 13.75 in. | 34.925 cm |
| Minimum elevation (low-level head) | 3.125 in. | 7.938 cm |
| Vertical beam travel | 46.878 in. | 119.063 cm |
| Lift capacity | 500 lb. | 227 kg |
| Lifts per charge | 7 | |
| Length | 56.5 in. | 140.97 cm |
| Width (wheels in) | 26.5 in. | 67.31 cm |
| Width (wheels out) | 32 in. | 81 cm |
| Height (operating) | 38.625 in. | 98.108 cm |
| Height (folded) | 25 in. | 63.5 cm |

### Standard Accessories

*Note:* These accessories should come with the Fisher #10 dolly:

**Figure 14.6a**   Fisher #10 Crab Dolly.

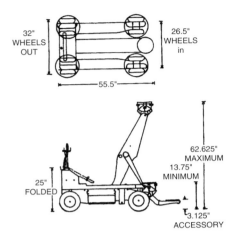

**Figure 14.6b** Fisher #10 Crab Dolly.

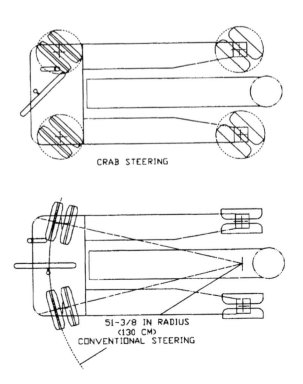

**Figure 14.6c** Fisher #10 Crab Dolly.

- Two seats
- Two front boards (elephant ears or pork chops)
- Two high side boards (36 in. long)
- Two low side boards (20-1/2 in. long)
- One battery rack
- Two push posts
- Two carry handles (nickname: can openers)
- One knee bumper
- One power cord
- Front pins

### Optional Accessories

- Straight (square) track: 20 ft., 16 ft., 10 ft., 8 ft., 4 ft., 3 ft., or 2 ft.
- Curved track: 10-ft. diameter, 20-ft. diameter, 30-ft. diameter, or 70-ft. diameter
- Rotating offsets (four models to choose from)
- Low-level heads (two- or four-way level-type models)
- 45-degree seat offset
- 90-degree seat offset
- Seat riser
- Rotating seat
- Beam step standing platform
- Camera offsets: 10 in. or 24 in. (nickname: Ubangie)
- Universal adapter (converts a Mitchell base into a Ball base)
- Camera risers: 3 in., 6 in., or 12 in.
- 90-degree camera angle plate
- Round track adapter wheel set (boggie wheels)
- Diving boards (48 in. long)
- Lamp adapter
- Front track platform (low board with roller wheels)
- Front porch (high board that hooks on front of the dolly)
- Ice skates
- Center mount kit (for large jib arms)
- Soft wheels (used as a softening effect)
- Monitor rack
- Cue board

### T.O.T.

Most dollies either fold or allow removal of the grips working end (stearing handle and arm control value) for a 360-degree shot.

**T.O.T.**
Put the back lifting bars in a Fisher #10, then stand on them; this will offset the weight enough to lift up the front of the dolly to get up a curb.

**T.O.T.**
When you push the dolly, always put down a tape mark every time you park the dolly. A lot of times the director of photography will say, "Go to that last mark." I will usually have three or four different color tapes already torn with tabs ready for such an occasion.

## Fisher #9 Crab Dolly

See Figure 14.7.

**Figure 14.7**  Fisher #9 Crab Dolly (Grip working end).

## Specifications

| | | |
|---|---|---|
| Maximum elevation (without riser) | 61.875 in. | (157.163 cm) |
| Minimum elevation (unaided) | 15 in. | (38.1 cm) |
| Minimum elevation (low-level head) | 3.75 in. | (9.525 cm) |
| Vertical beam travel | 46.875 in. | (119.063 cm) |
| Lift capacity | 500 lb. | (226.8 kg) |
| Lifts per charge | 5 | |
| Length | 67 in. | (170.18 cm) |
| Width | 30.375 in. | (77.153 cm) |
| Height (operating) | 36.625 in. | (93.028 cm) |
| Height (folded) | 19.250 in. | (48.895 cm) |
| Minimum turning radius (for conventional steering) | 51.355 in. | (130.493 cm) |
| Carrying weight | 445 lb. | (201.85 kg) |
| Maximum load capacity | 900 lb. | (408.23 kg) |

## Features

- Three-way steering system: crab, conventional, and steering
- 80 to 240 volts AC or DC

## Standard Accessories

- High (36 in.) and low (20-1/2 in. [52 cm]) side boards
- Interchangeable front boards
- Adjustable seats
- Push posts
- Carry handles
- Power cord
- Front pins
- Battery rack
- Knee board

## Optional Accessories

- 3-in., 6-in., and 12-in. risers
- 10-in. and 24-in. camera offsets
- Fisher rotating (nickname: Ubangie)
- 90-degree angle plates
- Pan/tilt adapters
- Monitor rack
- Low-level head
- Seat offset
- Seat risers
- Seat platform

- Extended high side boards
- Track trucks (for Fisher, Matthews, Elemack, and Dexter straight tracks)
- Straight track (round or square)
- Track ramps
- Shipping case

See Figures 14.8 through 14.48.

### *Fisher Camera Dolly Accessories*

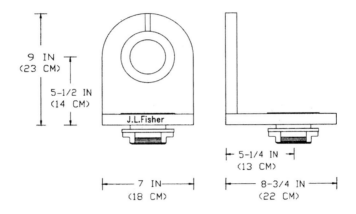

**Figure 14.8** 90-degree Angle Plates.

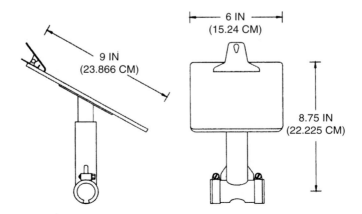

**Figure 14.9** Cue board.

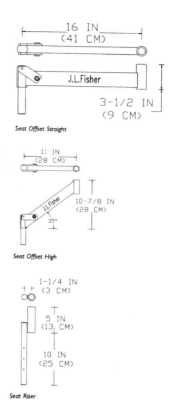

**Figure 14.10** Offset (straight) and offset (high) seat riser.

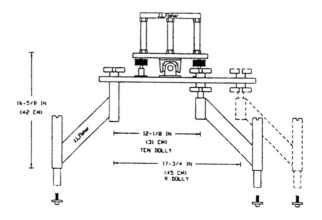

**Figure 14.11** Center mount kit.

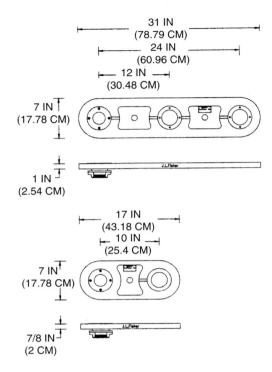

**Figure 14.12** Offsets (nicknamed "Ubangie").

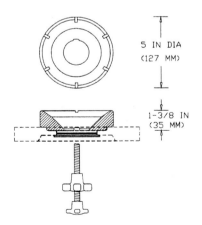

**Figure 14.13** Ballmount Adapter (A.K.A. Euro ball mount adapter).

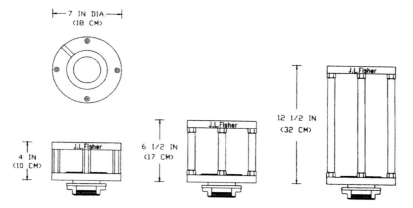

**Figure 14.14**   Rishers, 4″, 6-1/2″, and 12-1/2″.

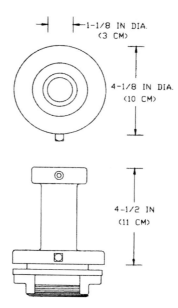

**Figure 14.15**   Adapter for 1-1/8″ lamp pin.

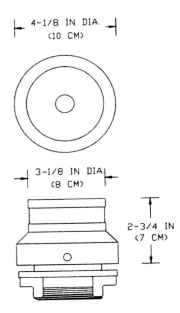

**Figure 14.16** Adapter for spider head.

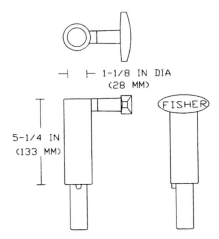

**Figure 14.17** Lamp adapter.

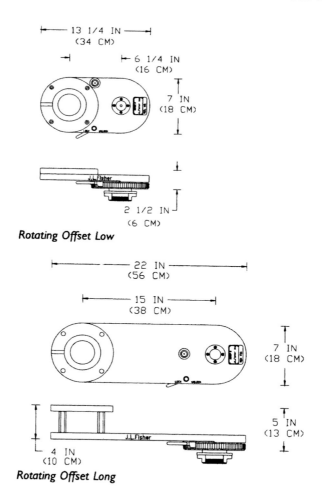

*Rotating Offset Low*

*Rotating Offset Long*

**Figure 14.18** Rotating offsets.

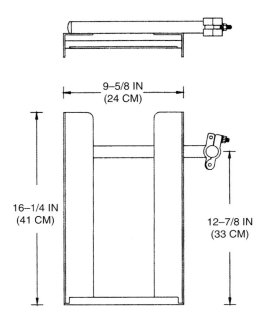

**Figure 14.19** Monitor Rack (MRD).

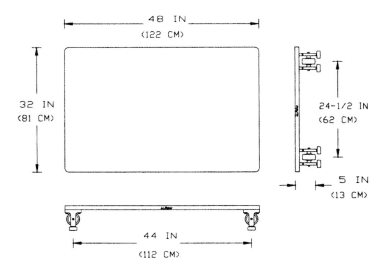

**Figure 14.20** Scooter Board (SCO).

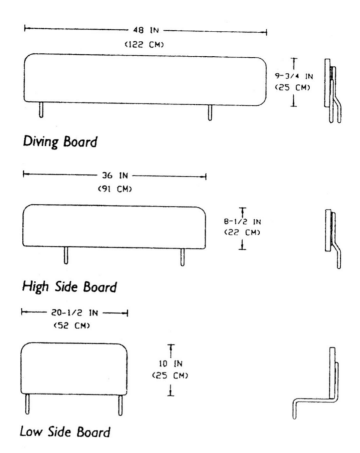

48 IN
(122 CM)

9-3/4 IN
(25 CM)

*Diving Board*

36 IN
(91 CM)

8-1/2 IN
(22 CM)

*High Side Board*

20-1/2 IN
(52 CM)

10 IN
(25 CM)

*Low Side Board*

**Figure 14.21**  Side Boards.

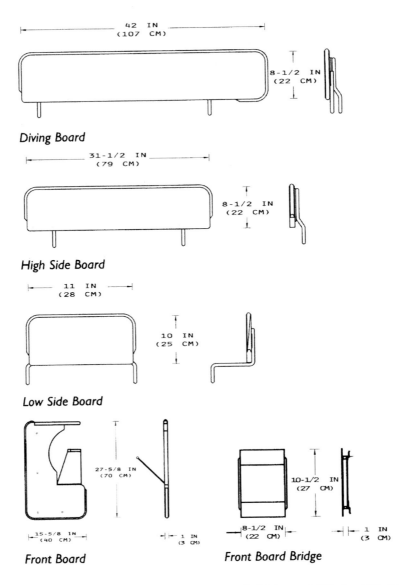

Diving Board

High Side Board

Low Side Board

Front Board

Front Board Bridge

**Figure 14.22** Fisher #11 Crab Dolly Front Boards (nicknamed "Elephant Ears").

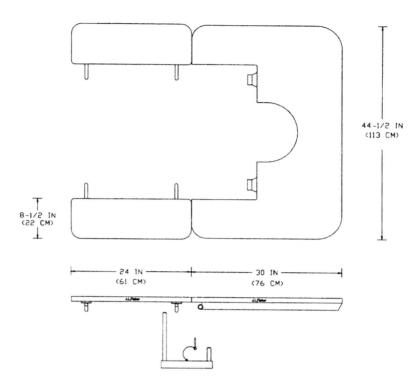

**Figure 14.23** Front Porch (FP & H).

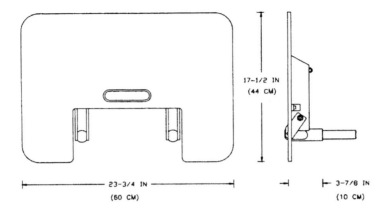

*Model 9 Dolly Platform*

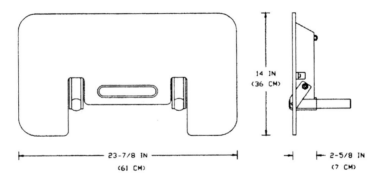

*Model Ten Dolly Platform*

**Figure 14.24** Dolly Platforms.

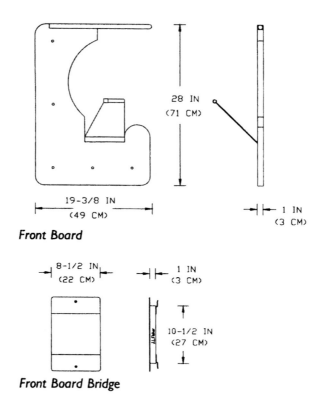

**Front Board**

**Front Board Bridge**

**Figure 14.25** Front Board and Bridge.

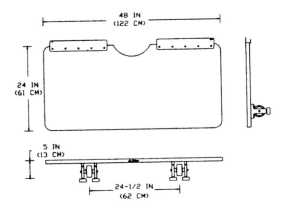

*Front Track Platform*

**Figure 14.26** Front Track Platform (FTPE).

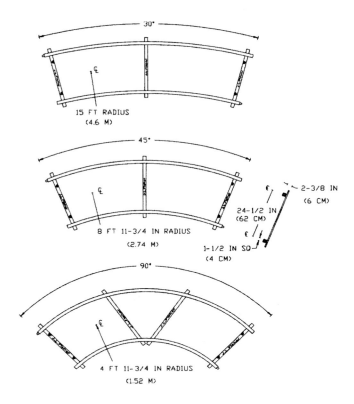

**Figure 14.27** Square curved track.

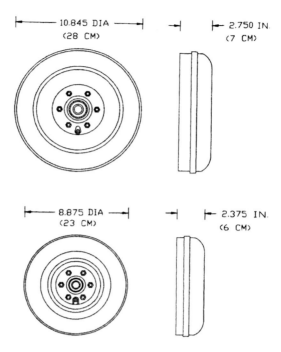

|← 10.845 DIA →| (28 CM)  |← 2.750 IN. (7 CM)

|← 8.875 DIA →| (23 CM)  |← 2.375 IN. (6 CM)

**Figure 14.28**  Pnuematic wheels (PNE).

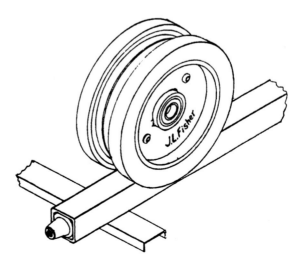

**Figure 14.29**  Square tube wheels on square tube track.

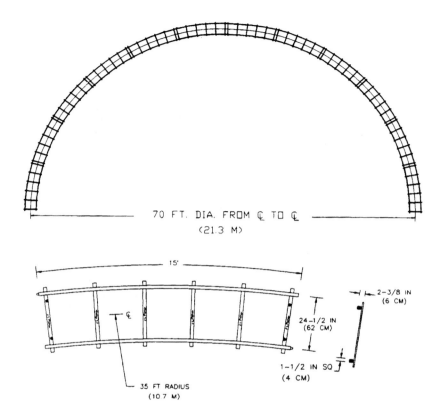

**Figure 14.30** 70 ft. diameter curved track (CS7) square tube.

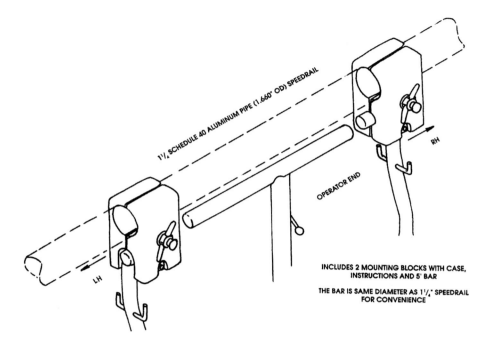

1¼ SCHEDULE 40 ALUMINUM PIPE (1.660" OD) SPEEDRAIL

RH

OPERATOR END

LH

INCLUDES 2 MOUNTING BLOCKS WITH CASE,
INSTRUCTIONS AND 5' BAR

THE BAR IS SAME DIAMETER AS 1¼" SPEEDRAIL
FOR CONVENIENCE

**Figure 14.31** Push bar for #9, 10, and 11 dollies.

## Shotmaker Blue Goes Above and Beyond You Know Who.

### SPECIFICATIONS

*eagle* by shotmaker

| | |
|---|---|
| Minimum length (A) | 45 in. |
| Maximum length (B) | 51 in. |
| Minimum width (C) | 29 in. |
| Maximum width (D) | 39 in. |
| Minimum height (E) | 17 in. |
| Maximum height (F) | 54 in. |
| Arm travel (G) | 38 1/2 in |
| Minimum turn radius | 32 1/2 in. |
| Usable track gauge | 24 1/2 in. |
| | 29 1/2 in. |
| Lifting capacity (recommended) | 360 lbs |
| Minimum working pressure | 1617 p.s.i. |
| Maximum working pressure | 2800 p.s.i. |
| Maximum arm lifts | 3 |
| (with accumulator fully charged) | |
| Weight (without accessories) | 396 lbs. |
| Charge time in Electronic Mode | 70 sec |
| Power Supply | 220        110 |
| | 50Hz or 60Hz |

### SPECIFICATIONS

*hawk* by shotmaker

| | |
|---|---|
| Minimum length (A) | 35 1/2 in. |
| Maximum length (B) | 49 in. |
| Minimum width (C) | 22 in. |
| Maximum width (D) | 35 1/2 in. |
| Minimum height (E) | 15 1/2 in. |
| Maximum height (F) | 51 in. |
| Arm travel (G) | 35 1/2 in |
| Minimum turn radius | 35 in. |
| Usable track gauge | 24 1/2 in. |
| Lifting capacity for camera head | 100 lbs |
| Lifting capacity for hoisting arm | 300 lbs |
| Minimum working pressure | 890 p.s.i. |
| Maximum working pressure | 2900 p.s.i. |
| Maximum arm lifts | 3 |
| (with accumulator fully charged) | |
| Weight (without accessories) | .320 lbs. |
| Charge time in Electronic Mode | 45 sec |
| Power Supply | 50Hz or 60Hz |

### SPECIFICATIONS

*falcon* by shotmaker

| | |
|---|---|
| Minimum length (A) | 34 in. |
| Maximum length (B) | 44 in. |
| Minimum width (C) | 22 in. |
| Maximum width (D) | 35 in. |
| Minimum height (E) | 17 in. |
| Maximum height (F) | 46 1/2 in. |
| Arm travel (G) | 29 1/2 in. |
| Minimum turn radius | 24 1/2 in. |
| Usable track gauge | 17 in. |
| | 24 1/2 in. |
| | 29 1/2 in. |
| Lifting capacity (recommended) | 132 lbs |
| Minimum working pressure | 855 p.s.i. |
| Maximum working pressure | 1854 p.s.i. |
| Maximum arm lifts | 4 |
| (with accumulator fully charged) | |
| Weight (without accessories) | 270 lbs. |
| Charge time in Electronic Mode | 70 sec |
| Power Supply | 220        110 |
| | 50Hz or 60Hz |

**Figure 14.32** Shotmaker Blue specifications.

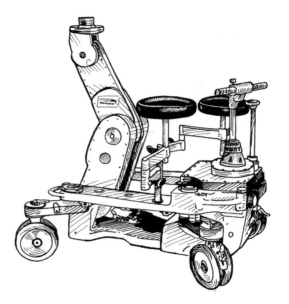

**Figure 14.33**  Eagle.

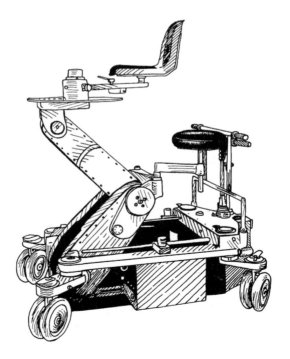

**Figure 14.34**  Hawk.

**Figure 14.35a**   Falcon.

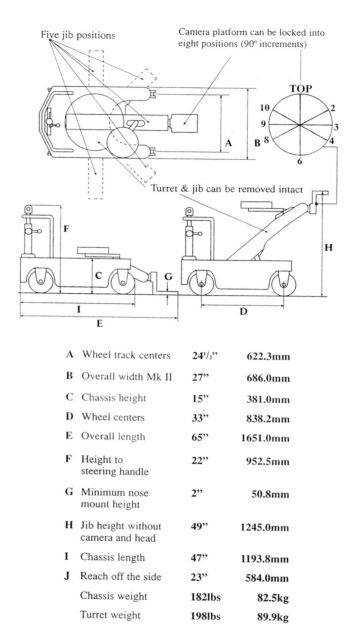

| | | | |
|---|---|---|---|
| **A** | Wheel track centers | 24¹/₂" | 622.3mm |
| **B** | Overall width Mk II | 27" | 686.0mm |
| **C** | Chassis height | 15" | 381.0mm |
| **D** | Wheel centers | 33" | 838.2mm |
| **E** | Overall length | 65" | 1651.0mm |
| **F** | Height to steering handle | 22" | 952.5mm |
| **G** | Minimum nose mount height | 2" | 50.8mm |
| **H** | Jib height without camera and head | 49" | 1245.0mm |
| **I** | Chassis length | 47" | 1193.8mm |
| **J** | Reach off the side | 23" | 584.0mm |
| | Chassis weight | 182lbs | 82.5kg |
| | Turret weight | 198lbs | 89.9kg |

**Figure 14.35b**  Frazer dolly.

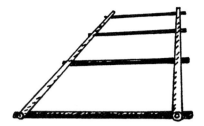

**Figure 14.36** Round track.

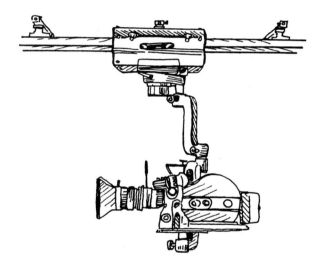

**Figure 14.37** Filou track system (top mount/slung position).

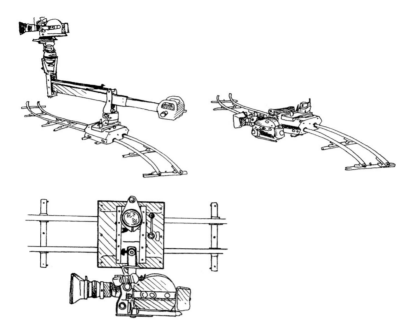

**Figure 14.38**  Filou track system (bottom/underslung and side mount positions).

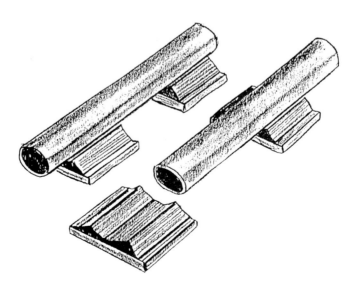

**Figure 14.39**  Track connectors (Modern Studio Equipment).

**Figure 14.40**   Portable track wheels (Modern Studio Equipment).

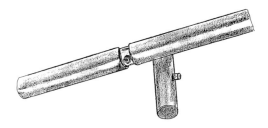

**Figure 14.41**   Pipe track connectors (Modern Studio Equipment).

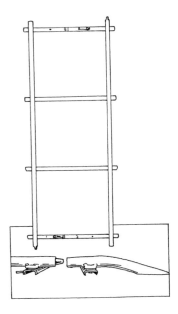

**Figure 14.42**   Starter track (chapman/Leonard).

**Figure 14.43**   Wheelchair dolly (Modern Studio Equipment).

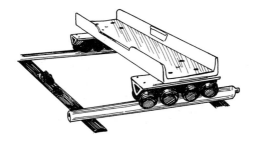

**Figure 14.44**   Channel wheels for tracks (Modern Studio Equipment).

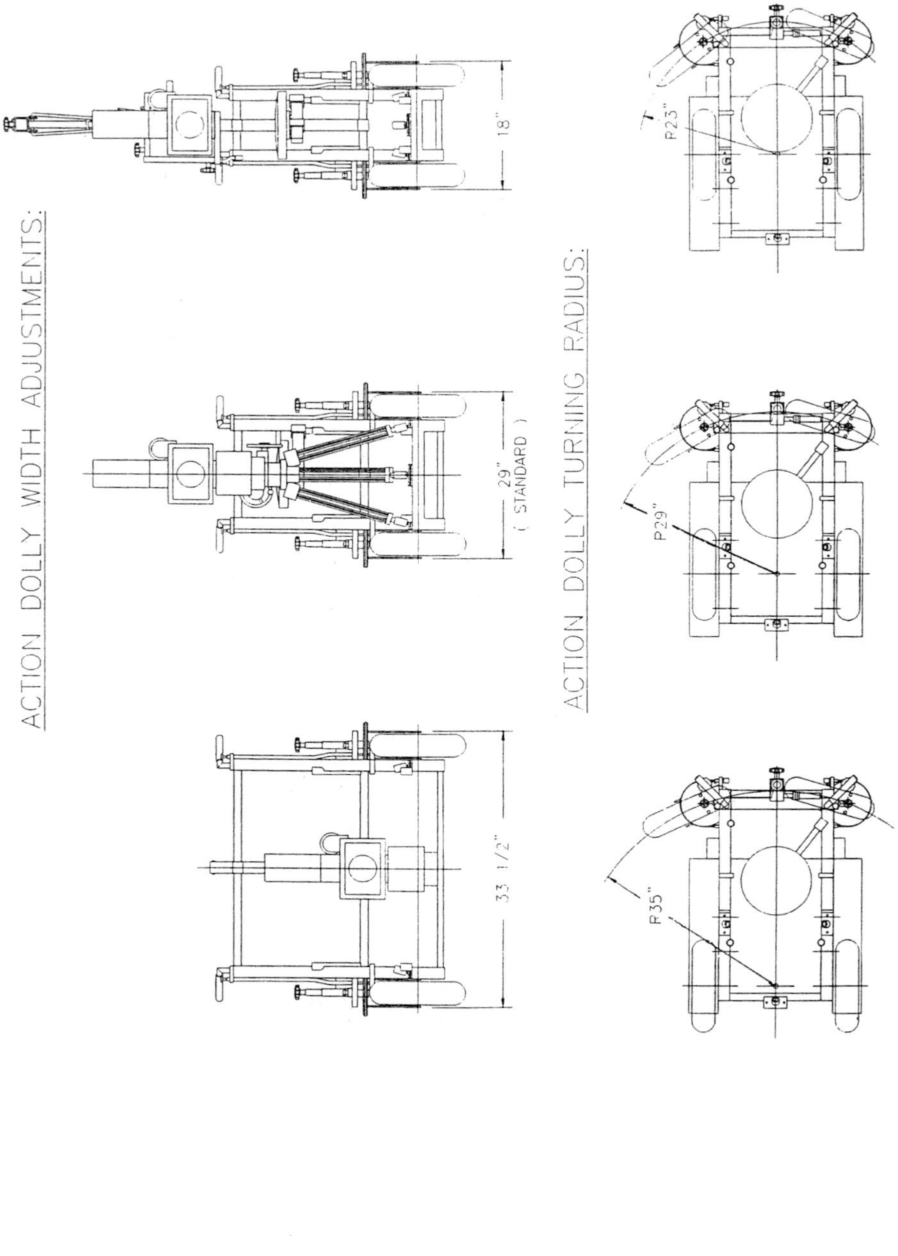

ACTION DOLLY WIDTH ADJUSTMENTS:

18"

29" ( STANDARD )

33 1/2"

ACTION DOLLY TURNING RADIUS:

R 23"

R 29"

R 35"

**Figure 14.45** Action dolly (Backstage Equipment).

ACTION DOLLY CAMERA OPTIONS:

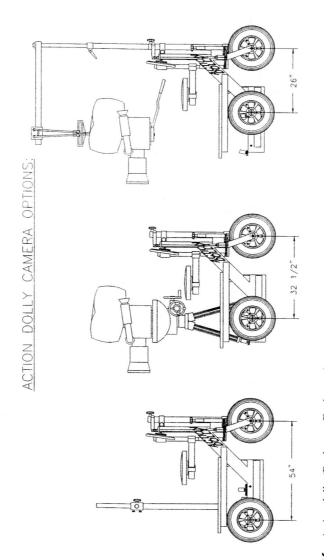

**Figure 14.46** Action dolly (Backstage Equipment).

**Figure 14.47**   Bazooka (Modern Equipment).

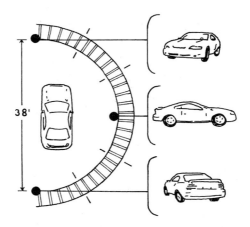

**Figure 14.48**   70 ft. track (J.L. Fisher Co.).

# Chapman Pedolly

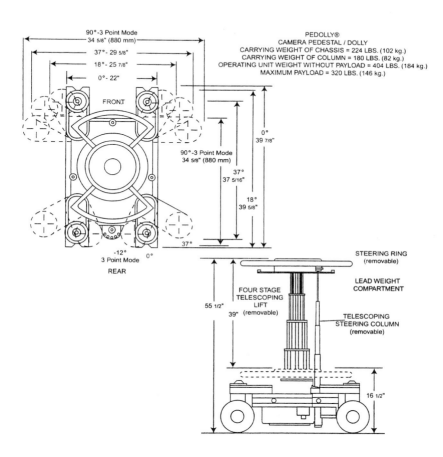

PEDOLLY®
CAMERA PEDESTAL / DOLLY
CARRYING WEIGHT OF CHASSIS = 224 LBS. (102 kg.)
CARRYING WEIGHT OF COLUMN = 180 LBS. (82 kg.)
OPERATING UNIT WEIGHT WITHOUT PAYLOAD = 404 LBS. (184 kg.)
MAXIMUM PAYLOAD = 320 LBS. (146 kg.)

**PEDOLLY ACCESSORIES**

Pedolly Wood Crate (Shipping & Storage)
Pedolly 7" Seat Offset
Pedolly Full Support Seat w/Back
Pedolly Steering Attachment
Pedolly Push Bar
Pedolly Battery Tray
Pedolly Adjustable Battery Tray - (3 Pieces)
Pedolly Precision Seat Offset
Pedolly Soft Tires - (Set of 8)
Pedolly Electronic Shifter
Pedolly Push Bar Offset
Pedolly Sideboards - (Set of 3)

Pedolly Sideboard Extension - (Set of 6)
Pedolly Weather Cover
Pedestal Mitchell Adapter - 3"
Pedestal Mitchell Adapter - 6"
Pedestal Mini Monitor Bracket
Pedestal 18" Column Riser
Pedestal Center Post Insert
Pedestal Column Star Base
Pedestal Pressure Regulator & Hose
Pedestal Nitrogen Bottle-Large
Pedestal Nitrogen Bottle Kit
Pedestal Small Steering Ring
Pedestal 4 Bolt 6" Riser

**Figure 14.49**  Chapman Pedolly.

### SPECIFICATIONS

| | | |
|---|---|---|
| Minimum Camera Mount Height | 16 1/2 in. | 42 cm |
| Maximum Camera Mount Height | 55 1/2 in. | 1.4 m |
| Vertical Travel | 39 in. | 99 cm |
| *Payload Range | 20 - 320 lbs. | 9 - 145 kg |
| **Maximum Payload with Center Post Insert | 1,100 lbs. | 500 kg |
| Number of Stages in Column | 4 | |
| Steering Ring Diameter | 28 in. | 71 cm |
| Column Diameter (when Removed) | 16 5/8 in. | 42 cm |
| Column Charging Pressure | 70 - 385 psi | |
| Chassis Width - Legs at 0 Degree Position | 22 in. | 56 cm |
| Chassis Width - Legs at 18 Degree Position | 25 7/8 in. | 66 cm |
| Chassis Width - Legs at 37 Degree Position (Track Position) | 29 5/8 in. | 75 cm |
| Chassis Width - Legs at 90 Degree Position (3 Point Mode) | 34 5/8 in. | 880 mm |
| Minimum Chassis Width | 22 in. | 56 cm |
| Minimum Chassis Length | 33 5/16 in. | 85 cm |
| Minimum Turning Radius | 27 1/2 in. | 70 cm |
| Carrying Weight of Chassis | 224 lbs. | 102 kg |
| Carrying Weight of Column | 180 lbs. | 82 kg |
| Total Weight | 404 lbs. | 184 kg |
| Operational Weight of Unit w/ Center Post Insert (w/o Payload) | 305 lbs. | 139 kg |

### OTHER PEDOLLY FEATURES

- Longer Tilt Line
- Open Access To Wheels for Maintenance
- Lock Column at Any Height (Cam Lock)
- Special Tire Compound Reduces Squeaking
- Can Be Used Indoors and Outdoors
- PEDOLLY Has Wheel Brakes
- Easily Replaced Steering Column
- Split Chassis Is Adjustable for Different Loads
- Split Chassis - with Dampened 3 Point Suspension and 4 Wheeled Stability

- Electronic Shifting of Steering
- Removable Lift Columns
- Securable to Floors or Platforms
- Can Be Used on Standard Track
- Interchangeable Hard or Soft Tires
- Virtually Silent Operation
- Changeable Leg Positions
- Easily Adjusted Cable Guards
- 22 Inch Steering Ring Available
- Seating Capability

*Payload Includes All Items (i.e. Man, Camera, Platform, Turret, Crane Arm, etc.) on Column.
**Payload Includes All Items (i.e. Man, Camera, Platform, Turret, Crane Arm, etc.) on Base Mount.

*It is advised that the user of Chapman/Leonard equipment check with the manufacturer for the latest updates on *all* equipment.

**Figure 14.49** (continued) Pedolly features and specifications.

## Chapman Peewee

See Figure 14.50.

## Chapman Super Peewee IV

See Figure 14.51.

## Chapman Hustler

See Figure 14.52.

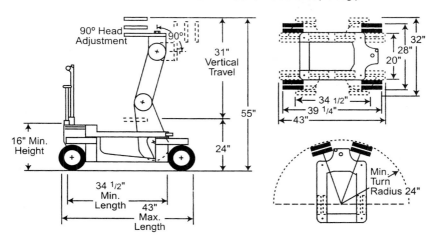

PEEWEE®
CAMERA DOLLY
CARRYING WEIGHT = 280 LBS. (127 kg.)
MAXIMUM PAYLOAD = 250 LBS. (114 kg.)

**PEEWEE ACCESSORIES**

PeeWee Grip Pouch
PeeWee Front Board
PeeWee Narrow Sideboard
PeeWee Wide Sideboard
PeeWee Standing Board
PeeWee Drop Down Sideboard
PeeWee Battery Box
PeeWee Levon Tracking Bar (Narrow)
PeeWee Tracking Bar (Wide)
PeeWee Rader Walk-Around Package
PeeWee Excalibur Case - (Set of 2)
PeeWee Soft Tires - (Set of 8)
PeeWee Pneumatic Tires - (Set of 8)
PeeWee Lifting Bars - (Set of 2)
PeeWee Square Track Tires - (Set of 8)
PeeWee Accessory Cart
PeeWee Heating System
3" Camera Riser - Mitchell 100
6" Camera Riser - Mitchell 100
12" Camera Riser - Mitchell 100
18" Camera Riser - Mitchell 100
24" Camera Riser - Mitchell 100
38" Camera Riser - Mitchell 100
3" Mitchell Riser with 24" Offset
Dolly Rain House
Open 4" Mitchell 4-Way Leveling Head

12" Mitchell Riser with 12" Offset
16" Camera Extension / 2 Cam Plate
24" Camera Extension / 2 Cam Plate
36" Camera Extension / 2 Cam Plate
Dolly Seat Pocket Light Adapter - 1 1/8"
3" Mitchell/Mitchell Male Adapter
3" Mitchell/Mitchell Female Adapter
3' Variable Extension - Panther
Euro / Mitchell Swing Head
Dolly Swivel Seat with Back Rest (Long Post)
Dolly Swivel Seat with Back Rest (Short Post)
Dolly Swivel Seat
Dolly Seat Complete
12" Dolly Seat Riser
Seat Offset Arm Short Post
Camera Swing Head & Case
Euro Camera Swing Head & Case
EVA (Electronic Valve Actuator)
Vibration Isolator & Case
Speed Rail Push Bar Adapter - (Set of 2)
Box of Wedges (FLORIDA ONLY)
Box of Shims (FLORIDA ONLY)
Box of Cribbing (FLORIDA ONLY)
Tire Holder - Short
Tire Holder - Tall
Underslung Seat Offset Arm

**Figure 14.50** Peewee accessories.

## SPECIFICATIONS

| | | |
|---|---|---|
| Maximum Camera Mount Height (without Risers) | 55 in. | 1.4 m |
| Maximum Camera Mount Height (with Standard 12" Riser) | 67 in. | 1.7 m |
| Minimum Camera Mount Height (without Riser) | 24 in. | 61 cm |
| Minimum Camera Mount Height with PeeWee 90 Degree Plate | 3 in. | 8 cm |
| Vertical Travel | 31 in. | 79 cm |
| *Maximum Payload | 250 lbs. | 114 kg |
| **Maximum Payload with High Post Kit | 1,100 lbs. | 500 kg |
| Maximum Boom Lifts (Fully Charged) | 4 Lifts | |
| Chassis Maximum Length (Wheels Fully Extended) | 43 in. | 109 cm |
| Chassis Minimum Length (Wheels Fully Retracted) | 34 1/2 in. | 88 cm |
| Minimum Chassis Height for Transportation | 16 in. | 41 cm |
| Chassis Width - Legs at 0° Position | 20 in. | 51 cm |
| Chassis Width - Legs at 17° Position (Pneumatic Tire Position) | 23 1/2 in. | 60 cm |
| Chassis Width - Legs at 45° Position | 28 1/2 in. | 71 cm |
| Chassis Width - Legs at 90° Position (Sideways or Scissor Track Position) | 32 in. | 81 cm |
| Steering Post Height | 35 in. | 89 cm |
| Minimum Turn Radius | 24 in. | 61 cm |
| Minimum Door Width PeeWee Can Be Carried Through | 16 in. | 41 cm |
| Carrying Weight | 280 lbs. | 127 kg |
| Standard Operational Weight | 329 lbs. | 150 kg |
| Operational Weight w/ High Post Kit (w/o Payload) | 386 lbs. | 178 kg |

## OTHER PEEWEE FEATURES

- PEEWEE Incorporates Brakes on Rear Wheels
- Variable Chassis Leg Adjustment Cam-Lock Chassis
- Hardened Stainless Steel Bushings
- Compact and Lightweight for Travel and Storage

- Vertical Arm Travel
- Planetary Gear-Driven Arm
- Rear Controlled Steering
- Corrected Steering Geometry

*Payload Includes All Items (i.e. Man, Camera, Platform, Turret, Crane Arm, etc.) on Arm.
**Payload Includes All Items (i.e. Man, Camera, Platform, Turret, Crane Arm, etc.) on Base Mount.

*It is advised that the user of Chapman/Leonard equipment check with the manufacturer for the latest updates on *all* equipment.

**Figure 14.50** (continued) Peewee features and specifications.

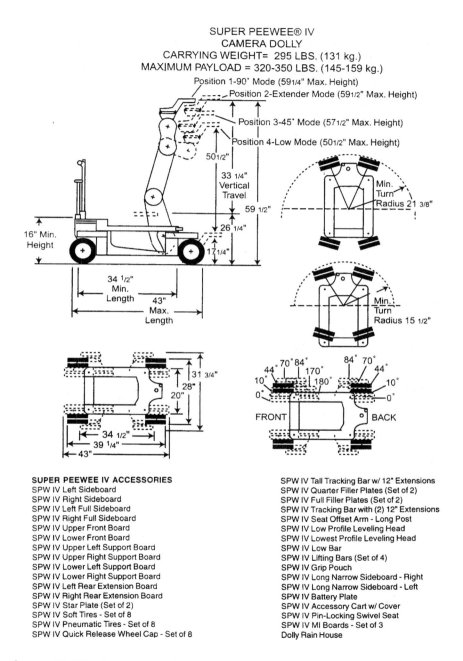

SUPER PEEWEE® IV
CAMERA DOLLY
CARRYING WEIGHT= 295 LBS. (131 kg.)
MAXIMUM PAYLOAD = 320-350 LBS. (145-159 kg.)

Position 1-90° Mode (59 1/4" Max. Height)
Position 2-Extender Mode (59 1/2" Max. Height)
Position 3-45° Mode (57 1/2" Max. Height)
Position 4-Low Mode (50 1/2" Max. Height)

50 1/2"

33 1/4"
Vertical
Travel

59 1/2"

26 1/4"

16" Min.
Height

17 1/4"

Min.
Turn
Radius 21 3/8"

34 1/2"
Min.
Length

43"
Max.
Length

Min.
Turn
Radius 15 1/2"

31 3/4"
28"
20"

70° 84°          84° 70°
44°       170°        44°
10°      180°       10°
0°                     0°

FRONT          BACK

34 1/2"
39 1/4"
43"

**SUPER PEEWEE IV ACCESSORIES**

SPW IV Left Sideboard
SPW IV Right Sideboard
SPW IV Left Full Sideboard
SPW IV Right Full Sideboard
SPW IV Upper Front Board
SPW IV Lower Front Board
SPW IV Upper Left Support Board
SPW IV Upper Right Support Board
SPW IV Lower Left Support Board
SPW IV Lower Right Support Board
SPW IV Left Rear Extension Board
SPW IV Right Rear Extension Board
SPW IV Star Plate (Set of 2)
SPW IV Soft Tires - Set of 8
SPW IV Pneumatic Tires - Set of 8
SPW IV Quick Release Wheel Cap - Set of 8

SPW IV Tall Tracking Bar w/ 12" Extensions
SPW IV Quarter Filler Plates (Set of 2)
SPW IV Full Filler Plates (Set of 2)
SPW IV Tracking Bar with (2) 12" Extensions
SPW IV Seat Offset Arm - Long Post
SPW IV Low Profile Leveling Head
SPW IV Lowest Profile Leveling Head
SPW IV Low Bar
SPW IV Lifting Bars (Set of 4)
SPW IV Grip Pouch
SPW IV Long Narrow Sideboard - Right
SPW IV Long Narrow Sideboard - Left
SPW IV Battery Plate
SPW IV Accessory Cart w/ Cover
SPW IV Pin-Locking Swivel Seat
SPW IV MI Boards - Set of 3
Dolly Rain House

**Figure 14.51**  Super Peewee IV accessories.

**SPECIFICATIONS**

| | | |
|---|---|---|
| Maximum Camera Mount Height (Position 1-90º Mode) | 59 1/2 in. | 1.5 m |
| Minimum Camera Mount Height (Position 1-90º Mode) | 26 1/4 in. | 67 cm |
| Vertical Boom Travel (Position 1-90º Mode) | 33 1/4 in. | 85 cm |
| Maximum Camera Mount Height (Position 2-Extender Mode) | 59 1/2 in. | 1.5 m |
| Minimum Camera Mount Height (Position 2-Extender Mode) | 18 1/4 in. | 46 cm |
| Vertical Boom Travel (Position 2-Extender Mode) | 41 1/4 in. | 1 m |
| Maximum Camera Mount Height (Position 3- 45º Mode) | 57 1/2 in. | 1.5 m |
| Minimum Camera Mount Height (Position 3- 45º Mode) | 24 1/4 in. | 62 cm |
| Vertical Boom Travel (Position 3- 45º Mode) | 33 1/4 in. | 85 cm |
| Maximum Camera Mount Height (Position 4-Low Mode) | 50 1/2 in. | 1.3 m |
| Minimum Camera Mount Height (Position 4-Low Mode) | 17 1/4 in. | 44 cm |
| Vertical Boom Travel (Position 4-Low Mode) | 33 1/4 in. | 85 cm |
| Minimum Camera Mount Height (Low Bar Setup w/ Lowest 4-Way Leveling Head) | 4 in. | 10 cm |
| Maximum Camera Mount Height (Low Bar Setup w/ Lowest 4-Way Leveling Head) | 37 1/4 in. | 95 cm |
| NOTE: LOWEST SETUP 11/2" REFER TO SPW IV USERS GUIDE | | |
| Chassis Width - All Legs at 0º (Use in Tight Quarters) | 20 in. | 51 cm |
| Chassis Width - All Legs at 10º (Pneumatic or 880 mm Track Position) | 25 in. | 64 cm |
| Chassis Width - All Legs at 44º (Track Position) | 28 in. | 71 cm |
| Chassis Width - All Legs at 70º (Tread and Wheel Base are Equal -'S' Position) | 31 in. | 79 cm |
| Chassis Width - All Legs at 84º (Sideways or Scissor Track Position) | 31 3/4 in. | 81 cm |
| Chassis Width - Front Legs at 84º/Rear at 0º (3 Point Solid Tire Position) | 31 3/4 in. | 81 cm |
| Chassis Width - Front Legs at 84º/Rear at 10º (3 Point Pneumatic Tire Position) | 31 3/4 in. | 81 cm |
| Chassis Width - Front Legs at 180º/Rear at 0º (Compact Solid Tire Position) | 20 in. | 51 cm |
| Chassis Width - Front Legs at 170º/Rear at 10º (Compact Pneumatic Tire Position) | 25 in. | 64 cm |
| Steering Post Height | 38 in. | 97 cm |
| Minimum Chassis Length | 34 1/2 in. | 88 cm |
| Maximum Chassis Length | 43 in. | 109 cm |
| *Maximum Payload with Accumulator Charge at 2,400psi | 320 lbs. | 145 kg |
| *Maximum Payload with Accumulator Charge at 2,600psi | 350 lbs, | 159 kg |
| **Maximum Payload with High Post Kit | 1,100 lbs. | 500 kg |
| Maximum Number of Lifts on a Single Charge | 5 Lifts | |
| Accumulator Charging Time (Empty to Full) | 60 sec. | |
| Carrying Weight | 295 lbs. | 131 kg |
| Operational Weight w/ High Post Kit (w/o Payload) | 391 lbs. | 178 kg |

*Payload Includes All Items (i.e. Man, Camera, Platform, Turret, Crane Arm, etc.) on Arm.
**Payload Includes All Items (i.e. Man, Camera, Platform, Turret, Crane Arm, etc.) on Base Mount.

**Figure 14.51** (continued) Super Peewee IV features and specifications.

## OTHER SUPER PEEWEE IV FEATURES (CONTINUED)

- Revolutionary new three mode transmission featuring conventional, crab and round steering that can be shifted while the dolly is moving or stationary, without the dolly operator's hands leaving the steering handle. This transmission has the ability to be adjusted to provide perfect steering geometry when re-configuring the chassis to its various leg positions. No other transmission has been able to do this.
- The Super PeeWee® IV now provides for much less maintenance.
  - (a) The need for air bleeding has been eliminated.
  - (b) Corrosion resistance has been dramatically improved.
  - (c) All exposed working joints have been sealed.
  - (d) Far greater precision greatly reduces the need for adjustments. All adjustments, if required by operator's specific desires, can be done externally without removing bolted covers or lids.
  - (e) Steering chain adjustments have been virtually eliminated, dramatically reducing maintenance time.
  - (f) Larger hydraulic capacity requires less recharging.
  - (g) Greater strength reduces the possibility of damage.
  - (h) Modular design of steering transmission and shifting linkage facilitates quick and easy replacements.

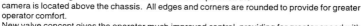
Above: New convenient location of Universal Stop Valve controls.

- New arm design provides greater operator clearance, while assuring greater rigidity, smoothness, speed and added vertical travel. This new trim arm design also allows for lower camera setups when the camera is located above the chassis. All edges and corners are rounded to provide for greater operator comfort.
- New valve concept gives the operator much improved control, providing for greater speed with added precision.
- Stop valve now requires no tools to make adjustments. Accessibility is now directly in front of the dolly operator, providing for quick and easy adjustments.
- Improved Universal Head performance is now achieved. Added arm precision, a control cylinder and a middle rib, provides major gains in safety and rigidity.
- Improved arm performance is exhibited with five full strokes of the arm on a single charge, while still achieving added vertical travel. The rigidity has been dramatically increased. The profile has been streamlined, providing added clearance for lower lens levels when operating over the chassis. This new design also adds to operator comfort. The new internal drive mechanism is smoother and maintenance free.
- Improved valve design provides for smoother, faster and quieter arm control. The dolly operator control has been significantly improved.
- The Super PeeWee® IV has a new sideboard system. Feedback from thousands of users and our own survey has led to this new design that provides complete walk-a-round ability at both the high and low levels.
- The Super PeeWee® IV now comes with built-in heat control for the hydraulic system to maintain a minimum hydraulic oil temperature of 70º F, thus providing constant performance even in the coldest environment.
- Leg positions have been improved to enhance performance by providing:
  - (a) **0º** position for **narrowest configuration with standard tires.**
  - (b) **10º** position for **narrowest configuration with pneumatic tires** OR for **side mounting the dolly on 880mm track.**
  - (c) **44º** position for **standard 24½" track** alignment and **general all-around use.**
  - (d) **84º** position for **maximum lateral stability** or for **side mounting dolly on 24½" track.**
  - (e) **Front legs at 84º, rear legs at 0º**. This is the **three point contact position** for standard tires which is great for outdoor use on rough terrain.
  - (f) **70º** position where Tread and Wheel Base are Equal, called the **S** position.
  - (g) **Front legs at 84º, rear legs at 10º**. This is the **three point contact position** for pneumatic tires which is great for outdoor use on rough terrain.
  - (h) **Front legs at 180º** and the **rear legs at 0º** provides the **most compact dolly configuration with Standard Solid Tires**, making the Super PeeWee® IV efficient, even in especially tight quarters.
  - (i) **Front Legs at 170º** and **rear legs at 10º** provides the **most compact dolly configuration with Pneumatic Tires**, making the Super PeeWee® IV efficient, even in especially tight quarters.

\*It is advised that the user of Chapman/Leonard equipment check with the manufacturer for the latest updates on *all* equipment.

**Figure 14.51** (continued) Super Peewee IV features.

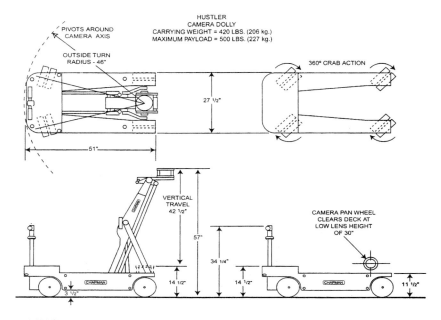

HUSTLER
CAMERA DOLLY
CARRYING WEIGHT = 420 LBS. (206 kg.)
MAXIMUM PAYLOAD = 500 LBS. (227 kg.)

PIVOTS AROUND
CAMERA AXIS

OUTSIDE TURN
RADIUS - 46"

360° CRAB ACTION

27 1/2"

51"

VERTICAL
TRAVEL
42 1/2"

CAMERA PAN WHEEL
CLEARS DECK AT
LOW LENS HEIGHT
OF 30"

57"

34 1/4"

14 1/2"        14 1/2"        11 1/2"

3 1/2"

## HUSTLER ACCESSORIES

Drop Down / Z Plate
Hustler Steering Extension
Hustler Mitchell 4-Way Leveling Head
Hustler Grip Pouch
Hustler Short Sideboard Pin
Hustler Medium Sideboard Pin
Hustler High Level Front Board
Hustler Front Board
Hustler Standing Board
Hustler Narrow Sideboard
Hustler Wide Sideboard
Hustler Grease Gun
Hustler Large Grease Gun
Hustler Push Bar - (Set of 2)
Hustler AR Battery Tray
Hustler Extended Push Bar (Set of 2)
Hustler Track Wheel Attachment & Ramps
Hustler Steadicam Z Plate
Hustler III Steadicam Platform Package
Hustler Heating System (Advanced Notice Required)
3" Camera Riser - Mitchell 100
6" Camera Riser - Mitchell 100
12" Camera Riser - Mitchell 100
18" Camera Riser - Mitchell 100
24" Camera Riser - Mitchell 100
38" Camera Riser - Mitchell 100
Open 4" Mitchell 4-Way Leveling Head

3" Mitchell Riser with 24" Offset
12" Mitchell Riser with 12" Offset
16" Camera Extension / 2 Cam Plate
24" Camera Extension / 2 Cam Plate
36" Camera Extension / 2 Cam Plate
Dolly Seat Pocket Light Adapter - 1 1/8"
3" Mitchell/Mitchell Male Adapter
3" Mitchell/Mitchell Female Adapter
3' Variable Extension - Panther
Euro / Mitchell Swing Head
Dolly Swivel Seat with Back Rest
Dolly Swivel Seat
Dolly Seat Complete
12" Dolly Seat Riser
Seat Offset Arm Short Post
Camera Swing Head & Case
Euro Camera Swing Head & Case
EVA (Electronic Valve Actuator)
Vibration Isolator & Case
Speed Rail Push Bar Adapter - (Set of 2)
Box of Wedges (FLORIDA ONLY)
Box of Shims (FLORIDA ONLY)
Box of Cribbing (FLORIDA ONLY)
Tire Holder - Short
Tire Holder - Tall
Underslung Seat Offset Arm
Dolly Rain House

**Figure 14.52** Hustler accessories.

## SPECIFICATIONS

| | | |
|---|---|---|
| Camera Mount Height (without Risers) | 57 in. | 1.4 m |
| Camera Mount Height (with Standard 12" Riser) | 69 in. | 1.8 m |
| Minimum Camera Mount Height (without Risers) | 14 1/2 in. | 37 cm |
| Minimum Camera Mount Height (with Standard 12" Riser) | 26 1/2 in. | 67 cm |
| Vertical Travel | 42 1/2 in. | 1.1 m |
| *Maximum Payload | 500 lbs. | 227 kg |
| Maximum Boom Lifts (Fully Charged) | 6 Lifts | |
| Chassis Length | 51 in. | 1.3 m |
| Chassis Width | 27 1/2 in. | 70 cm |
| Steering Post Height | 34 1/4 in. | 87 cm |
| Front Deck Height | 11 1/4 in. | 29 cm |
| Rear Deck Height | 14 1/2 in. | 37 cm |
| Minimum Turn Radius | 46 in. | 1.2 m |
| Accumulator Charging Time (110 A.C. and D.C.) | under 60 sec. | |
| Accumulator Charging Time (Hand Pump) | 2 min. | |
| Carrying Weight | 420 lbs. | 191 kg |
| Standard Operational Weight (w/o Payload) | 454 lbs. | 206 kg |

## HUSTLER FEATURES

- Hustler Camera Dolly Incorporates a Hydraulic Lift
- Hustler Has Both Crab and Conventional Steering
- Hustler Dolly Works on Straight or Curved Tubular
  Track with the Hustler Track Wheel Attachments
- Hustler II Incorporates a Hand Brake System
- Many Accessories Available
- Sealed Hydraulic System

*Payload Includes All Items (i.e. Man, Camera, Platform, Turret, Crane Arm, etc.) on Arm.

*It is advised that the user of Chapman/Leonard equipment check with the manufacturer for the latest updates on *all* equipment.

**Figure 14.52** (continued) Hustler features and specifications.

## Chapman Hustler II

See Figure 14.53.

## Chapman Hustler III

See Figure 14.54.

## Chapman Hybrid

See Figure 14.55.

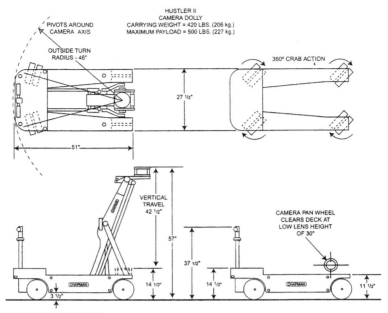

## HUSTLER ACCESSORIES

Drop Down / Z Plate
Hustler Steering Extension
Hustler Mitchell 4-Way Leveling Head
Hustler Grip Pouch
Hustler Short Sideboard Pin
Hustler Medium Sideboard Pin
Hustler High Level Front Board
Hustler Front Board
Hustler Standing Board
Hustler Narrow Sideboard
Hustler Wide Sideboard
Hustler Grease Gun
Hustler Large Grease Gun
Hustler Push Bar - (Set of 2)
Hustler AR Battery Tray
Hustler Extended Push Bar (Set of 2)
Hustler Track Wheel Attachment & Ramps
Hustler Steadicam Z Plate
Hustler III Steadicam Platform Package
Hustler Heating System (Advanced Notice Required)
3" Camera Riser - Mitchell 100
6" Camera Riser - Mitchell 100
12" Camera Riser - Mitchell 100
18" Camera Riser - Mitchell 100
24" Camera Riser - Mitchell 100
38" Camera Riser - Mitchell 100
Open 4" Mitchell 4-Way Leveling Head

3" Mitchell Riser with 24" Offset
12" Mitchell Riser with 12" Offset
16" Camera Extension / 2 Cam Plate
24" Camera Extension / 2 Cam Plate
36" Camera Extension / 2 Cam Plate
Dolly Seat Pocket Light Adapter - 1 1/8"
3" Mitchell/Mitchell Male Adapter
3" Mitchell/Mitchell Female Adapter
3' Variable Extension - Panther
Euro / Mitchell Swing Head
Dolly Swivel Seat with Back Rest
Dolly Swivel Seat
Dolly Seat Complete
12" Dolly Seat Riser
Seat Offset Arm Short Post
Camera Swing Head & Case
Euro Camera Swing Head & Case
EVA (Electronic Valve Actuator)
Vibration Isolator & Case
Speed Rail Push Bar Adapter - (Set of 2)
Box of Wedges (FLORIDA ONLY)
Box of Shims (FLORIDA ONLY)
Box of Cribbing (FLORIDA ONLY)
Tire Holder - Short
Tire Holder - Tall
Underslung Seat Offset Arm
Dolly Rain House

**Figure 14.53**  Hustler II accessories.

## SPECIFICATIONS

| | | |
|---|---:|---:|
| Camera Mount Height (without Risers) | 57 in. | 1.4 m |
| Camera Mount Height (with Standard 12" Riser) | 69 in. | 1.8 m |
| Minimum Camera Mount Height (without Risers) | 14 1/2 in. | 37 cm |
| Minimum Camera Mount Height (with Standard 12" Riser) | 26 1/2 in. | 67 cm |
| Vertical Travel | 42 1/2 in. | 1.1 m |
| *Maximum Payload | 500 lbs. | 227 kg |
| Maximum Boom Lifts (Fully Charged) | 6 Lifts | |
| Chassis Length | 51 in. | 1.3 m |
| Chassis Width | 27 1/2 in. | 70 cm |
| Steering Post Height | 37 1/2 in. | 95 cm |
| Front Deck Height | 11 1/4 in. | 29 cm |
| Rear Deck Height | 14 1/2 in. | 37 cm |
| Minimum Turn Radius | 46 in. | 1.2 m |
| Accumulator Charging Time (110 A.C. and D.C.) | under 60 sec. | |
| Accumulator Charging Time (Hand Pump) | 2 min. | |
| Carrying Weight | 420 lbs. | 191 kg |
| Standard Operational Weight (w/o Payload) | 454 lbs. | 206 kg |

## OTHER HUSTLER II FEATURES

- Hustler II Is Nickel Plated for Easy Maintenance
- Hustler II Incorporates the Universal Stop Valve System
- Hustler II Incorporates a Built-In Track Wheel System
- Hustler II Incorporates a Hand Brake System
- Many Accessories Available
- Operates in Both Crab and Conventional Steering
- **Optional AR Battery Tray Accessory**

- Extended Steering Column
- Hustler II Has Improved Faster Arm
- Swift Brake and Valve Controls
- Works on Standard Tubular Track
- Sealed Hydraulic System

*Payload Includes All Items (i.e. Man, Camera, Platform, Turret, Crane Arm, etc.) on Arm.

*It is advised that the user of Chapman/Leonard equipment check with the manufacturer for the latest updates on *all* equipment.

**Figure 14.53** (continued) Hustler II specifications and features.

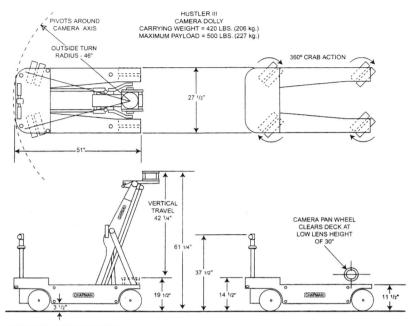

## HUSTLER ACCESSORIES

Drop Down / Z Plate
Hustler Steering Extension
Hustler Mitchell 4-Way Leveling Head
Hustler Grip Pouch
Hustler Short Sideboard Pin
Hustler Medium Sideboard Pin
Hustler High Level Front Board
Hustler Front Board
Hustler Standing Board
Hustler Narrow Sideboard
Hustler Wide Sideboard
Hustler Grease Gun
Hustler Large Grease Gun
Hustler Push Bar - (Set of 2)
Hustler AR Battery Tray
Hustler Extended Push Bar (Set of 2)
Hustler Track Wheel Attachment & Ramps
Hustler Steadicam Z Plate
Hustler III Steadicam Platform Package
Hustler Heating System (Advanced Notice Required)
3" Camera Riser - Mitchell 100
6" Camera Riser - Mitchell 100
12" Camera Riser - Mitchell 100
18" Camera Riser - Mitchell 100
24" Camera Riser - Mitchell 100
38" Camera Riser - Mitchell 100
Open 4" Mitchell 4-Way Leveling Head

3" Mitchell Riser with 24" Offset
12" Mitchell Riser with 12" Offset
16" Camera Extension / 2 Cam Plate
24" Camera Extension / 2 Cam Plate
36" Camera Extension / 2 Cam Plate
Dolly Seat Pocket Light Adapter - 1 1/8"
3" Mitchell/Mitchell Male Adapter
3" Mitchell/Mitchell Female Adapter
3' Variable Extension - Panther
Euro / Mitchell Swing Head
Dolly Swivel Seat with Back Rest
Dolly Swivel Seat
Dolly Seat Complete
12" Dolly Seat Riser
Seat Offset Arm Short Post
Camera Swing Head & Case
Euro Camera Swing Head & Case
EVA (Electronic Valve Actuator)
Vibration Isolator & Case
Speed Rail Push Bar Adapter - (Set of 2)
Box of Wedges (FLORIDA ONLY)
Box of Shims (FLORIDA ONLY)
Box of Cribbing (FLORIDA ONLY)
Tire Holder - Short
Tire Holder - Tall
Underslung Seat Offset Arm
Dolly Rain House

**Figure 14.54** Hustler III accessories.

**SPECIFICATIONS**

| | | |
|---|---|---|
| Camera Mount Height (without Risers) | 61 1/4 in. | 1.6 m |
| Camera Mount Height (with Standard 12" Riser) | 73 1/4 in. | 1.9 m |
| Minimum Camera Mount Height (without Risers) | 19 1/2 in. | 50 cm |
| Minimum Camera Mount Height (with Standard 12" Riser) | 31 1/2 in. | 80 cm |
| Minimum Camera Mount Height with Standard 90º Plate | 3 1/2 in. | 9 cm |
| Vertical Travel | 42 1/4 in. | 1.1 m |
| *Maximum Payload | 500 lbs. | 227 kg |
| Maximum Boom Lifts (Fully Charged) | 6 Lifts | |
| Chassis Length | 51 in. | 1.3 m |
| Chassis Width | 27 1/2 in. | 70 cm |
| Steering Post Height | 37 1/2 in. | 95 cm |
| Front Deck Height | 11 1/4 in. | 29 cm |
| Rear Deck Height | 14 1/2 in. | 37 cm |
| Minimum Turn Radius | 46 in. | 1.2 m |
| Accumulator Charging Time (110 A.C. and D.C.) | under 60 sec. | |
| Accumulator Charging Time (Hand Pump) | 2 min. | |
| Carrying Weight | 420 lbs. | 191 kg |
| Standard Operational Weight (w/o Payload) | 454 lbs. | 206 kg |

**OTHER HUSTLER III FEATURES**

- Hustler III Is Nickel Plated for Easy Maintenance
- Hustler III Incorporates the Universal Stop Valve System
- Hustler III's Newly Designed King Pin System Allows for Fluid Movement on Straight or Curved Tubular Track
- Operates in Both Crab and Conventional Steering
- **Optional Universal Head Mount** for Convenient, Quick Placement of the Camera
- Extended Steering Column
- Hustler III Has Improved Faster Arm
- Hustler III has a Hand Brake System
- Swift Brake and Valve Controls
- Many Accessories Available
- Sealed Hydraulic System

*Payload Includes All Items (i.e. Man, Camera, Platform, Turret, Crane Arm, etc.) on Arm.

*It is advised that the user of Chapman/Leonard equipment check with the manufacturer for the latest updates on *all* equipment.

**Figure 14.54** (continued) Hustler III specifications and features.

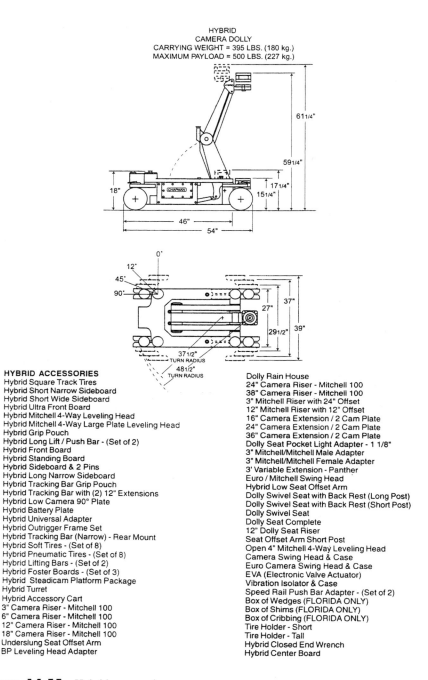

**HYBRID ACCESSORIES**
Hybrid Square Track Tires
Hybrid Short Narrow Sideboard
Hybrid Short Wide Sideboard
Hybrid Ultra Front Board
Hybrid Mitchell 4-Way Leveling Head
Hybrid Mitchell 4-Way Large Plate Leveling Head
Hybrid Grip Pouch
Hybrid Long Lift / Push Bar - (Set of 2)
Hybrid Front Board
Hybrid Standing Board
Hybrid Sideboard & 2 Pins
Hybrid Long Narrow Sideboard
Hybrid Tracking Bar Grip Pouch
Hybrid Tracking Bar with (2) 12" Extensions
Hybrid Low Camera 90° Plate
Hybrid Battery Plate
Hybrid Universal Adapter
Hybrid Outrigger Frame Set
Hybrid Tracking Bar (Narrow) - Rear Mount
Hybrid Soft Tires - (Set of 8)
Hybrid Pneumatic Tires - (Set of 8)
Hybrid Lifting Bars - (Set of 2)
Hybrid Foster Boards - (Set of 3)
Hybrid Steadicam Platform Package
Hybrid Turret
Hybrid Accessory Cart
3" Camera Riser - Mitchell 100
6" Camera Riser - Mitchell 100
12" Camera Riser - Mitchell 100
18" Camera Riser - Mitchell 100
Underslung Seat Offset Arm
BP Leveling Head Adapter

Dolly Rain House
24" Camera Riser - Mitchell 100
38" Camera Riser - Mitchell 100
3" Mitchell Riser with 24" Offset
12" Mitchell Riser with 12" Offset
16" Camera Extension / 2 Cam Plate
24" Camera Extension / 2 Cam Plate
36" Camera Extension / 2 Cam Plate
Dolly Seat Pocket Light Adapter - 1 1/8"
3" Mitchell/Mitchell Male Adapter
3" Mitchell/Mitchell Female Adapter
3' Variable Extension - Panther
Euro / Mitchell Swing Head
Hybrid Low Seat Offset Arm
Dolly Swivel Seat with Back Rest (Long Post)
Dolly Swivel Seat with Back Rest (Short Post)
Dolly Swivel Seat
Dolly Seat Complete
12" Dolly Seat Riser
Seat Offset Arm Short Post
Open 4" Mitchell 4-Way Leveling Head
Camera Swing Head & Case
Euro Camera Swing Head & Case
EVA (Electronic Valve Actuator)
Vibration Isolator & Case
Speed Rail Push Bar Adapter - (Set of 2)
Box of Wedges (FLORIDA ONLY)
Box of Shims (FLORIDA ONLY)
Box of Cribbing (FLORIDA ONLY)
Tire Holder - Short
Tire Holder - Tall
Hybrid Closed End Wrench
Hybrid Center Board

**Figure 14.55** Hybrid accessories.

| | | |
|---|---|---|
| Maximum Camera Mount Height (with Standard 12" Riser) | 73 in. | 1.9 m |
| Maximum Camera Mount Height (without Risers) | 61 1/4 in. | 1.6 m |
| Minimum Camera Mount Height | 15 1/4 in. | 39 cm |
| Minimum Camera Mount Height with Hybrid Low Camera 90 Degree Plate | 1 in. | 3 cm |
| Vertical Travel | 44 in. | 1.1 m |
| *Maximum Payload | 500 lbs. | 227 kg |
| **Maximum Payload with High Post Kit | 1,900 lbs. | 863 kg |
| Maximum Boom Lifts (Fully Charged) | 5 Lifts | |
| Chassis Maximum Length (Wheels Fully Extended) | 54 in. | 1.4 m |
| Chassis Minimum Length (Wheels Fully Retracted) | 46 in. | 1.2 m |
| Minimum Chassis Height for Transportation | 18 in. | 46 cm |
| Chassis Variable Widths - Legs in | 27 in. | 69 cm |
| Chassis Variable Widths - Legs at 12 Degree Track Position | 29 1/2 in. | 75 cm |
| Chassis Variable Widths - Legs at 45 Degrees | 37 in. | 89 cm |
| Chassis Variable Widths - Legs at 90 Degrees | 39 in. | 99 cm |
| Steering Post Height | 36 in. | 91 cm |
| Minimum Turn Radius | 37 1/2 in. | 95 cm |
| Accumulator Charging Time (110 A.C. and D.C.) | under 60 sec. | |
| Accumulator Charging Time (Hand Pump) | 2 1/2 min. | |
| Minimum Door Width Hybrid Can Be Carried Through | 18 in. | 46 cm |
| Carrying Weight | 395 lbs. | 180 kg |
| Standard Operational Weight (w/o Payload) | 463 lbs. | 210 kg |
| Hybrid w/ High Post Kit Operational Weight (w/o Payload) | 501 lbs. | 227 kg |

### OTHER HYBRID II FEATURES

- The Hybrid II Incorporates the Universal Stop Valve System
- The Hybrid II Is Nickel Plated for Less Maintenance
- Works on Both Straight or Curved Track
- Interchangeable Soft, Hard or Pneumatic Tires for Different Terrain
- Hybrid II Incorporates Brakes on Rear Wheels

- Cam-Lock Chassis Legs
- Enclosed King Pin System
- Variable Camera Head
- Variable Chassis Legs
- Compact and Lightweight

*Payload Includes All Items (i.e. Man, Camera, Platform, Turret, Crane Arm, etc.) on Arm.
**Payload Includes All Items (i.e. Man, Camera, Platform, Turret, Crane Arm, etc.) on Base Mount.

*It is advised that the user of Chapman/Leonard equipment check with the manufacturer for the latest updates on all equipment.

**Figure 14.55** (continued) Hybrid II specifications and features.

## Chapman Hybrid II
See Figure 14.56.

## Chapman Hybrid III
See Figure 14.57.

## Chapman Sidewinder
See Figure 14.58.

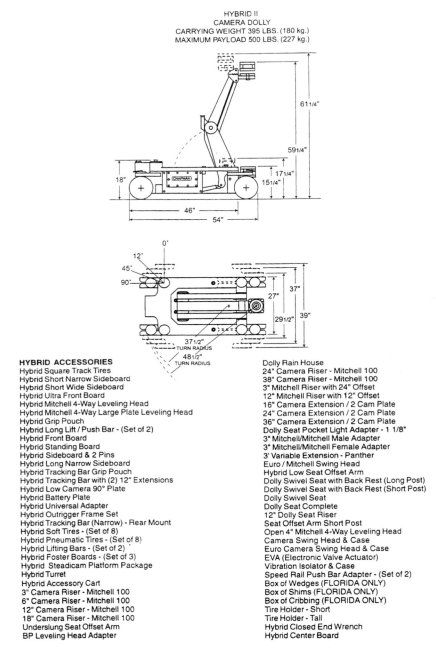

HYBRID II
CAMERA DOLLY
CARRYING WEIGHT 395 LBS. (180 kg.)
MAXIMUM PAYLOAD 500 LBS. (227 kg.)

**HYBRID ACCESSORIES**

Hybrid Square Track Tires
Hybrid Short Narrow Sideboard
Hybrid Short Wide Sideboard
Hybrid Ultra Front Board
Hybrid Mitchell 4-Way Leveling Head
Hybrid Mitchell 4-Way Large Plate Leveling Head
Hybrid Grip Pouch
Hybrid Long Lift / Push Bar - (Set of 2)
Hybrid Front Board
Hybrid Standing Board
Hybrid Sideboard & 2 Pins
Hybrid Long Narrow Sideboard
Hybrid Tracking Bar Grip Pouch
Hybrid Tracking Bar with (2) 12" Extensions
Hybrid Low Camera 90° Plate
Hybrid Battery Plate
Hybrid Universal Adapter
Hybrid Outrigger Frame Set
Hybrid Tracking Bar (Narrow) - Rear Mount
Hybrid Soft Tires - (Set of 8)
Hybrid Pneumatic Tires - (Set of 8)
Hybrid Lifting Bars - (Set of 2)
Hybrid Foster Boards - (Set of 3)
Hybrid Steadicam Platform Package
Hybrid Turret
Hybrid Accessory Cart
3" Camera Riser - Mitchell 100
6" Camera Riser - Mitchell 100
12" Camera Riser - Mitchell 100
18" Camera Riser - Mitchell 100
Underslung Seat Offset Arm
BP Leveling Head Adapter

Dolly Rain House
24" Camera Riser - Mitchell 100
38" Camera Riser - Mitchell 100
3" Mitchell Riser with 24" Offset
12" Mitchell Riser with 12" Offset
16" Camera Extension / 2 Cam Plate
24" Camera Extension / 2 Cam Plate
36" Camera Extension / 2 Cam Plate
Dolly Seat Pocket Light Adapter - 1 1/8"
3" Mitchell/Mitchell Male Adapter
3" Mitchell/Mitchell Female Adapter
3' Variable Extension - Panther
Euro / Mitchell Swing Head
Hybrid Low Seat Offset Arm
Dolly Swivel Seat with Back Rest (Long Post)
Dolly Swivel Seat with Back Rest (Short Post)
Dolly Swivel Seat
Dolly Seat Complete
12" Dolly Seat Riser
Seat Offset Arm Short Post
Open 4" Mitchell 4-Way Leveling Head
Camera Swing Head & Case
Euro Camera Swing Head & Case
EVA (Electronic Valve Actuator)
Vibration Isolator & Case
Speed Rail Push Bar Adapter - (Set of 2)
Box of Wedges (FLORIDA ONLY)
Box of Shims (FLORIDA ONLY)
Box of Cribbing (FLORIDA ONLY)
Tire Holder - Short
Tire Holder - Tall
Hybrid Closed End Wrench
Hybrid Center Board

**Figure 14.56** Hybrid accessories.

## SPECIFICATIONS

| | | |
|---|---|---|
| Maximum Camera Mount Height (with Standard 12" Riser) | 73 in. | 1.9 m |
| Maximum Camera Mount Height (without Risers) | 61 1/4 in. | 1.6 m |
| Minimum Camera Mount Height | 15 1/4 in. | 39 cm |
| Minimum Camera Mount Height with Hybrid Low Camera 90 Degree Plate | 1 in. | 3 cm |
| Vertical Travel | 44 in. | 1.1 m |
| *Maximum Payload | 500 lbs. | 227 kg |
| **Maximum Payload with High Post Kit | 1,900 lbs. | 863 kg |
| Maximum Boom Lifts (Fully Charged) | 5 Lifts | |
| Chassis Maximum Length (Wheels Fully Extended) | 54 in. | 1.4 m |
| Chassis Minimum Length (Wheels Fully Retracted) | 46 in. | 1.2 m |
| Minimum Chassis Height for Transportation | 18 in. | 46 cm |
| Chassis Variable Widths - Legs in | 27 in. | 69 cm |
| Chassis Variable Widths - Legs at 12 Degree Track Position | 29 1/2 in. | 75 cm |
| Chassis Variable Widths - Legs at 45 Degrees | 37 in. | 89 cm |
| Chassis Variable Widths - Legs at 90 Degrees | 39 in. | 99 cm |
| Steering Post Height | 36 in. | 91 cm |
| Minimum Turn Radius | 37 1/2 in. | 95 cm |
| Accumulator Charging Time (110 A.C. and D.C.) | under 60 sec. | |
| Accumulator Charging Time (Hand Pump) | 2 1/2 min. | |
| Minimum Door Width Hybrid Can Be Carried Through | 18 in. | 46 cm |
| Carrying Weight | 395 lbs. | 180 kg |
| Standard Operational Weight (w/o Payload) | 463 lbs. | 210 kg |
| Hybrid w/ High Post Kit Operational Weight (w/o Payload) | 501 lbs. | 227 kg |

## OTHER HYBRID II FEATURES

- The Hybrid II Incorporates the Universal Stop Valve System
- The Hybrid II Is Nickel Plated for Less Maintenance
- Works on Both Straight or Curved Track
- Interchangeable Soft, Hard or Pneumatic Tires for Different Terrain
- Hybrid II Incorporates Brakes on Rear Wheels

- Cam-Lock Chassis Legs
- Enclosed King Pin System
- Variable Camera Head
- Variable Chassis Legs
- Compact and Lightweight

*Payload Includes All Items (i.e. Man, Camera, Platform, Turret, Crane Arm, etc.) on Arm.
**Payload Includes All Items (i.e. Man, Camera, Platform, Turret, Crane Arm, etc.) on Base Mount.

*It is advised that the user of Chapman/Leonard equipment check with the manufacturer for the latest updates on *all* equipment.

**Figure 14.56** (continued).

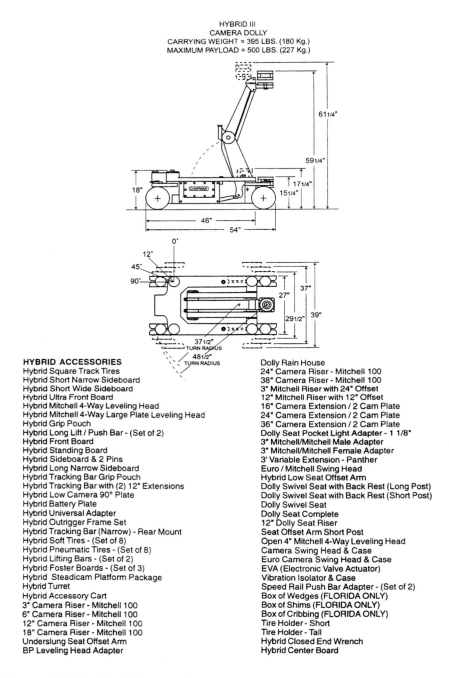

HYBRID III
CAMERA DOLLY
CARRYING WEIGHT = 395 LBS. (180 Kg.)
MAXIMUM PAYLOAD = 500 LBS. (227 Kg.)

**HYBRID ACCESSORIES**
Hybrid Square Track Tires
Hybrid Short Narrow Sideboard
Hybrid Short Wide Sideboard
Hybrid Ultra Front Board
Hybrid Mitchell 4-Way Leveling Head
Hybrid Mitchell 4-Way Large Plate Leveling Head
Hybrid Grip Pouch
Hybrid Long Lift / Push Bar - (Set of 2)
Hybrid Front Board
Hybrid Standing Board
Hybrid Sideboard & 2 Pins
Hybrid Long Narrow Sideboard
Hybrid Tracking Bar Grip Pouch
Hybrid Tracking Bar with (2) 12" Extensions
Hybrid Low Camera 90° Plate
Hybrid Battery Plate
Hybrid Universal Adapter
Hybrid Outrigger Frame Set
Hybrid Tracking Bar (Narrow) - Rear Mount
Hybrid Soft Tires - (Set of 8)
Hybrid Pneumatic Tires - (Set of 8)
Hybrid Lifting Bars - (Set of 2)
Hybrid Foster Boards - (Set of 3)
Hybrid  Steadicam Platform Package
Hybrid Turret
Hybrid Accessory Cart
3" Camera Riser - Mitchell 100
6" Camera Riser - Mitchell 100
12" Camera Riser - Mitchell 100
18" Camera Riser - Mitchell 100
Underslung Seat Offset Arm
BP Leveling Head Adapter

Dolly Rain House
24" Camera Riser - Mitchell 100
38" Camera Riser - Mitchell 100
3" Mitchell Riser with 24" Offset
12" Mitchell Riser with 12" Offset
16" Camera Extension / 2 Cam Plate
24" Camera Extension / 2 Cam Plate
36" Camera Extension / 2 Cam Plate
Dolly Seat Pocket Light Adapter - 1 1/8"
3" Mitchell/Mitchell Male Adapter
3" Mitchell/Mitchell Female Adapter
3' Variable Extension - Panther
Euro / Mitchell Swing Head
Hybrid Low Seat Offset Arm
Dolly Swivel Seat with Back Rest (Long Post)
Dolly Swivel Seat with Back Rest (Short Post)
Dolly Swivel Seat
Dolly Seat Complete
12" Dolly Seat Riser
Seat Offset Arm Short Post
Open 4" Mitchell 4-Way Leveling Head
Camera Swing Head & Case
Euro Camera Swing Head & Case
EVA (Electronic Valve Actuator)
Vibration Isolator & Case
Speed Rail Push Bar Adapter - (Set of 2)
Box of Wedges (FLORIDA ONLY)
Box of Shims (FLORIDA ONLY)
Box of Cribbing (FLORIDA ONLY)
Tire Holder - Short
Tire Holder - Tall
Hybrid Closed End Wrench
Hybrid Center Board

**Figure 14.57**  Hybrid III accessories.

## SPECIFICATIONS

| | | |
|---|---:|---:|
| Maximum Camera Mount Height (with Standard 12" Riser) | 73 in. | 1.9 m |
| Maximum Camera Mount Height (without Risers) | 61 1/4 in. | 1.6 m |
| Minimum Camera Mount Height | 15 1/4 in. | 39 cm |
| Minimum Camera Mount Height with Hybrid Low Camera 90 Degree Plate | 1 in. | 3 cm |
| Vertical Travel | 44 in. | 1.1 m |
| *Maximum Payload | 500 lbs. | 227 kg |
| **Maximum Payload with High Post Kit | 1,900 lbs. | 863 kg |
| Maximum Boom Lifts (Fully Charged) | 5 Lifts | |
| Chassis Maximum Length (Wheels Fully Extended) | 54 in. | 1.4 m |
| Chassis Minimum Length (Wheels Fully Retracted) | 46 in. | 1.2 m |
| Minimum Chassis Height for Transportation | 18 in. | 46 cm |
| Chassis Variable Widths - Legs in | 27 in. | 69 cm |
| Chassis Variable Widths - Legs at 12 Degree Track Position | 29 1/2 in. | 75 cm |
| Chassis Variable Widths - Legs at 45 Degrees | 37 in. | 89 cm |
| Chassis Variable Widths - Legs at 90 Degrees | 39 in. | 99 cm |
| Steering Post Height | 36 in. | 91 cm |
| Minimum Turn Radius | 37 1/2 in. | 95 cm |
| Accumulator Charging Time (110 A.C. and D.C.) | under 60 sec. | |
| Accumulator Charging Time (Hand Pump) | 2 1/2 min. | |
| Minimum Door Width Hybrid Can Be Carried Through | 18 in. | 46 cm |
| Carrying Weight | 395 lbs. | 180 kg |
| Standard Operational Weight (w/o Payload) | 463 lbs. | 210 kg |
| Hybrid w/ High Post Kit Operational Weight (w/o Payload) | 501 lbs. | 227 kg |

## OTHER HYBRID III FEATURES

- Hybrid III Incorporates the Universal Stop Valve System
- Hybrid III has a Built-in Automatic Hydraulic Oil Heating System
- Interchangeable Soft, Hard or Pneumatic Tires for Different Terrain
- Works on Both Straight or Curved Track
- Hybrid III Is Nickel Plated
- Hybrid III Incorporates Brakes on Rear Wheels

- Cam-Lock Chassis Legs
- Compact and Lightweight
- Enclosed King Pin System
- Variable Camera Head Mount
- Variable Chassis Legs

*Payload Includes All Items (i.e. Man, Camera, Platform, Turret, Crane Arm, etc.) on Arm.
**Payload Includes All Items (i.e. Man, Camera, Platform, Turret, Crane Arm, etc.) on Base Mount.

*It is advised that the user of Chapman/Leonard equipment check with the manufacturer for the latest updates on *all* equipment.

**Figure 14.57** (continued) Hybrid III specifications and features.

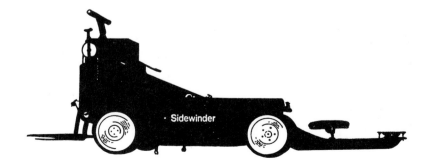

**Figure 14.58** Sidewinder.

## SPECIFICATIONS

| | | |
|---|---|---|
| Lens Height (Turret and Camera) | 9 ft. | 2.7 m |
| Base Mount Height | 5 ft. 6 in. | 1.7 m |
| Vertical Travel | 5 ft. | 1.5 m |
| Minimum Lens Height (Extension Setup) with Gear Head and Leveling Device | 22 in. | 56 cm |
| Minimum Lens Height (without Gear Head) Adapter Available | 12 in. | 30 cm |
| Maximum Lens Height with Sidewinder Setup (Leveling Head Only) | 7 ft. 6 in. | 2.3 m |
| Low Lens Height with Same Setup | 30 in. | 76 cm |
| *Maximum Payload | 900 lbs. | 409 kg |
| Maximum Horizontal Reach (with Extension) | 38 in. | 97 cm |
| Chassis Length | 64 in. | 1.6 m |
| Minimum Chassis Height | 41 in. | 1 m |
| Chassis Width (with Special or Pneumatic Tires) | 38 3/4 in. | 98 cm |
| Tread | 26 in. | 66 cm |
| Wheel Base | 42 in. | 1.1 m |
| Normal Operating Weight | 1,450 lbs. | 659 kg |

## OTHER SIDEWINDER FEATURES

- Operates on 8 Wheels (Power Delivered to 4)
- Dual Rocker Suspension (8 Wheels to 3 Point Suspension)
- Operates in Both Crab and Conventional Steering
- Selection of Turrets, Risers, Extensions and Aluminum Track
- On a Full Charge, Batteries Allow 24 Hours Use
- Built-In Battery Charger (110v/220v)
- Hydraulic Floor Locks
- Dual Steering Control
- Automatic Valve Control
- Silent Operation

*Payload Includes All Items (i.e. Man, Camera, Platform, Turret, Crane Arm, etc.) on Base Mount.

*It is advised that the user of Chapman/Leonard equipment check with the manufacturer for the latest updates on *all* equipment.

**Figure 14.58** (continued) Sidewinder features and specifications.

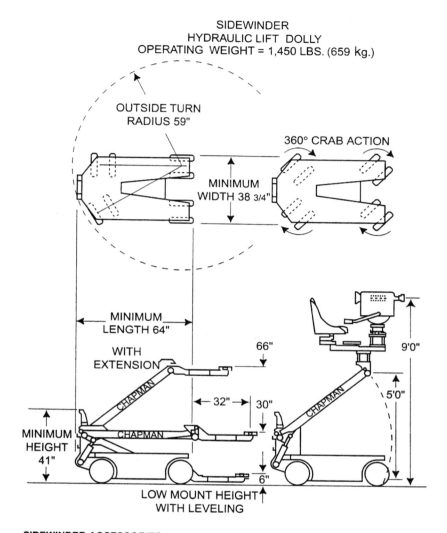

SIDEWINDER
HYDRAULIC LIFT DOLLY
OPERATING WEIGHT = 1,450 LBS. (659 kg.)

OUTSIDE TURN
RADIUS 59"

360° CRAB ACTION

MINIMUM
WIDTH 38 3/4"

MINIMUM
LENGTH 64"

WITH
EXTENSION

66"

9'0"

32" 30"

5'0"

MINIMUM
HEIGHT
41"

CHAPMAN

CHAPMAN

CHAPMAN

6"

LOW MOUNT HEIGHT
WITH LEVELING

**SIDEWINDER ACCESSORIES**
6" Mitchell Riser
Sidewinder Sideboard
Sidewinder Pneumatic Tires - (Set of 8)
Sidewinder Solid Tires - (Set of 8)
Sidewinder Extension Arm - 2'
Rear 14" Seat Arm w/Seat - Sidewinder
Sidewinder Standing Board

*It is advised that the user of Chapman/Leonard equipment check with the manufacturer for the latest updates on
*all* equipment.

**Figure 14.58**   (continued) Sidewinder accessories.

# Precision Cadillac Track

See Figure 15.1.

---

## Chapman Lencin

See Figure 15.2.

# Precision Cadillac Track

Precision Cadillac Track is extruded from structural marine alloy. Rigidity is 10 times greater than conventional tube track. Precision Cadillac Track is available in 2¹/₂" and 3" heights. Having a twin-pin joining system, it offers zero gap and deflection, thus giving you the smoothest tracking shots ever, particularly with long lenses.

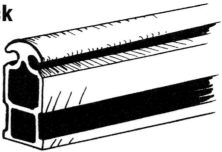

*Specifications*

| | Folding Length | |
| --- | --- | --- |
| | **Feet** | **Meters** |
| 3' Straight | 5'1" | 1.5 |
| 5' Straight | 7'2" | 2.1 |
| 8' Straight | 10'2" | 3.0 |
| 10' Straight | 12'2" | 3.7 |
| 12' Straight | 14'2" | 4.3 |
| 30 Curve | 6'6" | 1.98 |
| 2-5' Sections = | | |
| 20' Dia. Circlei | | |

| | Track Width | |
| --- | --- | --- |
| | **Feet** | **Meters** |
| With Standard Sleepers | 24¹/₂" | 0.6 |
| With Expandable Sleepers | | |
| 1st Position | 24¹/₂" | 0.6 |
| 2nd Position | 28" | 0.7 |
| 3rd Position | 34¹/₂" | 0.8 |

Precision Cadillac Track offers unique custom curves, folding 30 degree curves and non-folding 45 degree curves. It is a low profile, multi-wheel dolly and crane track that is compatible with Fisher and standard wheel applications. This large curve track is ideal for shooting car commercials and music videos.

Precision Cadillac Track is lower, lighter, stronger and more cost effective than other track.

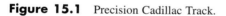

**Figure 15.1**  Precision Cadillac Track.

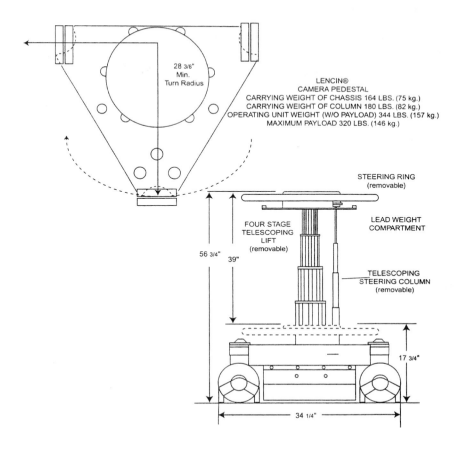

**LENCIN ACCESSORIES**
Lencin Seat Offset with Wheel
Lencin Wood Crate (Shipping & Storage)
Lencin Soft Tires - (Set of 6)
Lencin Battery Tray
Lencin Weather Cover
Pedestal Mitchell Adapter - 3"
Pedestal Mitchell Adapter - 6"
Pedestal Nitrogen Bottle-Large

Pedestal Mini Monitor Bracket
Pedestal 18" Column Riser
Pedestal Center Post Insert
Pedestal Column Star Base
Pedestal Pressure Regulator & Hose
Pedestal Nitrogen Bottle
Pedestal Small Steering Ring
Pedestal 4 Bolt 6" Riser
Pedestal Nitrogen Bottle Kit

**Figure 15.2** Lencin accessories.

**SPECIFICATIONS**

| | | |
|---|---|---|
| Minimum Camera Mount Height | 17 3/4 in. | 45 cm |
| Maximum Camera Mount Height | 56 3/4 in. | 1.4 m |
| Vertical Travel | 39 in. | 1 m |
| *Payload Range | 20-320 lbs. | 9 - 146 kg |
| **Maximum Payload with Center Post Insert | 1,100 lbs. | 500 kg |
| Steering Ring Diameter | 30 in. | 76 cm |
| Number of Stages in Column | 4 | |
| Carrying Weight of Chassis | 164 lbs. | 75 kg |
| Carrying Weight of Column | 180 lbs. | 82 kg |
| Total Weight | 344 lbs. | 157 kg |
| Operational Weight of Unit w/ Center Post Insert (w/o Payload) | 245 lbs. | 111 kg |
| Minimum Chassis Width | 34 1/4 in. | 87 cm |
| Minimum Turning Radius | 28 3/8 in. | 72 cm |
| Column Diameter (when Removed) | 16 5/8 in. | 42 cm |
| Chassis Minimum Height (without Column) | 14 1/2 in. | 37 cm |
| Column Minimum Height (when Removed) | 16 1/2 in. | 42 cm |

**OTHER LENCIN FEATURES**

- Open Access to Wheels for Maintenance
- Lock Column at Any Height (Optional Cam Lock)
- Special Performance Enhancing Tire Compound
- Can Be Used Indoors and Outdoors
- Track Ready, for Use on Straight Track Only
- Incorporates Both Crab and Conventional Steering
- Low Maintenance
- 22 Inch Steering Ring Available

- Removable Column
- Securable to Floors or Platforms
- Interchangeable Wheels-Hard or Soft
- Easily Adjusted Cable Guards
- Easily Replaced Steering Column
- Virtually Silent Operation
- LENCIN Has A Wheel Brake

*Payload Includes All Items (i.e. Man, Camera, Platform, Turret, Crane Arm, etc.) on Column.

**Payload Includes All Items (i.e. Man, Camera, Platform, Turret, Crane Arm, etc.) on Base Mount.

*It is advised that the user of Chapman/Leonard equipment check with the manufacturer for the latest updates on *all* equipment.

**Figure 15.2** (continued) Lencin specifications and features.

# Fluid and Remote Heads

*Fluid heads* in cameras give hands-on control. They are designed with springs and lubricants that give the camera operator a pan and tilt movement. They usually have adjustment levers or collars that can restrict or lessen the friction of each head—sort of like an adjustable power steering unit. Each operator will prefer a certain "feel" that enhances his or her movement of the camera. There are several designs out there in the film world; I will show you some of what I see used daily.

*Remote heads* are electronic heads that attach to cranes, dollies, or rigs. They are fast becoming preferred over having a person riding a crane and operating the camera. They have control wheels, a joystick, or even a fluid-type head with sensors on it to operate the remotely controlled head. They are sometimes located up to 100 feet from the operator. On a set, I am often asked what remote heads I want to use because the production personnel want to place an order to hold a particular piece of equipment. I give them my standard answer: "I'll tell you as soon as I talk to the DP and find out what camera they are using and how high a crane or jib is supposed to be." The weight of each camera is usually not the main factor but is one of several factors. Another factor is the length (or how high the camera is supposed to go). The longer the arm of a crane, the less weight can be put on the receiving end. You have to know the weight of the remote head and the weight of the camera. Always use your worst-case scenario (*e.g.*, the heaviest the remote might be rigged with extensions; the heaviest the camera will be with a zoom and the largest _lm magazine). Plan for the worst and then design for the best.

Some cranes may take a lot of weight, but they must have added cable strength. This is wonderful for safety, but it makes the crane wider, which could be a problem in a tight spot. You may not get the desired movement on the crane shot. The remote head may be the type that can be reduced in overall size; by using certain remotes, you can squeeze down the size (adjust the unit to a smaller size) for use on a shot; for example, if you want a high shot on a set that drops as the actor approaches a door, opens it, and walks in, then the remote head used could actually enter an adjoining living room window and go inside with the actor.

So now you can see why there is no one easy answer to the question of which remote heads should be used. First, you have to know what shots are desired. After you have planned out the shot, you now have to find out what equipment is available. Sometimes shots may have to be reconsidered because of the unavailability of equipment or funds. I have worked with production companies when, through no fault of their own, equipment suddenly does not show up, and then they are told:

"Oh, by the way, we do not have that in stock." As the grip in this situation, you have to ensure that the substituted equipment will work and is safe.

## Flight Head

See Figures 16.1 and Figure 16.2.

## Hot Head

See Figure 16.3.

## Kenworthy Snorkel Camera Systems (Remote)

The Kenworthy Snorkel (Figure 16.4) is the perfect device to maneuver. It is a special designed tube with the mirror attached to one end. It was designed to travel through close areas. For example, suppose you are shooting a fast-food commercial. After an extreme closeup of a hamburger, you want to then rotate to a huge cup in frame, then to the fries. The snorkel will help you film shoot in such tight areas. The downside is it's extremely heavy weight (about 350 pounds). You will probably need to mount it on a small stage crane; whatever you mount it on, make sure when you first set up the Snorkel system that the unit can handle the weight. Fortunately, the Snorkel system always comes with an able technician. Not only does the snorkel get into tiny places, but it also delivers its own look (almost a three-dimensional effect) for film, I am told. Other pieces of equipment are available, but this one is a major problem solver.

## Libers III

See Figure 16.5.

## Oppenheimer Spin-Axis 360 Head (Remote)

The Spin-Axis 360 Head (Figure 16.6) is the all-new motorized third-axis system from Oppenheimer Camera Products of Seattle. The system is lightweight, exceptionally robust, and built to a standard that allows it to carry virtually any modern 35-mm, 16-mm, or video camera.

## FLIGHT HEAD w/ AUTO-ROBOT CRANE
### (Four Axis Gyrostabilized System)

**SPECIFICATIONS**          (Flight Head and Auto-Robot Crane - Item # 6020)

| | | |
|---|---|---|
| Unit Weight | 580 lb. | 263.6 kg |
| (Max. Configuration with Arri 453 camera and 70 mm Zoom Lens | | |
| FIZ Wireless Control and Two Batteries) | | |
| Shipping Weight for Complete System | 1500 lb. | 681.8 kg |
| Maximum Payload for Auto-Robot Crane | 120 lb. | 54.5 kg |
| Maximum Speed Approved for Base Vehicle | 65 mph | 100 kph |
| Angular Speed of Boom Control | 25 deg./sec. | |
| Power (10 hour job w/ 216 Gel Batteries) | 30 v, 7 A DC | |
| Setup Time | Approximately 1-2 Hours | |

### OTHER FLIGHT HEAD / AUTO=ROBOT FEATURES

- The Flight Head Can Be Mounted on Lenny Arms, Dollies, Super Nova & Apollo Mobile Cranes, or Any Standard Mitchell Mount.
- The Flight Head Can Be Mounted on the Auto-Robot Crane or Shock Absorber System. This Setup Can Also Be Mounted on Cars, Boats and Cranes.
- The Flight Head Offers Automatic Backpan Compensation to Simplify Tough Following Shots.
- The Flight Head Has a Unique Ability to Dutch, Pan, Tilt and Zoom with a Single Operator. The Auto-Robot Crane Allows Remote Control of the Crane Arm.
- Gyrostabilized Head Corrects the Horizon, while Allowing Motion of the Head's Base.
- Operates with Hand Wheels or Joy Stick.
- Can Be Used with a Variety of Motion Picture and Video Cameras, Including Panavision 65 mm Cameras
- Trained Tech Necessary with Every Rental

*It is advised that the user of Chapman/Leonard equipment check with the manufacturer for the latest updates on *all* equipment.

**Figure 16.1a**   Flight Head specifications and features (Chapman/Leonard Equipment).

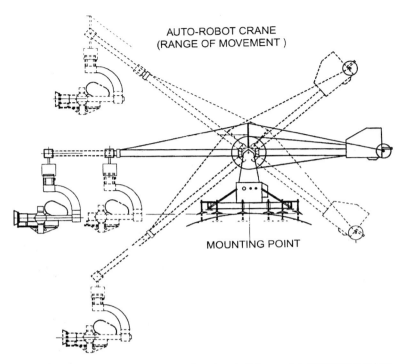

AUTO-ROBOT CRANE
(RANGE OF MOVEMENT )

MOUNTING POINT

*It is advised that the user of Chapman/Leonard equipment check with the manufacturer for the latest updates on *all* equipment.

**Figure 16.1b** Flight Head—range of movement.

FLIGHT HEAD and AUTO-ROBOT CRANE
(Four Axis Gyrostabilized System)
Maximum Payload: 120 lb. (54.5 kg)
Unit Weight 1,500 lb. (681.8 kg)

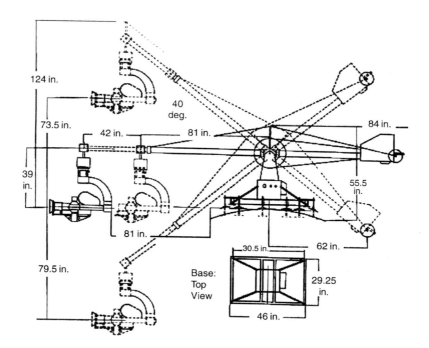

124 in.

40 deg.

73.5 in.

42 in.        81 in.

84 in.

39 in.

55.5 in.

81 in.

79.5 in.

Base: Top View

30.5 in.    62 in.

29.25 in.

46 in.

**FLIGHT HEAD AND AUTO-ROBOT STANDARD PACKAGE AND ACCESSORIES**
Joystick (Pan, Tilt, Dutch and Zoom) and Wheels Control (Pan and Tilt)
2 Monitors
Preston FiZ Lens System
8 Batteries (10 Hours) - For Flight Head
4 Batteries (20 Hours) - For Auto Robot
Cables (up to 130 ft.)
3 Chargers -110 ac
Battery Maintainer
Padding Kit
Straps
Transport Cart
Shipping Cases
Wireless Intercom w/3 Headsets
Wireless Intercom Headset (w/ Item #8200)
Flight Head Shock Absorber - 3 Axis
Chapman/Leonard Battery Pack
Chapman/Leonard Battery Charger - 110v
Chapman/Leonard Battery Charger - 220v

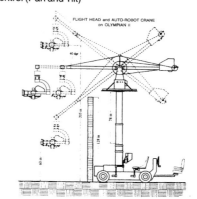

FLIGHT HEAD and AUTO-ROBOT CRANE
on OLYMPIAN II

*It is advised that the user of Chapman/Leonard equipment check with the manufacturer for the latest updates on *all* equipment.

**Figure 16.1c** Flight Head.

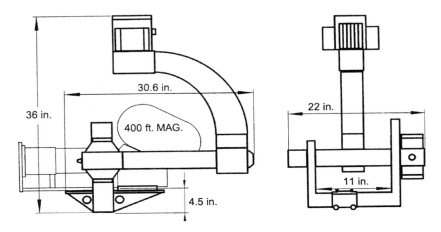

FLIGHT HEAD
(Three Axis Gyrostabilized Remote Head)
Maximum Payload: 66 lb. (30 kg)

**FLIGHT HEAD SYSTEM STANDARD PACKAGE AND ACCESSORIES**
Joystick (Pan, Tilt, Dutch and Zoom) and Wheels Control (Pan and Tilt)
2 Monitors
Preston FiZ Lens System
8 Batteries (10 Hours)
Cables (up to 130 ft.)
3 Chargers -110 ac
Battery Maintainer
Shipping Cases
Wireless Intercom w/3 Headsets
Wireless Intercom Headset (w/ Item #8200)
Flight Head Shock Absorber - 3 Axis
Chapman/Leonard Battery Pack
Chapman/Leonard Battery Charger - 110v
Chapman/Leonard Battery Charger - 220v

*It is advised that the user of Chapman/Leonard equipment check with the manufacturer for the latest updates on
all equipment.

**Figure 16.2** Flight Head.

## FLIGHT HEAD
*(Third Axis Gyrostabilized Remote Head)*

### SPECIFICATIONS

| | | |
|---|---|---|
| Height | 36 in. | 91.5 cm |
| Width | 22 in. | 55.9 cm |
| Depth | 30.6 in. | 77.7 cm |
| Weight | 55 lbs. | 25 kg |
| Shipping Weight for Complete System | 850 lbs. | 386.4 kg |
| Payload Capacity (Recommended) | 66 lbs. | 30 kg |
| Range of Movement: | | |
| Pan | Unlimited | |
| Tilt | 75º Positive to 165º Negative | |
| Roll | 95º Left or Right | |
| Maximum Usable Focal Length | 250 mm | |
| Mounting Base | Standard Mitchell | |
| Dynamic Stabilization Error | No more than 3 Arc Minutes | |
| Maximum Angular Speed | 120 Degrees / sec. | |
| Maximum Angular Acceleration | 120 Degrees / sec. / sec. | |
| Regular Current | 2.5 amps | |
| Operating Temperature | 14º F to 122º F | |
| Power Supply: | | |
| AC | 110 / 220 v     50 - 60 Hz | |
| DC | 22 - 32 v | |
| Regular Current | 2.5 amps | |
| Operating Temperature | 14º F to 122º F | |
| Setup Time | Approximately 1 Hour | |

### OTHER FLIGHT HEAD FEATURES

- The Flight Head Can Be Mounted on Lenny Arms, Super Nova & Apollo Mobile Cranes, for Increased Versatility in Camera Movement, Especially with Dual Axis Movements.
- The Flight Head Can Be Mounted on the Auto-Robot Crane. This Setup Can Be Mounted on Cars, Boats and Cranes.
- The Flight Head Offers Automatic Backpan Compensation to Simplify Tough Following Shots.
- The Flight Head Has a Unique Ability to Dutch, Pan and Tilt with a Single Operator. The Auto-Robot Crane Allows Remote Control of the Crane Arm.
- Gyrostabilized Head Corrects the Horizon, while Allowing Motion of the Head's Base.
- Operates with Gear Head or Joy Stick.

**Figure 16.2** (continued) Flight Head specifications.

# HOT HEAD
## REMOTE CAMERA
### (with Preston System)

**SPECIFICATIONS**

|  | Hot Head S/NTS | | HD Hot Head | |
|---|---|---|---|---|
| Height | 2 ft. 3 in. | 68 cm | 2 ft. 3 in. | 68 cm |
| Width | 1 ft. 3 in. | 37 cm | 1 ft. 7 in. | 47 cm |
| Depth | 11 in. | 27 cm | 11 in. | 27 cm |
| Weight | 44 lbs. | 20 kg | 48 lbs. | 22 kg |
| Total Shipping Weight | 374 lbs. | 170 kg | 410 lbs. | 186 kg |
| Load Capacity | 154 lbs. | 70 kg | 176 lbs. | 80 kg |
| Voltage | 24v DC | | 24v DC | |
| Maximum Speed | 2.5 sec. per 360° | | 2.5 sec. per 360° | |
| Minimum Speed | 17 min. per 360° | | 17 min. per 360° | |
| Number of Slip Rings | 34 | | 34 | |
| Number of Limit Switches | 2 Tilt & Pan | | 2 Tilt & Pan | |
| Riser Size | 4.38 in. | 11.11 cm | 4.38 in. | 11.11 cm |
| Riser Size | 8.63 in. | 21.9 cm | 8.63 in. | 21.9 cm |

**OTHER HOT HEAD FEATURES**

- Rotates 360° with Most Types of Film and Video Cameras
- Can Be Used with Film Magazines up to 1,000 ft. in Size
- Rotates a Continuous 360° Pan and Tilt with Lenses up to 10:1
- Smooth Pan and Tilt with Your Choice of Handwheel or Joystick
- Joystick Control System Offers One Man Pan/Tilt, Zoom and Focus
- F.I.Z. Controls Come with Witness Camera, Viewing Monitors and Mobile Control Cart
- Works on All Types of Crane Arms
- Smooth, Silent Performance
- Remote Head Technician Available upon Request
- Can Be Used with a Variety of Motion Picture and Video Cameras

© 2000, Chapman / Leonard Studio Eq., Inc.

*It is advised that the user of Chapman/Leonard equipment check with the manufacturer for the latest updates on *all* equipment.

**Figure 16.3** Hot Head specifications.

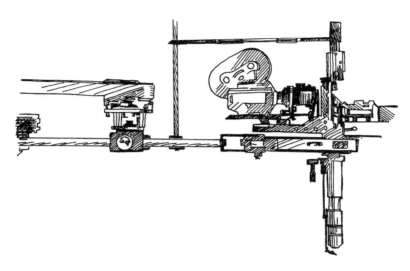

**Figure 16.4** Ken Worthy Snorkel.

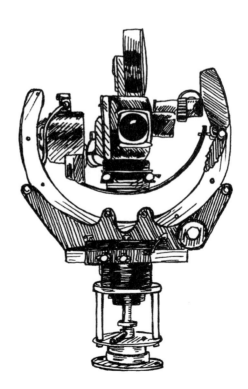

**Figure 16.5a** Liber III Head.

**Figure 16.5b** Libra III 3 axis control system.

**Figure 16.6** Oppenheimer Spin-Axis 360° Head Remote.

## Pearson Fluid Head

See Figures 16.7 and 16.8.

## Power Pod

See Figure 16.9.

## Weaver/Steadman Fluid Head

See Figure 16.10.

## Weaver/Steadman's "ds Remote™"

See Figure 16.11.

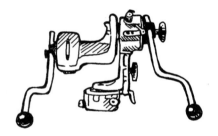

**Figure 16.7**   Pearson Fluid Head.

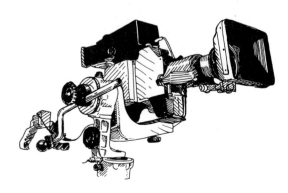

**Figure 16.8**   Pearson Fluid Head.

## *POWER POD*
### *(REMOTE CAMERA SYSTEM)*

### SPECIFICATIONS

| | | |
|---|---:|---:|
| Height (w/o Riser) | 1 ft. 7 in. | 48 cm |
| Width | 11 1/4 in. | 29 cm |
| Depth | 1 ft. 4 3/4 in. | 43 cm |
| Weight | 40 lbs. | 18 kg |
| Shipping Weight w/ Case for Complete System | 492 lbs. | 224 kg |
| Load Capacity (Recommended) | 60 lbs. | 27 kg |
| Voltage | 12, 24 & 30 v DC | |
| Maximum Speed | 3 sec per 360° | |
| Minimum Speed | 16 min. per 360° | |
| Number of Slip Rings | 4 rated at 9 amps | |
| Number of Limit Switches | 1 Tilt Access | |
| Riser Size | 300 mm & 150 mm | |

### OTHER POWER POD FEATURES

- Rotates 360° with Most Types of Film and Video Cameras
- Works on All Types of Arms
- Can Be Used with Film Magazines up to 1000 ft. in Size
- Smooth, Silent Performance
- Can Rotate a Continuous 360° Pan and Tilt with Lenses up to 10:1
- Smooth Pan and Tilt with Your Choice of Handwheels or Joystick
- F.I.Z. Controls Come with Witness Camera and Viewing Controls
- Trained Technician Available upon Request
- Can Be Used with Arriflex and Panavision 65mm Cameras

*It is advised that the user of Chapman/Leonard equipment check with the manufacturer for the latest updates on *all* equipment.

**Figure 16.9**   Power Pod specifications.

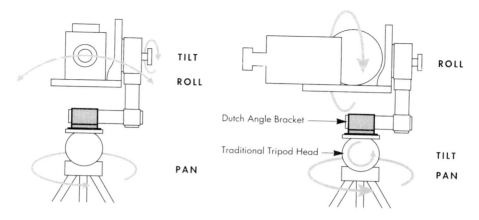

**Figure 16.10a** Weaver/Steadman Head.

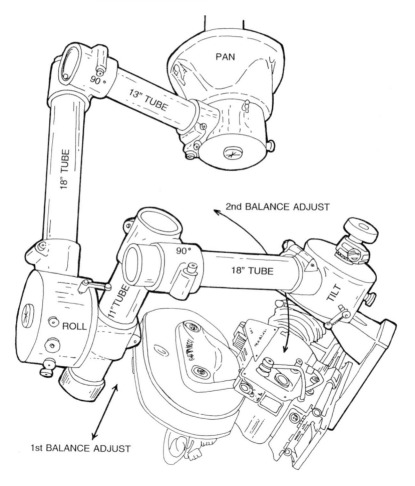

**Figure 16.10b** Weaver/Steadman Head.

## WEAVER STEADMAN'S "ds Remote™"
### CAMERA SYSTEM
### (with Preston System)

### SPECIFICATIONS

| | | |
|---|---:|---:|
| 2-Axis Height (Minimum Configuration) | 2 ft. 1 in. | 63.5 cm |
| 2-Axis Width (Minimum Configuration) | 1 ft. 9 in. | 53.4 cm |
| 2-Axis Depth (Minimum Configuration) | 1 ft. | 30.5 cm |
| 3-Axis Height (Minimum Configuration) | 2 ft. 8 in. | 81.3 cm |
| 3-Axis Width (Minimum Configuration) | 2 ft. 2 in. | 66 cm |
| 3-Axis Depth (Minimum Configuration) | 2 ft. 1 in. | 63.5 cm |
| 2-Axis Weight | 61 lb. | 27.7 kg |
| 3-Axis Weight | 93 lb. | 42.3 kg |
| 2-Axis Payload Capacity (Recommended) | 120 lb. | 54.5 kg |
| 3-Axis Payload Capacity (Recommended) | 90 lb. | 40.9 kg |
| Electronic Limit Switches (Both Directions) | Pan, Tilt & Roll | |
| Pan, Tilt & Roll Movement | 360° Continuous | |
| Speed Range (Pan, Tilt & Roll) | 3 sec. to 24 hr. | |
| Number of Slip Rings | 120 | |
| Mounting Base | Standard Mitchell | |
| Outputs at Camera | BNC 75 Ohm (x3) | |
| | 12 volts @ 2 amps for video (x2) | |
| | 12 or 15 volts @ 10 amps peak (x2) | |
| | 24 or 30 volts @ 15 amps peak | |
| Lens Control Systems | Preston Fi+Z and Arri Lens Control | |
| Outputs Spare for Client's Use | Two Channels 2 amps | |
| | Five Channels 2 amps | |
| Link between Head & Controls (Single Cable Capability) | 50 ft. - 800 ft | 15 m - 244 m |
| Supply Voltage Range | 48 volts DC, 90-240 volts AC | |
| Power for Head @ 48 volts DC | 1.6 - 10 amps Peak | |

### OTHER WEAVER STEADMAN FEATURES

- Rotates 360° with All Common Film & Video Camera
- Can Be Used with All Common 1,000 ft. Film Magazines
- F.I.Z. Come with Witness Camera & Viewing Controls
- Can Be Used with Arriflex & Panavision 65mm Cameras
- Open Side Chassis for Tight Camera Positioning
- User Friendly, Quick, Simple Setup and Arrangement
- Modular Components for Optimal Size & Camera Placement
- Can Rotate a Continuous 360° Pan, Tilt and Roll with Lenses up to 10:1
- Smooth Pan, Tilt and Roll with Your Choice of Handwheels or Fluid PTR

- Pan, Tilt & Roll Movement in Any Direction
- Trained Tech Available upon Request
- Works on All Types of Arms
- Smooth, Silent Performance
- Powers Arriflex 435 at High Speed
- Instant Record and Playback

*It is advised that the user of Chapman/Leonard equipment check with the manufacturer for the latest updates on *all* equipment.

**Figure 16.11** Weaver/Steadman's "ds Remote" specifications.

# General Tricks of the Trade

**T.O.T.**
Most equipment trucks are usually no higher than 12 ft., 6 in., and most telephone or electrical wires are no lower than 13 ft., 6 in., but this is not written in stone: "Measure it safely."

**T.O.T.**
Listen like a field mouse, but be ready to spring like a leopard when needed. This proves two things: (1) You are paying attention (good for points), and (2) you can anticipate what is needed (better for call-backs). Trust me on this. This practice works for any profession.

**T.O.T.**
Play the sag load (that is, the weight of the light unit that is being rigged) when you rig. Add a little extra pull, then let it sag into place.

**T.O.T.**
Sometimes the key grip is considered the unofficial safety expert.

**T.O.T.**
Before removing any set wall, check to see if the seams have been cut or if there are any lights or braces on it.

**T.O.T.**

When hanging a painted backing or translight on a stage, you may not have any place to tie off the grommets from the sides. Drop a rope from the perms about 3 feet from each side of the backing or translight, then nail the rope to the floor. Make the rope as tight as possible. Now tie off the backing sides from the grommets to the rope.

**T.O.T.**

Put a Styrofoam cup over a sprinkler head in a building to deflect heat from a lamp under it.

**T.O.T.**

Use P-tons (little spikes with rings or holes on them) in cracks in asphalt for tie-offs.

**T.O.T.**

Never knock, talk down, or disrespect any crew member you are working with or have worked with. You may have to work with them again.

**T.O.T.**

*Never* safety, rig, or tie off any equipment to a fire sprinkler line.

**T.O.T.**

I recommend that you get yourself a personal headset. There are two good types. One is like what the Secret Service uses; the headset wraps over one ear with a clip-on mic to attach to your shirt. The other type has an over-the-ear headset with a mic attached.

**T.O.T.**

Always keep your eye on the key grip and the director of photography. Learn to listen for their voices in the middle of a crowd. Try to remember what style of lighting they do and anticipate if a flag or scrim is needed.

**T.O.T.**

A stand extension works in place of a short rod (norms pin).

**T.O.T.**

Use sunglasses if no contrast filter is around to check for clouds. Hold the sunglasses at arm length and look at the *reflection only* of the sky and the clouds in the shaded glass. Never look directly at the sun!

**T.O.T.**

Don't move, and don't talk to or make eye contact with actors, during filming.

**T.O.T.**

Always carry ear plugs in your personal bag.

**T.O.T.**

Ensure that all electrical open-ends are taped off. An electrician will or should do it.

**T.O.T.**

P.O.V. (point of view) is what a person sees from his or her perspective.

**T.O.T.**

When you are working on a set, I suggest that you wear dark clothing to avoid reflection problems.

**T.O.T.**

Cut pieces of 1/8-in. plywood to line the sides and bottom inside of a milk crate. This will prevent equipment from protruding and getting jammed.

**T.O.T.**

Know the placement of all fire extinguishers on the set.

**T.O.T.**

Safety all objects (lights, clamps, etc.) so they will swing away from the center of the set toward the set wall if they fall. This will keep an object, we hope, from hitting the talent.

**T.O.T.**

Wrap all rope and cable in a clockwise direction. This way the next technician will wrap it in the same direction, preventing tangles. Wrap rope in a 2-ft. loop and cable in a 14- to 16-in. loop—about the size of a basketball hoop.

**T.O.T.**

Put a safety rope on all lights that are hung.

**T.O.T.**

Know all your exits on stage.

**T.O.T.**

To measure approximately how much time is left before the sun sinks behind a mountain or building at sunset, extend your hand and arm toward the sun, place your lower fingers on top of the horizon or mountain range, then count the number of fingers between the horizon line and the bottom of the sun. The thickness of each finger represents about 10 to 15 minutes. It's just a ball-park guess, but this really works. Be sure to wear your shades! Also, do not do this if your eyes are sensitive. *Remember:* Never look directly at the sun.

**T.O.T.**

When you use sailboats (weighted base with a telegraphic tube with a pulley and rope attached to the upper end) for backings (and sometime translights), you should use a rope to tie the center off high in the perms to keep it from sagging.

**T.O.T.**

Use whatever is available to get the shot. I once needed a long dolly shot in front of a peru (a small swamp boat) in the Louisiana swamps. The actor would be standing in his small craft and using a long rod to push himself off the swamp floor. It was supposed to be a slow-paced movement. The director wanted a long, slow move down the center of the bayou. A boat would rock, creating unwanted camera action; instead, I used two floating platforms that were square and flat-bottomed. I placed the camera, the cameraperson, and the camera assistant on the camera platform, which was tied to the front platform where the excess camera gear and two grips were. A 600-foot rope was tied to a tree down the bayou. I pulled the rope, setting the pace asked for by the cameraperson. I am not telling you this to show how clever I am, but I am telling you this to illustrate that film making is never a perfect world.

**T.O.T.**

When you measure doors to determine if they are wide enough to pass equipment through, be sure to watch out for the hinged side of the door, which makes the doorway smaller than it at first appears. For example, Bank of America's 70-in. double-wide door may actually be only 54 in. when it is open. Always measure a door in the position it will be in when you are going through it.

**T.O.T.**

Use a can of Dust-Off® to blow away chalk lines.

**T.O.T.**

Here is something for you to chew on as a grip: "Say what you mean, mean what you say, but do not say anything mean." Mom was right, if you do not have anything nice to say, do not say anything. I can promise you this: If and when you do let your mouth run, it *will* come back to bite you in your behind in this or any business.

**T.O.T.**

To *pan* means to rotate the camera right or left.

**T.O.T.**

The yellow or red lines 4 feet from stage walls on stage indicate the "no block zone." This zone must be left free and clear in case the stage fills with thick black smoke, preventing people from seeing where they are or how to get out. The 4-foot "no block zone" allows people to make their way to any wall and feel their way to an emergency exit.

**T.O.T.**

Use a rubber-coated lead in a swimming pool. It will not mark the gunite (plaster). It can be rented from the Fisher Dolly Company or a crane company.

# Glossary

Here are some terms or words that you might hear daily in the course of your stay in the film and television business. A few of these words may be exclusive to the grip department, but for the sake of understanding the overall flavor of a working set, you should be aware of some general words that are used almost daily. Here is an example: You are a grip who was asked to work the *sticks* for the camera department. The AD yells "tail slate!" or your may hear "grab a Gary Coleman, with a postage stamp, and put an ear on the third zip light" or "lamp right next to the egg crate, then drop some beach on that hog trough before they pull the buck." "Say what?" you ask.

ABBY SINGER  The shot before the last shot.

AGE  This technique is used to make a new object, such as a mailbox, look older and to create a used look, such as old clothes, a sign, etc.

AMBIANCE  Sound recorded in the area where the filming was done. This "quiet" sound is added to set the mood of a scene.

BABY  A 1000-watt lamp.

BACK TO ONE  Go to your start position.

BACKING  A scenic piece behind a set window or open door; also called a *drop*. A photographed or painted canvas background used on movie or video sets seen outside windows or doors.

BAIL  The "U"-shaped metal arm that a movie lamp sits on. The bottom of the "U" has either a male pin or female receiver for attachment to a stand or hanger device.

BASE CAMP  The place where all the production vehicles are located—sort of like a mobile headquarters.

BASTARD SIDE  A term used for stage right.

BATTENS  Two pieces of wood (1 × 3 in. or 2 × 4 in.) attached to the top of a cloth drop or backing in a sandwich configuration to hold it up.

BEACH  Slang for a sandbag.

BEAVER BOARD  Usually a eighth apple box with a baby plate nailed onto it used for placing a lamp at low angles; also called a *skid plate*.

BECKY  A fixed-length mount bracket much like a trombone. The wall attachment has feet that are the only things that adjust. The receiver is a fixed height (about a foot down using the bottom pin).

BELLY LINES  Ropes strung (usually about 10 feet apart) under a large silk, grifflon, or black.

BLACKS   Drapes used to hide or mask areas not to be shown on film or stage.

BLOCK AND FALL   A rope-and-pulley system that allows a heavy object to be lifted with less pulling force.

BLOCKING   A rehearsal for actors and camera movement.

BOOGIE WHEELS   Wheels that do not usually come standard with a dolly. They are used to adapt a dolly to a specialty track, such as a pipe dolly, sled dolly, or tube track. Several types or sets of boogie wheels are available.

BOOTIES   Surgical-style paper shoes worn over street shoes when walking on a dry painted surface to prevent mars or scuffs.

BOSS PLATE   A metal plate attached to the stage floor of a set to hold a set wall or scenery in place.

BOTTOMER   Flag off or block unwanted light from the bottom of a light source; also called a *bottom shelf*.

BOUNCE   Light that has been redirected first. It is directed onto foam core, a show card, or any other surface and redirected (bounced) onto the subject. (See *fill light*.)

BRANCH-A-LORIS   A limb or branch from a tree placed in front of a light to create a pattern.

BROWNIE   Nickname for the camera.

BRUTE   A carbon arc lamp that runs on 225 amps.

B-TEAM   The stand-ins used for blocking and lighting a scene.

BUCK   Usually refers to a car that has been cut in half or the roof cut off for filming the inside of the vehicle, such as showing a center console or dashboard.

BULL PEN   Slang word used for the area where all the grip equipment is staged (set up); also called *staging area*. It is usually located as close as possible to the set.

BUTTERFLY KIT   Assorted nets, silks, solids, and grifflons used for light control; generally, they are mounted on 5 × 5 ft. or 6 × 6 ft. frames. Frames 12 × 12 feet or 20 × 20 feet are also commonly called butterfly kits, although they more accurately are described as *overhead kits*. The term "butterfly" now generally means a kit containing one each of a single, double, silk, solid, frame, and grifflon.

CAMERA LEFT   A direction to the left of what the camera sees.

CAMERA RIGHT   A direction to the right of what the camera sees.

CANS   Headsets used to hear what is being recorded for the film.

CEILING PIECE   A frame built from flat 1 × 3 in. lumber with luan gussets covered on one side with muslin cloth (usually seamless).

CELO   A cucoloris made of wire mesh material used to create a pattern of bright and dark spots when placed in front of a light.

CHARLIE BAR   A strip of wood, 1 to 6 in. wide × 3 ft. long, with a pin attached that is used to create shadows on an object (long, thin flags; gobos).

CHEATING   Avoiding an object for a better shot—moving it from the camera's view.

CHECKING THE GATE   Inspecting the camera pressure plate, which holds the film in place, for any film chips, dirt, or debris. This task is conducted after each scene.

CHERRY-PICKER   See *condor*.

CHROMATRAN   Looks like a giant photographic slide that is lit from the back. Chromatrans come in all sizes, from small to 30 × 100 ft. or larger. They are usually pictures of city landscapes, but they can be countrysides, airports, whatever. There are daytime and nighttime chromatrans/translights. They are usually transported rolled up in a large cardboard tube and hung from grommets.

CLAPPER/LOADER   Another name for a camera assistant.

CLEAR LUMBER   Lumber without knots in it; it is normally used for dolly track.

CLEAT   A point at which to tie off a rope; usually an "X"-shaped or cross-shaped piece of wood nailed to a stage floor.

CLOTHESLINE   When a rope or cable is strung about neck height (like the old clothesline days). If a clothesline is needed, always hang some tape from it to mark it visually so no one gets hurt.

COLOR TEMPERATURE   The warmth or coolness of a light is measured in degrees Kelvin. 5600 K is considered daylight (blue), and 3200 K is a tungsten (or white) light.

COME-A-LONG   A hand-cranked cable that can pull heavy objects closer together, like a wrenching block and fall.

CONDOR   A machine with a telescoping arm, which will also boom up, down, left, or right; also called a *cherry-picker*. Used frequently for lighting platforms.

COURTESY FLAG   A flag set for the director, director of photography, talent, agency, or anyone who needs shading.

COVE   When you tent a window or doorway to make it night during the day.

CRAFT SERVICES   A table of food set out for the entire film cast and crew.

CROSSING   A term yelled out by anyone who crosses in front of a lens when there is not any filming going on but the cameraperson is looking through the eyepiece; it is considered a courtesy to the cameraperson.

CUT   Refers to setting a flag in front of a light to cut or remove the light from an object. There are two types: (1) a hard or sharp cut, which produces a hard shadow close to the object; and (2) a soft cut, where the flag or scrim is held closer to the light source.

CYC-STRIPS   One or several lamps placed in one housing fixture.

DAILIES   Film shot the previous day which is shown to the director, cameraperson, and crew so they can review that day's work to ensure that no reshoots are necessary. Sometimes called *rushes*.

DAPPLE   Shadow effect made with a branch with leaves on it.

DEAL MEMO   A written paper describing the compensation you have agreed to for your service.

DECK POLES   Pointed sticks about 4.5 ft. long that are stuck in the holes along green beds (chain-hung working platforms from the rafters, a.k.a. perms) and to which arms and flags are attached.

DINGO   A small branch-a-loris.

DOWN STAGE   Closer to the camera or audience.

DP   Director of photography.

DUTCH ANGLE   To lean the camera sideways, either left or right, to film in that position.

EAR   A flag mounted on the side of a light to block light; also called a *sider*.

EARS ON   Turn on your handheld walkie-talkie.

EASY-OUT   Tool that looks like a reverse drill and is used to get out broken bolts. After drilling with a small bit, put the easy-out in the hole and twist out.

EGG CRATE   A soft light control frame that directs light without allowing it to spill off the subject. Looks sort of like a rectangle box with several dividers spaced evenly in it.

EYE LIGHT   The eyes are given a sparkle light; also called an *obie light*.

E-Z-UP   A popup-style tent that is usually 8 × 8 ft. or 10 × 10 ft., although larger and smaller sizes are available.

FEATHER   Effect achieved by setting a flag in front of a light source; moving the flag closer to or farther away from the source will feather, soften, or harden the shadow on the surface of an object.

FILL LIGHT   Light added to the opposite side of a subject to fill in the shadows made from the *key light*.

FIRST TEAM   The talent, the actors that will be filmed, the A-team.

FLARE   When a light shines into the camera lens, it will flare or cause a glare on the film.

FLASHING   Term called out before someone takes a flash photo; this lets the gaffer know that one of his lights has not burned out.

FLOAT A FLAG   To handhold a flag as the camera is moved, to float with the camera and block unwanted light flares. A *floater* is a handheld flag or net that moves with an actor during a take.

FLOOD   Spreads light to the overall subject.

FLOPPY   A 4 × 4 ft. floppy-type flag made of a white-out bounce material; excellent for bounce/fill.

FLY IT OUT   Pull it out of the scene.

FLYING IN   The object asked for is being fetched in an extremely quick manner.

FLYING THE MOON   A bunch of lights hung on pipes shaped into a box frame. A muslin (rag) cover is wrapped around the frame, and it is flown over an exterior location by a cable on a crane.

FRAME LINE   The edges (top or bottom or sides) of what the camera will pick up.

FREEBIE   A film project for which the crew usually receives no pay. (It is a way to give something back to the industry for being so good to you.)

FRESNEL   The glass lens in front of a movie lamp used to spread or focus the light.

F-STOP   A measurement of the lens aperture. Lenses are rated by speed (how much light they can gather); a lens that can film with a minimum of F/1.4 is considered faster than a lens that films with a minimum of F/8; for example, F/1.4 requires less light for a correct exposure, and F/8 requires more light for a correct exposure.

FULLER'S EARTH   Used to make blowing dust in the background or to dust down or age a person or object.

GAFFER   Head electrician.

GAFFER TAPE   Adhesive tape similar to duct tape; also called *grip tape* or *cloth tape*.

GARY COLEMAN   A short C-stand, about 20 in. tall.

GEL   Transparent cellophane material used for changing the color of a light, either for visual effect or for film exposure correction.

GHOST LIGHT   A single large light bulb mounted on its own wooden stand. Usually left on a stage that is not being used because it is believed to keep friendly spirits illuminated and evil spirits away and because it helps people see the set objects lying on an unlit stage.

GOBO HEAD   A clamping device for holding equipment; also called a *grip head* or *C-stand head*.

GRAZE   Go to the craft services food table.

GREEK IT OUT   To disguise a word to make a logo unrecognizable. For example, Coke might become Ooko AA Cola.

GREENBEDS   Platforms hung from chains from the rafters called perms.

GRIP HEAD   A C-stand head used as a clamping device; also called a *gobo head*.

GRIP RADIO TALK   "10-100" means you are going to the restroom; "10-4" means you understand; "what's your 20?" is asking where are you?

GRIP TAPE   Adhesive tape similar to duct tape; also called *gaffer tape* or *cloth tape*.

HAIR IN THE GATE   When a piece of debris or film chip is lodged in the corner of the pressure plate gate. In case that chip or bit of debris may have scratched the film emulsion, the last shot is reshot (sort of like insurance).

HAND SHOES   Leather gloves.

HARDMARKS   Permanent objects or tape marks placed by the camera assistant.

HEADACHE   Duck! Something has fallen from overhead.

HEMP   Rope, usually 1/4 to 1 in.

HERO   The product featured in a commercial, such as a perfectly prepared hamburger, a toy, or a color-corrected label. Whatever it is, it is perfect (hero) for the shot for filming a commercial.

HIGHLIGHT   Used to brighten an area of an object or to emphasize an interesting part with light.

HISTORY   Something that has been removed from the set or lost; it is only a memory, gone, a vapor.

HMI LAMP   (H, mercury; M, metals; I, halogen components) Metal halide lamp that usually burns at 5600 K (also known as *blue light*).

HODS   A bead board, three-side light bounce, usually made from polystyrene (bead board). About 18 in. long × 12 in. wide, with a 12 × 12-in. cap on one end.

HOG TROUGH   An "L"- or "V"-shaped brace made with two sticks of 1 × 3-in. lumber; used when nails, screws, or glue must be applied. The brace makes an otherwise flimsy piece of 1 × 3-in. board stronger by giving it a backbone.

HOT SET   Don't move anything, because more filming is to be done.

IDIOT CHECK   Before leaving a location, sending a grip out to search for any equipment that may have been left behind on a set after a shoot was finished.

INCANDESCENT LAMP   A lamp with a 3200 K temperature (also called *white light*).

JUICER   Electrician, sparks.

JUNIOR   A 2000-watt lamp.

KICK   A sparkle off an object or person that may be desirable or may require removal.

KILL THE BABY   Turn off the 1-kilowatt lamp.

KNEE CAPS   Heads up! Equipment coming through.

KODAK MOMENT   A chance to take a picture with the talent (actors and actresses). Same as a *photo op*.

LACE-OUT   Laying out of equipment so it can be easily counted, such as during a prep or wrap day on a stage or when returning from a shoot.

LANYARD   Cord attached to a tool so it cannot be dropped when it is being used high in overhead perm.

LEAK   A small amount of light that has gotten past the flag or gobo.

LEGAL MILK CRATE   Not stolen from a store; a crate that has been rented or bought.

LENSER   A shade for the lens, such as a flag or a shade attached to the camera (called an *eyebrow*).

LEXAN   Plastic material that comes in 4 × 8 ft. sheets in many different thicknesses (*e.g.*, 1/8 in., 1/4 in., 1/2 in., 1 in.); used to protect cameras and personnel from explosions. It is optically clear and highly recommended.

LIMBO TABLE   A table that has a 90-degree sweep; usually used for product shots. The back part stands straight up and then curves 90 degrees to form a table, on which the product is placed.

LINE OUT!   Called out from overhead when a rope or line is let out.

LOSE IT   Remove something from the set or from the surrounding area; it is no longer needed.

LUAN   Plywood-like material, usually about 1/8-in. thick, which is used to make set walls; can be a three-ply timber, which is still lightweight, paintable, and stainable. It is sometimes referred to as *Philippine mahogany*.

MAKE IT LIVE   Set the object in place.

MARTINI SHOT   Last film shot of the day. Slang for the next shot is "in a glass" (the wrap shot).

MICHAEL JACKSON   Taken from his song "Beat It"; means get out of the way.

MICKEY MOLE   A 1000-watt lamp.

MICKEY ROONEY   Nickname for a slight creep of the dolly; a small, slow movement.

MIGHTY MOLE   A 2000-watt lamp.

MOLELIPSO   A 1000- to 2000-watt lamp mainly used for performances; the spotlight.

MOS   (mitt out sound) Not a sound take or recording.

MOUSE   The shadow of a microphone.

MULLIONS    Strips of wood that hold panes of glass in a window; provide a French window effect.

ND (NEUTRAL DENSITY) FILTER    A soft, rolled gel; also comes in large plastic sheets as well as small glass rings for the camera. It is used to reduce the brightness of a lamp or light source (sort of like sunglasses).

NECK DOWN    Slang term for being hired from the neck down (don't think, just do).

NEGATIVE FILL    A black surface used to remove unwanted light close to the actor.

NET    The use of scrims (nonelectrical dimmers) to reduce the light shining on an object in small amounts.

NEW DEAL    Staring on a new setup when a scene is finished.

NG    No good.

NODAL POINT    The dead center of the camera lens if the camera was to rotate in a 360-degree twisting motion.

NOOK LIGHT    A 650- to 2000-watt light, on average.

OBIE LIGHT    A small light placed just on top of the camera to add a sparkle to the talent's eyes or used as a fill light.

ONE-LINER    A breakdown of the script that tells the crew what scenes will be shot that day; it provides scene numbers and a bit of the story line or actions that will occur.

ONSTAGE    Move toward the center of the set or stage.

OPERATOR    Camera operator; can also be the director of photography (DP), but usually these are two different people in film production.

OVERCRANKING    Speeds up the frame rate of film through the camera; when the film is processed and projected at normal speed (24 frames per second [fps]), the action appears in slow motion.

OVERHEAD KIT    Usually a 12 × 12 ft. or 20 × 20 ft. set of one each of a single, double, silk, solid, frame, and grifflon. Commonly referred to as a *butterfly kit*, although the term "overhead kit" is more descriptive.

OZONES    Open areas between the wood beams that make up the perms. This is the area that we throw ropes over to rig lights or greenbeds or to set wall tieoffs.

PAN    Rotate the camera left or right.

PARABOLIC REFLECTOR    The part of the lamp behind the glove (light bulb) used to gather and reflect the light onto a subject.

PHOTO FLOOD GLOBES    Normal-looking light bulbs that give off a brighter light (but have a short useful life).

PHOTO OP    A chance to have your picture taken with someone you would like to be seen with, such as an actor or actress.

PIPE GRID    A series of pipes, most often connected together for rigidity, that are usually hung by chains above a movie set.

PLAYBACK    Video recording of a scene just shot.

POOR MAN'S PROCESS    Can mean filming a stationary vehicle by passing a light, shadow, or background object by it, giving the impression that the vehicle is in motion; other techniques that work well include slightly shaking the vehicle or moving a lever under the frame of the car to give it a small jolt every so often.

POV   (point of view) What a person sees.

PRACTICAL   A fixture (light) in frame such as a table, floor, or wall lamp.

PREP   To prepare for a job—for example, to check out the equipment or camera to ensure that they are in good working order for the job that is about to begin.

P-TON   A sharp, flat peg with a ring welded to it for tying off a rope. It can be hammered into small cracks in cement or asphalt without inflicting much damage.

RAGS   Any of the following are referred to as rags because they do not usually have a permanent frame affixed to them: muslin (bleached or unbleached), nets (single or double), silk, solid, or grifflon.

REEFING   A way to properly fold a large rag (*i.e.*, grifflon, black, or any material that requires folding).

ROPE WRENCH   A knife for cutting rope.

SAIL BOATS   Used to hoist or fly a backing or translight, making it mobile.

SCAB PATCH   Two 2- × 4-in. × 16 ft. pieces of lumber, for example, are laid end to end to total 32 feet long, and a third equal-length piece of lumber is laid equally on the split line where the two 2 × 4's touch together. Also, a patch laid over a hole, like a bandage. Both examples are called *scabbing*. A *sandwich* is the same as a scab patch, except that it is nailed onto two sides with two pieces of scab lumber.

SCENE DOCK   A storage place for several wall flats. You can also temporarily store a removed wall on a set next to a working wall with hog troughs or set braces.

SCOUT   To go to different places or locations to check out an area.

SCRIMS   Net material or wire mesh that is put right in front of a light.

SEAMLESS PAPER   A wide roll of paper used for a background, such as that used in a portrait shot.

SET CONSCIOUSNESS   Be aware of what is where on the set. (This will make or break you. If you are not aware of where your equipment is when it is called for, you can look pretty bad.)

SET DECORATOR   The person who actually decorates a set with appropriate objects for the storyline. This will make a scene look real to the viewing audience.

SHEAVE   The wheel in a pulley on which the rope or wire rides.

SIDER   A flag mounted on the side of a light to block light; also called an *ear*.

SKID PLATE   Usually, an eighth apple box with a baby plate on it that is used for setting lamps at low angles; also called a *beaver board*.

SLEEPER TRACK   Framing track made from 4 × 8 ft. frames constructed from straight (not warped), kiln-dried lumber; used under the dolly or crane track to reinforce the foundation of the track for the dolly.

SLOW IT DOWN   (Take it down, knock it down) Reduce something; usually refers to bringing down the intensity of a light.

SNOOT   A device shaped like a funnel or coffee can hooked on the front of a lamp.

SOFFIT   The outcropping of a set wall or header where a movie light can be set.

SOFT   A gentle, pleasing light.

SOFT LIGHT   Ranges from 650 to 4000 watts, on average; also known as a *zip light*.

SOLDIER-UP   Setting up more stands in rows, ready for action.

SPAN SET   A loop of extremely strong material wrapped around a frame or beam that is hoisted up by a winch or crane; comes in 1- to 20-ft. loops but can be larger upon request.

SPARK   Electrician, juicer.

SPEED   The cameraperson or soundperson may call this out when they have their equipment running at the desired speed or operating revolutions per minute (rpm) for filming.

SPILL   Directing a light or natural sunlight onto an object and allowing the light to spill or leak off that object onto something else.

SPOT   Direct all light to one point on the subject.

SQUEEZER   An electrical dimmer.

SQUIB   A small explosive device (which can be activated accidentally by pressing the talk button on your walkie-talkie); used by special effects crews to make bullet holes or cause other damage during a scene.

STEVADOR   A hand truck.

STORYBOARDS   Cartoon-like drawings of the sequence of a shoot that indicate the required camera angles or framing.

TABLE IT   To set something on or parallel to the ground, such as a reflector or 12 × 12-ft. frame.

TAG LINES   Ropes usually made of 1/4-in. hemp that are tied to a lamp hanger (trapeze); used to pan or tie off a lamp, as well as to tie off rags on frames.

TAIL SLATE   Hitting the camera sticks after a scene has been shot. The slate is turned upside down, with the wording facing the lens, and then the hinged sticks are slapped together; also called *tail sticks*.

TAKE DOWN   Reducing the light on an object through the use of nets, scrims, or dimmers or by wasting or spilling some of the light.

TAKE   A scene that has been shot.

TALENT   The actors.

TEASER   Used to cut light (*e.g.*, a flag).

TILT   Move the camera up and down in a tilting motion.

TOENAIL   To put either a nail or screw in the edge of an object to secure it temporarily in place.

TOPPER   A flag, for example, used to block unwanted light from the top of a light source; also called a *top shelf*.

TRACK SYSTEM   An overhead track used to hang backings that be easily moved, changed, or replaced.

TRUSS   A triangular metal structure used to span a large area; sometimes called a *rock-and-roll truss*. Lights can be hung from trusses.

TURN ON TWO BUBBLES   Turn on two lights in the same lamp.

TWEENIE    A 650-watt lamp.

UPSTAGE    Move toward the back of the set or stage. (Term comes from older stages that had a higher, or raked, upward incline toward the rear or back wall, away from the audience.)

WAFF    To lightly fan, smoke, or move a curtain sheet. To create the effect of a breeze, with a hand fan.

WALL BRACE    A metal rod, the ends of which are flattened and have holes drilled through them; used to attach a set wall to a wood-slatted floor. Also, a *hog trough* can be used.

WALL FLAT    A scenic covered wall usually made from 1 × 3 in. lumber covered in a thin plywood-type material called Luan.

WALL JACK    A two-wheeled brace or jack used to transport a large set wall.

WALL SCONCE    A lamp hung on a wall; a practical fixture.

WARNER BROTHERS    An extreme closeup of a person; cropping a little off the top of the actor's head with a shadow or by the camera lens.

WASTE    Shining all the light on an object, then slowly turning the light so some of the light misses or falls off of the object.

WATCH YOUR BACK    Yelled by someone carrying equipment and approaching someone from behind.

WHIP-PAN    A fast pan of the camera that blurs the motion.

WIG-WAG    A red flashing light outside of a stage that indicates that filming is going on.

WILD WALL or WILD CEILING    Walls or ceiling panels that can be moved individually.

WING    Setting an object such as a flag in front of a light and then moving it away or closer in a semicircular motion.

WIPE    An image that moves across the frame during filming; used to hide a cut during editing.

WRAP    Putting away all equipment or quitting for the night. Go home.

ZIP CORD    A lightweight cord that looks like an extension cord. It comes in different gauges and colors, usually black, white, or brown, but can be ordered in other colors.

# Index